ONCE UPON A WEDDING

Stories of Weddings in Western Canada, 1860-1945,
For Better or Worse.

Nancy Millar

Once Upon A Wedding
Nancy Millar
© Copyright 2000, Bayeux Arts, Inc.

Published by

Bayeux Arts Incorporated

119 Stratton Crescent S.W.
Calgary, Alberta, Canada T3H 1T7

Design: Brian Dyson, Syntax Media Services

Printed in Canada

Canadian Cataloguing in Publication Data

Millar, Nancy.
   Once upon a wedding

   ISBN 1-896209-33-5

   1. Weddings-Canada, Western-History. I. Title
GT2713.A3W48 1999 392'.5'09712 C99-910710-0

The author gratefully acknowledges the support of
the Alberta Historical Resources Foundation

The publisher gratefully acknowledges the generous support of
The Alberta Foundation for the Arts, The Canada Council for the Arts,
and the Government of Canada through the Book Publishing Industry
Development Program.

Dedicated in memory
of Gaye Ross who
left us way too soon

Was it a year or lives ago
We took the grasses in our hands,
And caught the summer flying low
Over the waving meadow lands,
And held it there between our hands?
Bliss Carman (1861-1929)

Bayeux *Arts*

CONTENTS

Introduction

There was something I meant to do
when I got up   something
important   but   what was it
Yes. The jewelry.

I must find something for Susan:
mother's ring, perhaps the pretty pin.

Will she understand it
is to be a link
between mothers and daughters,
between us as women?
Maybe when she holds this trinket

she will imagine (as I sometimes do)
that we are all here: mothers
daughters   granddaughter
 a moving forest of shadowy
figures receding into
a veiling mist,
a forest standing tall
with strong roots entwining
as they brood above
the seeds they have dropped.

…from *A Day's Lifetime* by Marion Smith of Red Deer, Alberta

People keep asking me why I decided to write about weddings. In reply, I must babble on about weddings being history, how they contain so many stories of beginnings and middles and ends. How weddings are peak experiences; therefore people remember details about them—what they wore, what was said, what came next. Weddings are drama, theatre, a play by Shakespeare, I say. But none of my explanations work as well as Marion Smith's poem, A Day's Lifetime.

We *are* all here—mothers, daughters, granddaughters. Fathers, sons, grandsons. We are, as she says, forests with roots and seeds both, and what I want this book to do is to bring the roots and seeds closer together. Too often, generations remain shadowy to one another, removed. What a loss.

I was at a noon luncheon one day at a table with several young very smart working women. They were complaining about the pension plan offered by their employer. It was completely inadequate apparently, a product of incompetents who had no idea of the needs of women. So far, I could sympathize, but then one of them said, "You'd think women would have done something about this before now. Why do we have to do everything?" I nearly fell off my chair. Didn't they know what their mothers and grandmothers had done simply to survive, to make the kind of world where we could be at this luncheon wearing expensive suits and sipping wine? I was so flabbergasted I couldn't speak.

How could they not know:
> About the log shacks full of bed bugs
> And the crops that failed
> And the men who died in war
> And the women who died in childbirth?

How could they not know:
> About loneliness and isolation
> And making do and doing without
> And lard sandwiches and one orange in the Christmas stocking
> And sacrifices made to ensure a future for them?

How could they not know:
> About the battles for equal pay
> And day care and child care credits
> And shelters for the battered
> And maternity leave and student loans?

How could they not know that pension plans are a relatively new concept, that their foremothers and forefathers didn't even get old age pension?

I couldn't say all that. But it troubled me enormously. I felt as if I hadn't kept the faith. I hadn't spoken up for the pioneers. I had let them recede into the mist.

Well, no more. Following are stories that begin with a wedding but don't stay there. Some stories go forward, some backward, and some do both. The time frame is 1860-1945 in western Canada and the north. That covers a lot of history and a lot of space, but most of the important events in that period and place find expression in the weddings, one way or another. You'll see. Immigration, settlement, rebellions, heroes, sinners, lovers, politicians (some of whom are lovers), scandals, rubber boots—they're all there. And they're all real people. I'm not making any of this up, although our history is sometimes so cruel and hard that I'd rather be making it up. I did not. Our history is not a piece of cake, but it's not boring either. We should know it and be proud of it.

Enough preaching, although I would like to thank those who told me the stories of their own wedding or gave me information about weddings before their time. They had to trust I wouldn't make them look stupid or thoughtless. I tried to get the stories right—forgive small errors—but I don't think I got any of the big details wrong. I couldn't. I care passionately about those who came before and what they tried to accomplish, what they did accomplish. I measure myself against them and I come up short again and again. How could I be critical?

I also have to salute my own mother and daughter in this process. At my mom and dad's 50th wedding anniversary party, daughter Sheila was persuaded/cajoled/bullied into wearing her grandmother's wedding dress. It was a pretty print thing with three flounces, not fancy at all, but Sheila got compliments and finally asked mom, "Where did you get your dress, grandma?"

"From Eaton's Shopper," she said. There were no stores in the Peace River country of Alberta, so she sent away what little money she had, included her measurements, and asked Eaton's in Winnipeg to pick her out a dress. They did. A parcel arrived one day and there was her wedding dress—a pretty print thing with three flounces. Sort of a peachy color. She wore it and was glad of it. It was 1935, the depths of the Depression in western Canada.

"You mean you never saw your dress before you wore it?" Sheila was horrified.

I could have lectured her about poverty and life in an isolated northern neck of the woods. I could have given her chapter and verse about homesteading and good years and "next year." I could have explained that mom could never throw anything away in her lifetime "in case there was another depression." But none of it would have stuck like the story of grandma's wedding dress.

Sheila still has it. I think she knows by now that she's one of the links. She'd better know it or I may be reduced to lecturing yet! And speaking of lecturing, take care, all of you who don't know what came before. I may be at a table near you someday and this time I'm ready!

And now, as the old Newfoundland saying goes…"**If it is a wedding, let it be a wedding.**"

THE 1860s

Indians, missionaries, brides by the bushel, a good guy and a Prime Minister

1860s...Seven Wives For One Brother...

In 1860, the Canadian West was just that—west. In eastern Canada, there were Maritime provinces with distinctive names and legislative assemblies and all those civilized things. In the central part of the country, there was a Lower Canada and an Upper Canada and a lot of wars and all those civilized things. But beyond the Ontario border, there was just the west. Nobody really knew the measure of the place—the size, the length, the altitude, the population. It was just there, sort of a black hole into which a few explorers and fur traders disappeared once in awhile. And, oh yes, the Indians. They lived in the west but since nobody could count them or understand them or organize them into political parties, they too were lumped into the concept of "west."

The Great Lone Land, in other words. Mostly Indians, and not very many of them at that, maybe 250,000 or a few more people than live in Saskatoon, SK, now. Add to that number a few white folks who lived in the Red River area and a few more on the west coast. Otherwise, emptiness. And no weddings to speak of. I should end this chapter now.

But if the word "wedding" is taken to mean the process by which a man and woman, or a man and women, come to live together as a family unit, then of course there were weddings. It's just that, in native cultures, there was no standard practice. It cannot be said that every native wedding included this or that every time. Instead, every Indian band, clan or tribe had its own practices and those depended on a whole lot of other things. Had there been a recent inter-tribal war? If so, men and women might have been killed. New alliances would have to be made to look after children. Was there a shortage of men? If so, polygamy would be logical. Was there a shortage of buffalo? If so, who had time or energy to worry about changing partners? Was disease present in the camp? If so, other ceremonies would be more important, ceremonies invoking protection against the invisible killers. And so on.

Whether a standard practice or not, polygamy was common among western Indian tribes. Robert Rundle, one of the first missionaries to work in the west wrote matter-of-factly to his sister back in England, **"The chief who received me into the Blackfoot camp had seven wives. I believe there were two or three or perhaps four sisters amongst the number."** He lived among the Indians from 1840-1848.

Most marriages were arranged; often money and goods were exchanged. Mike Oka, a member of the Blood Indian band of southern Alberta, said in 1936 when he was 76 years old, **"We had no ceremonies of marriage. In the old days, we bought our wives. Many Indians had more than one wife. We were very strict with our young girls. Many were put to death or marked for life for unfaithfulness to their husbands. They might have the ends of their nose and ears cut off. When an Indian is found guilty of adultery, he leaves home to never come back, because he knows that the penalty for this crime is death. Some people think that being savages in the** old days we lived like animals. We respected and protected our younger women. We kept the seventh commandment although it was unknown to us then."

Not all Indians were so complimentary about the women in their midst. Samuel Hearne's native guide also had multiple wives—eight by some counts—and he had this to say about them, **"Women were made for labor; one of them can carry, or haul, as much as two men can. They also pitch our tents, make and mend our clothing, keep us warm at night, and in fact there is no such thing as travelling any considerable distance, or for any length of time, in this country without their assistance."** So far, so good, except that Matonabee also adds that, **" Women, though they do everything, are maintained at trifling expense for they always stand cook, the very licking of their fingers in scarce times, is sufficient for their subsistence."**

According to some historians, Plains Indian women could get rid of a husband by simply pitching his personal belongings out of her teepee. By modern standards, the wives of Hearne's guide should have given him the heave-ho for his cavalier attitude toward their hard work, but it wasn't that easy. There had to be good cause or else the woman's family would have a hard time arranging another liaison for her. Then there was the problem of violence. Male Indians were expected to fight; it was part of their culture and sometimes included their women. Maskepetoon, a Cree Indian chief, was reputed to have scalped one of his wives while she was still alive. Years later, he repented of his sins and took the Christian message to heart, so much so that he walked unarmed into an enemy's camp to demonstrate his peaceful intentions, only to be killed on the spot.

It was not a simple life, the Indian way of life, which is why it's hard to be definitive about wedding customs.

Some west coast Indian tribes, the Kwakiutl on Quadra Island for one, celebrated important weddings with potlaches. These were elaborate ceremonies of song, dance and gift giving and were a very important way of establishing status in the community. The family who could give the most gifts and serve the most food won, even if they had to live in poverty for years to come. This desire to give things away made no sense to the British administrators so potlaches were eventually outlawed, a restriction that was resented and often ignored by the native people.

Competition was part of a Chipewyan tradition in northern Alberta as well. There, men wrestled for their women whether the women wanted them or not. David Thompson spoke out against the practice but was told that strong men take women when they want them. **"What is a woman good for, she cannot hunt, she is only to work and carry our things,"** the native told him.

1860s...David Thompson and the Missus...

David Thompson was one of the good guys. A poor kid from London, England, he came out to Canada to work for the Hudson's Bay Company (HBC) but switched to the rival North West Company (NWC) when they promised he could make maps as well as trade furs. Mapmaking was his thing and the west was his place, being as it was, largely unmapped. Eventually, he plotted two million square miles of land, rivers, lakes, mountains and mountain passes. Even the ocean made it onto his maps because it was he who finally found a way through the Rockies to the mouth of the Columbia and thence to the Pacific. He was amazing but he belongs in a book on marriages because of Charlotte. After being in Canada for 15 years—from the age of 14 to 29, he took as his country wife Charlotte Small, herself but 14 years old. When other traders who took wives "a la façon du pays" registered their liaison, they would identify their Indian wife as a "**woman of the country**." Just that. No name. Not David Thompson. He insisted that Charlotte be named in the register.

Charlotte knew about country marriages; she was the daughter of one. Her father was an NWC man who left his Cree Indian wife and half breed children behind when he returned to England. That's what a lot of the fur traders did, live with one or sometimes a succession of native women; then drop them on their heads when it came time to go back to so-called civilization. Certainly, George Simpson, the governor of the combined NWC/HBC, did just that. Leaving behind at least two country wives and numerous "**bits of brown**," as he so thoughtfully referred to his mixed blood children, he returned to England, married cousin Frances and once back in Canada set himself and herself up as Emperor and Mrs. Simpson.

To be fair, country marriages could be a boon to the native wife as well as the European husband. He got someone to cook and make camp for him, to interpret the native languages and guide him through Indian territory while she got a better life than she might have had with her own people. Life was not a bowl of cherries for Indian women. They did the dirty work, the daily grind, and if a "country marriage" to a European fur trader meant a house, warm blankets, food supplies, education for their children, even hired help now and then, then it wasn't such a bad deal. Even when the fur trader or explorer moved on, the woman was often able to find another mate because she had stuff. She had some status. She was somebody. So it was a win/win thing in some cases.

Interestingly, it was a win/win thing as long as the "white" wives stayed out of the picture, but once they arrived, everything changed. Frances Simpson, for instance, would not eat at the same table or go to church with the country wives and children in the Red River settlement. When Colin Robertson tried to introduce his Metis wife to Mrs. Simpson, he was told that it was impossible. Suddenly, there were upper classes and lower classes and never the twain shall meet. Then things got rough for some of the country wives.

As for Charlotte, David remained her faithful defender. When they married—without clergy but in the fashion of the country—he wrote in his diary, **"My lovely wife is the blood of these people (the Cree), speaking their language and well educated in the English language which gives me a great advantage."**

About Cree marriages in general, he wrote, **"Their marriages are without noise or ceremony; nothing is requisite but the consent of the parties and the parents...When contrariety of disposition prevails, so that they cannot live peaceably together, they separate with as little ceremony as they came together and both parties are free to attach themselves to whom they will, without any stain on their characters."**

Apparently, there was no contrariety of disposition in the Thompson household for they stayed together through all his years of mapmaking, through 13 children and finally through some lean years in Quebec when Thompson lost his sight and his ability to support the family. It was an inglorious end to a glorious career but never did Thompson consider leaving Charlotte. In fact, one of the first things he did upon reaching civilization was find a preacher and marry Charlotte, a la façon de l'eglise. October 30, 1812.

He died in 1857, Charlotte followed a few months later. They're both buried in Mount Royal Cemetery in Montreal but only David is named on the marker. That must make him spin in his grave, but there's good news. Charlotte is to get her own marker in the new millenium.

1860s...Missionaries By God...

First the explorers discover there is a west. Then fur traders discover there's money to be made in beaver pelts from the west. Then the men who are posted in god-forsaken trading posts all over the west discover that life goes better with a country wife or two. Then a sort of society evolves—European fur traders, Indian country wives, mixed blood children, mixed mixed blood children and so on. It's a fur trade culture and it works in its own disorganized way.

But then the missionaries came. And the missionaries had very different ideas as to how people should live their lives and what's more, they didn't mind saying so. In fact, it was their duty, their God-given responsibility to bring the Christian message of hope and redemption to the Indians who had neither, or so it was supposed. Here's part of a journal written by Robert Rundle, the Wesleyan minister from England who worked with the natives of western Canada between 1840 and 1848. It's Easter Sunday, 1841, and he's with the Cree Indians around Fort Edmonton.

"As there had been many applications for Baptism of children and as I wished them to fully understand the nature of the Sacrament, I devoted some time in the morning service explaining the subject to them. I tried to show them what was

required of the parents in bringing children to have it performed. I felt a burden on my conscience till I had delivered it. I told them the responsibility must rest with themselves. Afterwards I talked to them on the observance of the Sabbath & took occasion to remark on our Lord's Ascension on that day. I spoke to them very closely and firmly on both subjects. In the evening, the subject was Philip the Eunuch, thereby I showed them what was required of adults coming to Baptism. Eight marriages today. Late when we had finished."

How the native interpreter explained Philip the Eunuch to the Indian congregation at that service is hard to imagine. In fact, the whole thing is hard to imagine. Easter Sunday in Fort Edmonton in 1841. Maybe five buildings total, otherwise bush and sky and river and Indians who had for centuries made sense of their lives with their own religious ceremonies, their own superstitions. And then this guy comes along and tells them they've got it all wrong. That some other white man died on a cross and that means that everyone will go to heaven as long as they're good and repent of their sins. And by the way, how about a proper marriage?

As far as one can tell, the Indians were remarkably patient with Rundle and his need to baptize and marry. They did both with great good cheer; sometimes in fact, did them over and over again.

Rundle stayed only eight years in the west, but he sincerely liked and respected the native people, travelling to their camps and staying with them rather than expecting them to come to a church in the wildwood. Toward the end of his time in western Canada, he despaired that some of his converts had been beguiled away by "popery"— by the Catholic church in other words, and he urged the mother church in England to send more missionaries at all speed to keep ahead of the popery.

Meanwhile, some of the Indians were indeed beguiled by popery and like the obliging folk they were, they allowed the beguiling Catholic priests to marry them again. Marrying seemed to please the various church people, so why not do it?

1860s...A Tiny Perfect Town...

While Rundle was travelling all over the west and teaching the lessons of Philip the Eunuch to the Plains Indians, William Duncan, a lay minister with England's Church Missionary Society, was making plans to stay put. As long as the Tsimshian Indians of northern BC were free to travel and meet temptation at every turn, they'd never overcome their heathen ways, he figured, so better to live together in one place, isolated from outside influence. Thus was established the model community in northern BC called Matlakatla. Duncan called the shots—in the name of God, of course—and taught his people the skills they needed to survive independently of the rest of the world. How to garden, preserve food, weave clothing, make soap, build buildings, worship the Lord. And it worked wonderfully for 20 years or so but the sin of pride caught up with Duncan when he began telling the Anglican Church just how they ought to conduct all of their missionary work. The church officials in turn told him that he wasn't the god of northern BC and should start training natives to take over the missionary work.

With that, he packed up his bags and moved with about a thousand faithful souls to Alaska where he established New Matlakatla. Again, he posted his 15 rules for living, none of which mentioned the institution of marriage directly but several of which couldn't hurt: Cease drinking intoxicating liquor, send your children to school, be clean, be industrious, be peaceful, be honest and oh yes, don't forget to pay the village tax.

1860s...Cleave to One Woman?

Meanwhile, back on the prairies, Father Albert Lacombe was leading a popery charge, not that he ever talked like that. Even though he established a Metis settlement at St. Albert near Edmonton and another at St. Paul des Cris, both complete with church, school and farm buildings, he was not the stay-at-home type. He liked nothing better than to be home on the range, ministering to Indians, Metis and white folk alike. Consequently, he did a lot of marrying, baptizing and burying, the three Christian sacraments most often called for in isolated areas.

Kathryn Hughes tells in her book, *The Black Robed Voyager*, about one of Father Lacombe's weddings. It seems that he began the process with an explanation of the meaning of Christian Catholic wedding. It means, he said to the native couple, that you must cleave to one another and be faithful only unto one another. That was bad news for the would-be bridegroom who said he could never make such a big promise, to cleave to his woman always. What if she gets out of hand, he asked?

She won't get out of hand because she will be a good Christian wife, Lacombe said, and checked it out with the waiting bride. She agreed. Still, the man couldn't bring himself to such a major commitment. Father Lacombe played his trump card. OK then, you won't be able to come to church anymore, he said.

That did it. The next morning, the reluctant bridegroom was waiting at the altar with his bride, and Fr. Lacombe began the service. The service progressed on cue until Lacombe got to the part about loving and cherishing until death does you part. Again, the bridegroom got all worked up. What will she do if she knows I can't send her away, he worried. She'll get entirely out of control.

So maybe she should leave you right now, Lacombe suggested.

The bridegroom considered his options. His woman had been with him for years; he was accustomed to her services. On the other hand, what if she exercised some muscle under the terms of the marriage vows? There was silence until finally, he said, **"No, I do not want that (her departure.) I have said I will marry her, and I will. But I want to speak my mind first about what trouble she may make for me**."

And they lived happily ever after, or so the story goes.

1860s...And Be Sure To Patch His Pants...

It is to be hoped that Sarah and William lived happily ever after too. They were married by Rev. Cochrane in the famous St. Andrews on the Red, the Anglican Church in the Red River settlement which by 1860 had enough people to produce several levels of society. There were the Selkirk settlers who came in 1810 and who thought themselves the cream of the crop. After all, hadn't they lived through the most incredible privations to establish themselves in this new country? Then there were the fur traders and their descendants who also thought they had suffered enough to be the cream of the crop. And then there were the ordinary folk like William and Sarah. At least, they must have been the ordinary folk for this is what Cochrane told them after they said their vows: **"Now, William, you must be kind to Sarah. See that she always has a pail of water on hand. Get in wood for her. Do not leave her to fetch it herself. And do not let the cupboards get empty. And you, Sarah, must be good to William and take care of him. Take care of William's clothes. Never let him come to church without his trousers being neatly patched."**

Other weddings in the emerging Red River settlement of Kildonan were much more elaborate and much longer. W.J. Healy in his book, *The Women of Red River*, reported that some lasted up to two weeks.

The process began on a Monday when the father of the bride delivered invitations in person to other members of the community. While he was out tramping around the countryside, other men prepared the beef and mutton roasts that would be hung on spits before the open fireplaces. Female relatives made bread, cakes and plum pudding. Weddings were a welcome break from the rigors of pioneering; everyone was glad to help.

By Thursday, everything had to be ready because Thursday was the day for weddings. The bride and groom led the procession to the church-sometimes walking, sometimes in horse drawn carrioles and cutters. Once there, they stood before the minister and said their vows. The solemnity of the occasion lasted only until the service was over, and then it was a race to the brides parents home, the better to eat and dance until the cows came home that night or the next. The dancing was so important and so pleasurable that many a young person wore out more than one pair of moccasins at a wedding dance—or wedding dances. Sometimes, two or three neighbors opened their homes for dancing so there would be room for everyone.

Then on the following Sunday, the young couple were kirked. In other words, they sat together in the front row at church, thus demonstrating their new status as grownup members of the church and community. This time, there was no racing to get back to the brides parents. It was Sunday. Sunday was Gods day—no foolishness allowed. There was another major feast but no dancing.

Fear not. There was dancing and merry-making at the home of the grooms parents the following Tuesday, after which the newly weds settled down and so did the community. Until the next wedding.

The Red River was the first part of the west to get missionaries, church headquarters and private church schools. In 1820, for example, the Rev. John West headed west and enroute performed a marriage for Thomas Bunn and Phoebe Sinclair, the first wedding, it is said, to be sanctioned by the Anglican church in western Canada. The next day, he baptized four of their five children, the fifth being away at school in Scotland. Thomas had had some practice with this marriage business having married first in England. That wife died and Thomas made the move to Canada to work for the Hudson's Bay Company (HBC) in northern Manitoba. There he took **"in the custom of the country"** a native wife only to have her die on him as well. It was then that he took up with Phoebe, the daughter of another HBC man and his native wife. She was 16 years of age; he was 43.

It would be nice to report that they lived happily ever after and perhaps they did as man and wife, but Thomas Bunn and the HBC governor, George Simpson, did not get along and Thomas had to take early retirement.

Rev. West had better luck with his job and was especially proud of the fact that he had presided over at least 65 formal marriages of HBC men and their country wives.

1860s...Bride in a Box...

Out on the west coast, Victoria was working away to become a tiny perfect piece of jolly old England. That process included some snobbery about who was white and who was not and who was halfway in between. Not that the lines could be drawn exactly because there was the Governor, you see. James Douglas was part Scot, part something else. His wife Amelia was part British, part Indian. They lived together without the benefit of clergy for nine years, imagine that, before legitimizing the relationship in the Anglican Church. So with a muddle like that at the top of the social scale, it didn't pay to get too snippy about Who's Who. Mind you, Douglas kept Amelia out of the social limelight and encouraged his children to live entirely in the white world.

Thus, the wedding of his oldest daughter Cecilia to Dr. John Sebastian Helmcken in 1852 was as grand as Victoria could manage. It would have been much less grand had the man in charge of transportation on that fateful day not been a French Canadian familiar with carrioles, the light sleds used in Quebec. Two feet of heavy new snow fell the night before the wedding, making it impossible for horses to pull the heavy cart that was supposed to bring the bride to the church. What to do? Make a carriole, of course, The charioteer commandeered a big dry goods box from the trading post, fixed some runners and a shaft beneath it with willow branches, lined it with a bright new blanket, hitched up the horses and delivered the bride. Better late than never.

Helmcken had a few anxious moments as he waited at the church. Years later, he wrote,

"The poor bridegroom is waiting impatiently in the mess room church—here's a pretty kettle of fish, but just then the tinkle of sleigh bells is heard and the bride and maids and drygoods box appear. The whole party hurry into the church, the ceremony proceeding. The clock strikes twelve just as the ring is put on the finger. The ceremony over, the bride and bridegroom leave the church to return to their parents' house for a good time and then the guns roar from the bastions. The bell in the middle of the fort rings—the dogs howl thereunder—the men fire muskets—all hurrah! Grog is served out all round, there is feasting, reveling and jollity and everybody, heart and soul, wishes the handsome, favorite and favored couple many happy new years."

It does sound wonderful—bells and muskets and grog and all. But the favored couple did not have many years or much happiness. Two of their children died as infants and were buried near their house in Victoria, "where the holly once grew," according to Helmcken's memoirs. Then after 13 years of marriage, Cecilia died in 1865 from a severe inflammation of the lungs, the Victoria paper explained. Probably tuberculosis. She was buried with her two babies who were moved from the holly bush.

Helmcken remained an influential member of BC society, one of those who negotiated their province's entry into Confederation.

1860s...The Marrying Kind...

The Hardisty family practically ran the Hudson's Bay Company and western Canada for some years—sons, grandsons, nephews, in-laws. They were everywhere and everywhere respected for their integrity and ability, but it must be said that they had some of the strangest weddings in the history of the west.

The first Hardisty to come to Canada was a stiff-necked Scot called Richard who insisted upon a legal wedding ceremony when he and Margaret Sutherland joined forces. Never mind that Margaret's mother, a native woman, and her father, another HBC Scot, lived together in the custom of the country. Richard would not go that route so waited until a senior HBC official was available to marry them. It was a civil service that was allowed in Hudson's Bay territory when no clergy were available.

So Richard and Margaret were properly married and had ten children. Their first born was William who, like father, like son, followed his dad into the service of the HBC and had a HBC official conduct his marriage to Mary Anne Allen. In 1857, he wrote this about his new wife: **"I was up at Fort Simpson in August and got married there in a very offhand way to a Miss Allen—she is an orphan, her parents having died when she was an infant—her education has been very much neglected, and it is my intention to send her to school for a year or two. It is a very unusual thing to send a Wife to school and no doubt will cause a laugh at my expense, but I don't care a fig and won't mind the expense, so long as she is enabled thereby to act her** part with credit in the society among which she is placed. As for the rest, the woman who I consider good enough to live with is good enough for my friends to look at."

Now there's a husband that modern women could be proud of! Such support and defiance of public opinion. And apparently, Mary Anne lived up to his expectations but he may not have lived up to hers. During a distinguished career with the HBC, he enjoyed his liquor a bit much and died fairly young as a result. However, their daughter Isabella, known as Belle, became the very model of a proper young woman and as such had a very proper wedding in Calgary in 1884. She was by that time living with her aunt and uncle, Eliza and Richard Hardisty.

This is how the newspaper reported it: **"Last evening, the youth and beauty of our town might be seen wending their way towards the Methodist Church where a scene of no common interest was being enacted—a marriage ceremony. The principals were James A. Lougheed, Esq., Barrister, and Miss Hardisty. The bride was waited upon by Miss Clara Hardisty, Calgary, and Miss McDougall of Morley. Messrs. Parlow and Andrews performed similar services for the groom. Before the hour, the building was packed, a number having to satisfy themselves with a peep through the windows. After the ceremony had been performed and the usual congratulations indulged in, a large company repaired to the residence of Chief Factor Hardisty where a sumptuous feast awaited. We extend our congratulations to the happy couple and wish them a happy sail o'er the sea of life."**

The happy couple did have a pretty good sail o'er the sea of life. They started out in a fairly modest vessel, a small house on Stephen Avenue, now 9th Avenue in Calgary. Even in their small house, they were much admired for the house had a bay window— the first of its kind in Calgary. People came from all over to see it. Eventually, the Lougheeds moved into Beaulieu, which truly was something to see! A grand sandstone mansion, it was more suited to the social responsibilities that came along with being a well-connected lawyer, then a Senator, then a Sir James Lougheed. Lady Belle did her part well, entertaining royals and politicians and rogues alike. She was a Hardisty, after all. She could cope.

Belle and James had four sons and two daughters. Son Edgar had son Peter and the rest is Alberta history since Peter Lougheed served as Alberta premier from 1971 to 1985.

But back to the Hardisty bunch. Son of the first Richard, the second Richard's marriage wasn't particularly interesting in that he married the daughter of a Methodist minister who saw to it that the pair had a proper wedding. But his bride was certainly interesting. She was Eliza McDougall, daughter of George McDougall, the Methodist missionary who established missions at Fort Edmonton, Victoria (later known as Pakan) and Morley. No stranger to life on the frontier, Eliza took her honeymoon trip in stride, according to a family friend who wrote, **"Her honeymoon trip by cart to Edmonton and saddle horse to Rocky Mountain House from Victoria was an event of historical**

fortitude that any present-day bride might well envy." That was in 1866. In the next few years, Richard and Eliza moved around from HBC post to post, ending up in Fort Edmonton in the Big House, the western headquarters of the HBC. Eliza was Edmonton's "first lady."

Richard managed to combine his HBC responsibilities, his own growing business empire and his job as Senator, but it meant he traveled constantly. That he missed his wife and was a fond husband is revealed in a letter he wrote from London, England. He's a bit grumpy about the English weather and being away from home. **"Now with all the love I can bestow on you and with the blessing of God resting on you in that land where the sun shines and where you can see trees, grass and water now and again, I pray you to remain contented and happy till it's God's pleasure for us to meet again. Your absent love, Richard."**

But it was Isabella Hardisty who topped them all when it came to marriages. She had three weddings, two living husbands, no divorce, two children and more money than you could shake a stick at. Or a finger. She was quite amazing.

Isabella was sister to William and Richard. She was with her parents at a northern HBC post in Labrador when love was in the air. Sister Mary was marrying Joseph McPherson, HBC, and Isabella was considering James Grant, also HBC. Everyone was HBC in some way or another around the Hardistys. To her brother, she wrote, **"I suppose I had better tell you that there is a bit of a favourite of mine, who has really so overturned all my preconceived notions on the subject of single happiness that he has really convinced me I might be more than tolerably happy in the home he has prepared for me, so that after this month if no accident should intervene, I will have changed my name from Hardisty to Grant."**

That letter is full of what would be called mixed messages now, but marry James Grant she did. Her own father conducted the service as he was the highest ranking HBC official at the post at the time. A baby boy followed, rather quickly, it was whispered, June 24, 1852. That winter, however, she declined to accompany James to his northern post and stayed instead with baby Jamesie at the Hudsons Bay trading post where Donald Smith was the chief in charge. Again, there was whispering but Isabella was adamant. She would not rejoin James; he was toast, and she stayed on in the vicinity of Donald Smith. By January 17, 1854, she delivered a baby girl, known at first simply as Maggie but gradually in correspondence with her family, she began to refer to the child as Maggie Smith.

The Hardisty relatives had a fit but Donald Smith and Isabella lived together as if everything were perfectly above board. The fact that they were in a remote Labrador post probably helped. Who was counting anyway? Gradually, she became Mrs. Smith in the official records.

However, Donald did want to regularize the relationship so he wrote off to HBC Governor Simpson and asked his advice. Turned out that Simpson approved of his choice of the spunky Isabella Hardisty so he came up with the argument that the first marriage had not been legitimate. The elder Hardisty did not have the authority to perform a marriage ceremony in Labrador in the colony of Newfoundland, he said. Only in areas where the HBC had sole control of the territory could its officers marry people. Therefore, the young couple should have had the ceremony repeated at the first opportunity but they hadn't done that. "**So far from taking that step, however, they separated by mutual consent, which was quite sufficient to annul any ties that existed between them as man and wife**," he wrote.

So that was that, no need for a divorce since there had never been a marriage, except that Donald continued to worry about it. What if there were problems concerning inheritance rights? Maggie was his daughter but she'd come along at a time when Isabella was still technically Mrs. Grant or maybe Miss Hardisty. Maybe they should get married, but they were still in the north, still far away from those who are authorized to do marriages. There was nothing for it but Donald Smith would have to conduct his own wedding. He was a Justice of the Peace for his area, he had been approved by the Anglican Bishop of Newfoundland to do weddings, so who better to do it? Thus, in June 1859, when daughter Maggie was five years old, Donald Smith conducted the marriage ceremony for himself and Isabella.

It was enough to silence the whispers, to please the Hardistys and to put Donald Smith's mind at ease for awhile. But then in the next 20 years, he became as rich as Rockefeller, bailed the CPR out of trouble when it looked as if the trains might not make it across Canada, ruled the HBC, controlled the bank of Montreal, had honors heaped upon him until in the end he and Isabella were no longer plain old Mr. And Mrs. Smith but Lord and Lady Strathcona. Once again, Donald got to worrying. What if his will was challenged on the basis that daughter Maggie was illegitimate when she was born? What if the wedding that he had performed on himself was not, after all, sufficient for the powers-that-be? What if…?

So they got married again. On March 9, 1896, when Donald was 75 and Bella 71, they were married in a civil ceremony at the Windsor Hotel in New York in the presence of two lawyers. Even that wasn't enough for Donald for when he lay dying, he once more explained to his solicitors just who was what and when, fudging the dates so that Maggie would seem legitimate. Then, as final defense, he added that he had been throughout this time a domiciled Scotsman and by Scottish law, children born to common law parents were considered legitimate.

His efforts seemed to pay off; there were no troubles with the will. And the marriage was a happy and solid one. Maggie was their only child; she and her five children inherited the bulk of the Smith fortune after Donald died in 1914, Jamesie Grant got his share, various of the other Hardisty connections got some, universities, hospitals, faithful servants, friends, all shared in the largesse.

1860s...Bundles of Dirty Laundry...

As a consequence of one little word—GOLD, thousands of men came from all over the world to the Cariboo in 1862 to get rich quick. A few succeeded—Billy Barker, Cariboo Cameron—but most did not. Gold makes men crazy; it doesn't make them rich, not very often anyway, which is why northern BC suddenly had a whole bunch of men setting up as farmers, ranchers, store keepers, hoteliers. Anything to make a living when the gold didn't pan out. To service this growing population, roads had to be carved out of the mountains and wilderness, ships had to be built to bring in supplies, and hospitals had to be built and law had to be maintained. And so on it went until BC became a place to be reckoned with. No longer just two small British colonies on the west coast. Now the place had length and breadth and height. Don't forget the height.

What it lacked was women. Alexander Grant Dallas, a Hudson's Bay Company official, wrote the following to the London Times in January, 1862.

"Permit me to draw attention to a crying evil—the want of women. I believe there is not one to every hundred men at the mines; without them the male population will never settle in this country and innumerable evils are the consequence. A large number of the weaker sex could obtain wages, with the certainty of marriage in the background.

The miner is not very particular—plain, fat and fifty even would not be objected to, while good looking girls would be the nuggets and prized accordingly. An immigration of such character would be a great boon to the colony as I am sure it would be to many under-paid and over-worked women who drag out a weary existence in the dismal streets and alleys of the metropolis."

There you have it—thousands of men scrabbling for gold and building a province, but nobody to wash the dishes and warm the bed. Bring on the Columbia Emigration Society in London, England. They came up with the obvious solution—take the women to the men. Or at least take them to the colony and see what might happen. As it happened, England had a surplus of women right then.

So at least three "brideships" set out for the colony. The first one made the mistake of docking in San Francisco enroute to Victoria. The women left the ship and were never seen again, California men being just as anxious for female company as the ones further north. The organizers of the next shipment on the Tynemouth didn't make that mistake again. The 62 women on board were not allowed off the ship until it finally arrived in Esquimalt harbor September 17, 1862. There, a reporter from the Colonist newspaper was allowed on board and wrote that **"they are mostly cleanly, well built, pretty looking women, ages varying from 14 to an uncertain figure; a few are young widows who have seen better days. Most appear to have been well raised and generally a superior lot to the women usually met with on emigrant vessels."**

Faint praise indeed, but the bachelors of BC could not be discouraged. They hung around the Esquimalt harbor trying to get a glimpse of the **"bundles of crinoline"** as the local newspaper dubbed the female newcomers. No luck there; the women were kept out of sight. It was only when they were transferred to another boat to bring them into Victoria harbor that the men waiting on shore finally got a look. Some held up gold nuggets and proposed as the women walked off the boat. Most just stood in awed silence as the women walked by. It was known that these were women selected by a respectable organization, a Christian organization. They were to be treated as ladies.

The men got another chance to check out the goods when the women were taken to the grounds of the Parliament building where great tubs of water had been set up so the **"bundles of crinoline"** could wash their crinolines and other assorted dirty clothes. They had been on the ship for some three months. No wonder they wanted to wash clothes but how they managed to wash their clothes—which must have included some items of a delicate nature—and still keep their reputations as respectable women who never even allowed a glimpse of stocking, let alone underwear, is hard to understand. Also, where did they hang the clothes to dry? No one seems to mention that essential detail. Did they take the wet clothes with them to the prospective employers and good church people who were housing them, or did they spread them out on the lawn in front of the Parliament buildings?

The Townsend sisters, Louisa and Charlotte, did not stoop to washing their clothes in public. From money and privilege in England, they had decided to come to the colony of British Columbia in search of adventure and husbands—but not just any husband. They had been raised as proper young ladies with French lessons and music lessons and servants to do the dirty work. They were not about to head into the bush as miners' wives, and certainly they weren't about to wash their own clothes in public. For that matter, they didn't need to since they had worn their old clothes on the voyage and then chucked them out a porthole when they arrived in Victoria. **"No one else on the ship had half the luggage we had,"** Louisa Townsend Mallandaine said years later.

Louisa was not impressed with her new country. **"Everyone said it would be so beautiful, but I didn't think it was beautiful at all,"** she said in an interview on her 90th birthday. **"I hated the rain and the mud. It was all awful. We had to carry sticks to put down in front of us to walk on or we would have sunk over our boots in mud. I cried myself to sleep every night."**

She's talking about New Westminster here. That's where her first hostess/employer lived. As if the mud wasn't bad enough, she had to do **"all kinds of awful tasks that I had never done before"** and what's more, she could never go out alone. There were always men parading up and down in front of the house hoping to catch a glimpse of her. One man kept flashing his gold. It was too much. She found another position as companion/ governess in Victoria.

Victoria was much more to her liking. She rode horseback, played the piano, played cricket, danced a lot, joined a choir and somewhere in there must have done the work of a companion. But not for long. She met Edward Mallandaine who had the same kind of background she did—British parents with good connections, the best schools, a classical education, etc. He proposed one day, they were married the next. Sister Charlotte was not at all pleased; she thought they should have had a bigger splash but Louisa was always rather pleased with her no-nonsense wedding. Years later, she still explained that she was married in the morning and went shopping in the afternoon.

Another brideship arrived the following year with more " bundles of crinoline" on board. Again, prospective bridegrooms thronged the docks and it wasn't long before connections were made. Martha Clay, for example, was scheduled to go into domestic service, but she caught the eye of Joseph Akerman from Salt Spring Island and was married within days. The first night on Salt Spring, she heard the most dreadful caterwauling and woke Joseph, fearing they'd been taken over by ghosts or the end of the world or something. **"Go back to sleep, Martha. 'Tis only wolves,"** he said.

Most of the women who came on the various brideships were soon married and most of them were a credit to their English mothers, just as the preacher had advised in a sermon soon after the Tynemouth arrived. **"Remember your religious duties and the duties to your employers**," he exhorted from the pulpit. **"Always and under any circumstance shape your conduct so that you might be a credit to your English mother. And when beset by sin and temptation, rely on a kind Providence for aid and comfort**."

And so they did, even when the wolves were howling.

1860s...No Wonder He Drank...

John A. Macdonald was neither from the west nor of the west, but he belongs in this book about western Canadian history and weddings for two reasons: he got married again in 1867 and his new wife thought western Canada was about as wonderful as anything could be. As well, he husbanded the creation of Canada in 1867. Not that the west cared one hoot about John A. Macdonald and his affairs at the time. The west was still this great unknown, a British possession all of it with British governors and British rules and British customs, unless you'd never heard of Britain in which case it was just this great unknown.

But back in eastern Canada, they'd gone about as far as they could go, or so they figured, as independent British colonies. Time, the politicians argued, for a coalition of colonies, a confederation. So, Ontario, Quebec, New Brunswick and Nova Scotia joined in one big happy family on July 1, 1867. They called themselves Canada and John A. Macdonald became the first Prime Minister.

As for the one big happy family part, it wasn't, so the job of prime minister was no bargain either. Even then, Quebec was mad at the other provinces. Nova Scotia wasn't happy either; at one point they almost left Confederation. Ontario groused about tax loads and patronage and Quebec. And so on it went, sounding very much like the politics of the late 1900's. No wonder John A. Macdonald drank to excess, or at least got the reputation for same. In fact, that's about all we hear about our first Prime Minister—that he was a boozer. Never do we hear about his home life which, if he was a boozer, may have had something to do with it.

His first wife was Isabella Clark, an invalid for 14 of the 15 years they were married. There's no clear explanation of what her trouble was, but it's obvious from letters that still exist that Isabella was constantly sick. This is what John writes to his sister in 1845 about a mix-up in rooms in a Baltimore hotel: **"The consequence of all this was great exhaustion and great suffering by Isabella. She was in great agony all night and the two following days, and was obliged to have recourse to opium, externally and internally, in great quantities. She had rather a better night of it last night and thinks herself able to take her pilgrim's staff in her hand today."**

To his mother, he writes in 1847 about the birth of their first child: **" She (Isabella) suffered for some hours tremendously when we called in Dr. Rodgers a physician celebrated for the use and application of the Lethena or somnific gas. She was too weak and her nerves in too disordered a state to give her enough to set her asleep, but from time to time, enough was administered to soothe her considerably. She suffered dreadfully all night and about 8 this morning was so weak that the Doctors determined to use the forceps as she was quite unable to deliver herself."**

The baby was healthy. Everyone was delighted. Macdonald's mother was given the honor of naming him so there was another John Alexander. But illness and death seemed to surround the family. Young John A. unaccountably died at the age of 13 months. In the meantime, Isabella continued her life of pain and sorrow. There's not one letter in the Macdonald collection that doesn't mention some new treatment, some new source of pain, frequent resort to opium, constant attention by doctors, leeching and blistering and other barbaric sounding forms of treatment, etc. How John ever managed to carry on his law practice and his political life is a mystery, and how Isabella ever managed to deliver a second baby is almost as mysterious, but Hugh John was born in 1850.

When he was seven years old, his mother died. She was 48.

Ten years after that, John remarried, much to the surprise of his family and friends who had tried matchmaking with no success at all. To them, it seemed as if John was confirmed in his bachelor state. But he met Agnes Bernard, the sister of his private secretary, on a street in London, England, in December 1866. Two months later, they were married and he brought her back to Canada as Lady Macdonald. She was 31; he was 52. Not quite May and December but close.

Agnes took to her new life like a duck to water. She entertained, she supervised, she redecorated, she charmed, she did all those things that prime minister's wives do. She even rode the cowcatcher on a train travelling through the Canadian Rockies, the better to see the glorious scenery with, she said. **"As for me, I have been to the summit of the Canadian Rocky Mountains by C.P.R. To Mount Stephen this side of the Pacific** slope and Kicking Horse Pass. It was by far the most interesting and delightful trip I ever made in my life. I traveled in the car platform or on the engine of the specials and was more than delighted with all I saw."

It seemed as if John might be in for a peaceful patch of his personal life at last, and then they had a baby—Margaret Mary Theodora, better known as Mary. Whether it happened in birth or in utero, Mary was born with severe physical handicaps. She was never to walk, never to have complete control of her hands, never to live a normal life. For a time, they feared her mind might also be compromised but it wasn't. She was just "childish" as her older half brother Hugh described her because she was treated that way.

Speaking of Hugh, he was cared for by various aunts and uncles until he went off to university to follow in his father's footsteps as a lawyer. It wasn't easy being the son of a famous man. When he married Jean who had two strikes against her—she was a widow and Roman Catholic—he and his father fell out completely for several years but there was some reconciliation when Mary Isabella was born, aka Daisy. Then Jean died—the Macdonald curse at work again. Then John Alexander Macdonald, the son of Hugh and his second wife, died as a young man. More of the curse. Hugh did not have a happy time until he got politics off his plate and became a magistrate in Winnipeg.

After Sir John A. Macdonald died in 1891, Agnes and Mary moved back to England, and when Agnes died in 1921, Mary was cared for by companions for another 12 years. Back in Canada, Hugh died in 1929, survived only by his daughter Daisy who, it is said in the official records, no longer had the Macdonald name so apparently doesn't count as a Macdonald descendant. Still, she's all there is.

THE 1870s

Life along the edges, mounties to the middle, the late bridegroom, and a gassy gift

The Harris/Douglas wedding, 1878, Victoria, BC

29

1872...Wilhemina Will...

The West in the 1870s was a place **"where men are men and women are back East,"** according to one newspaper wag of the time. About the few women who did move west with their husbands, he said many of them were unsuited for frontier life. **"They were shaped like hourglasses,"** he wrote later, **"with too many petticoats and too much hair. And they hadn't the faintest idea of how to hitch up a span of oxen."**

So much for woman's part in building the west. This guy should have hung around a little longer to see those selfsame women pin up their hair, remove some of the petticoats and learn to hitch a span of oxen. He might also have checked into the lives of the native women who carried a heavy load in more ways than one. Being a woman was not all that much fun in the early days what with birth and death and everything in between.

As far as settlement was concerned, it was still mostly happening on the edges of the west—along the BC coast and in the Red River area of Manitoba. In between were the Indian and Metis people, and for them the 1870s were a disaster. First of all, smallpox. The disease decimated whole villages. It was terrible. Father Lacombe, for one, roamed the prairies providing Christian burials for the victims of the awful disease, regretting always that he couldn't start with a different Christian sacrament. Then the buffalo disappeared as if they'd never been. Plains Indians couldn't live without them. They literally starved.

So, the government had to step in. Mind you, the government wanted to step in anyway because they now owned all the land formerly held by the Hudson's Bay Company. It was one thing for the HBC to leave the Great Lone Land alone, leave it to the animals and Indians, but the Canadian government wanted to fill it up with settlers. So they had to have agreements with the Indians. Thus the various Indian treaties across western Canada. One more loss for Indian people.

But the west was open for business, as they say now. Manitoba joined Confederation in 1870, BC in 1871. Canada was building, and if you build it, they will come.

Thomas Ellis came, for instance, and settled in the Okanagan. Six years later in 1872 with a house, barn and cattle to his name, he visited his old home in Ireland and while there married Wilhemina Wade. Did she know when she said her vows in the green gentle hills of Ireland that her first trip in Canada would be over the Dewdney Trail, a twisty narrow mountain road from Hope through the mountains to the Okanagan area? And did she know that once she got to the ranch, there wasn't a corner store within hundreds of miles nor a hospital nor another woman? One can't help but wonder what those guys promised in order to get themselves a bride. Anyway, Thomas and Wilhemina made a good job of their lives, built a huge ranch, introduced fruit farming to the area, had nine children (one of whom would become Mrs. Pat Burns), built a church and just generally ran the show in their part of the world.

1874...Lock, Stock and Mistress...

Percy Criddle had two major surprises for Alice when he married her in 1874 in England. First, he told his bride that he had a mistress in Germany and four, soon to be five, children by her. Secondly, he said, we're all moving to Canada—lock, stock, barrel, mistress and children. So over they came to southern Manitoba and established St. Albans, a home/school/cultural centre quite unlike anything experienced by most pioneer Manitobans. Art, science, philosophy, the classics—all were experienced by the Criddle children, several of whom went on to distinguish themselves in the professions.

1874...The Gift of Gassy Jack...

Next time you're in Vancouver, go stand by a lamppost on Water Street right across from the Seabus Terminal. Try to block out all the pavement and buildings around you. Think mud, tree stumps, piles of sawdust, a few buildings helter skelter along the shore, the rain forest looming beyond. This is called Hastings Mill. Wander a few blocks west to what is now known as Gastown. Stand by the statue of Gassy Jack Deighton who owned a grubby hotel on this site in the 1870's. Then look across Burrard Strait to North Vancouver. Know that in 1874, it was known as Moodyville and it too was a mess, just a few buildings holding back the forest. Named for a Mr. Moody, it could just as well have gotten its name from the mood of the place, dark and sombre.

It was in this setting that Abbie Lowell Patterson, aged 15 years and two months, was married on December 2, 1874, to Capt. Frederick William Jordan, master of the barque Marmion moored at the Hastings Mill dock. The marriage was the first Christian marriage of a European maiden and man on the site of Vancouver, or so the records at the Vancouver archives say. The first resident Methodist minister on the mainland, Rev. James Turner, conducted the ceremony, and created his own wedding certificate on a blank sheet of paper, there being no systems in place for more formal registration.

Abbie designed her own dress—a light beige gown, and arranged her long dark hair around the wax orange blossoms lent to her by the mill manager's wife. Miss Ada Miller, daughter of the only policeman for hundreds of miles around, was her bridesmaid but history does not tell us what she wore.

Gifts included a brooch and earrings, and more to the point a case of wine and whiskey from Gassy Jack. When you're in Gastown, remember the man who contributed so much cheer to Abbie and Fred's wedding. Along with the liquid refreshments, the guests were treated to a buffet laid out on a table made from a single board. Had the guests been seated, there would have been room for at least 20, the tree from which the table was made was that large. As it was, there was enough room and enough food on the table to feed all residents of Burrard Inlet at that time.

Meanwhile across the water at Moodyville, the school kids got the afternoon off because a small ship in the harbor decided to salute the newly weds with a constant barrage of cannon shot. There was so much noise and smoke, the teacher sent everyone home. The folks across the water at Hastings Mill couldn't hear the wedding salutes, but they could see the smoke and appreciate the thought.

After the groaning board, the bridal party and guests walked across the sawdust spit to the community's reading room where toasts were made, songs sung, violins played. And then Abbie and Fred walked out to the Marmion and three days later left for China.

Captain Jordan and the Marmion continued freighting on the seas. Abbie accompanied him much of the time and was on board with several of their young children when the Marmion, loaded to the gunnels with coal, went down in a storm off Cape Flattery on the Olympic Peninsula. Fortunately, they were rescued in small boats. There were six children eventually and eventually the family settled in San Francisco.

1876...Four Times Out Of the Trunk...

Meanwhile, 274 men, bound for hope and glory or at least adventure, left the Red River area to cross the prairies to become North West Mounted Policemen. Not that any of them knew what a North West Mounted Policeman was exactly; they just knew that the government, especially John A. Macdonald, thought the west needed some policing. Whiskey traders, for example, were making a bad situation worse, selling liquor to disheartened and displaced Indians. Go forth and fix it, the NWMP members were told, and to their credit, they did, mostly.

Adventure was theirs in full measure. What was missing were women. R.B. Nevitt, a young doctor at Fort Macleod, wrote to his fiancée in Toronto about a dance he had attended. **"I was the belle of the ball,"** he explained, **"the only one who could dance the lady's part with anything like decency, and consequently my hand was sought after."** Two other NWMP members resorted to the want ads in the Montreal Star: **"Two lonely Mounted Policemen desire to correspond with a limited number of young ladies for mutual improvement."** Apparently, mutual improvement was all you could hope for when separated by thousands of miles.

James Macleod who became the Commissioner of the NWMP managed to snag himself a wife in the first few years of NWMP existence, but it took awhile. Mary Drever took her wedding dress out of the trunk four times before she actually got to wear it at her wedding.

James Macleod rode into Lower Fort Garry in the Red River settlement of Manitoba in 1870, handsome as all get out in his uniform and his position as a member of Wolseley's militia, there to make the west safe for one and all. Eighteen year old Mary

Drever was not easily impressed but there was something about this guy that caught her. Certainly, she wasn't looking for a protector. She knew how to do that herself. A native of the Red River area, daughter of two strong pioneers, she was as self reliant as they come. She had even stared down some of Louis Riel's men and smuggled important papers past their nose during the battle with government surveyors and government policies in 1870.

James Macleod and Mary Drever saw a fair amount of one another through the winter and spring of 1871, so it was no surprise when they announced their engagement. That's when she wrote off to Scotland for a wedding dress, but by the time it arrived, her father was ill and James was posted back to Ontario. She couldn't be in two places at once so opted to stay with her dad. The engagement was off. The dress was put in storage.

Two years later, Prime Minister John A. Macdonald decided that what the west needed most of all was a police force and to that end, James Macleod would make a dandy superintendent third-in-command of what he was calling the North West Mounted Police. Once again, James rode into Winnipeg resplendent in uniform and authority, and once again, he and Mary decided to wed. Spring 1874, that's when it would happen for sure. But come spring, James was named assistant commissioner and assigned a large share of the task of getting men, horses, equipment, food and supplies across the trackless prairie to what would eventually be known as southern Alberta. In the spring of 1874, it was just the back of beyond.

So was the wedding. Mary put the dress back into the trunk.

By November, 1875, after 18 months away from one another, James decided the only way he could ever get away to marry Mary would be to resign from the force. So he wrote her, told her to get ready again, he'd be there shortly. But along came the government and made him Commissioner of the NWMP. The big cheese. He couldn't turn it down. Mary put the dress away.

Seven months later, June 1876, he figured he had the situation under control. Forts Calgary and Macleod were up and running, his men had the illegal whiskey trade under some control, the Indians were beginning to trust them and vice versa. Time surely for a wedding. But wait—this is the moment that Sitting Bull headed north to Canada after the massacre at Little Big Horn. American authorities threatened to move into Canada and take the Sioux by force. The Canadian government thought they maybe should fight back. The Sioux threatened to fight anybody who came near them, and so on. It was such an explosive situation that James headed directly to Ottawa to calm them down, and Inspector James Walsh headed into the midst of the Sioux Camp to calm them down. Everyone calmed, except perhaps Mary who had to put her dress away one more time.

Still, the situation offered one compensation. James was in the east. Maybe he could make a small detour into Winnipeg to marry Mary on his way back west. Which is what happened. He arrived in the morning of July 28, 1876, and within hours they were married. It could have been the equivalent of a royal wedding in the Red River area—the Drevers were well known, Mary's sisters had married prominent churchmen, James Macleod was by this time something of a hero— but no. This was a wedding that couldn't wait upon pomp and ceremony.

The Daily Free Press account a week later was brief and rather amazing in its choice of words: **"On Saturday last, Col. Macleod, C.M.G. accompanied by his adjutant, Captain Dalrymple Clarke, left for Pelly to assume his position as Commissioner of the North West Mounted Police. Macleod is well known in the Prairie Province, having accompanied Colonel (now Sir Garnet Joseph) Wolseley's Red River Expedition in 1870, in the capacity of Brigade Major; and all join in congratulating him on his new and well-deserved appointment. The marriage columns testify to a circumstance in this connection of particular interest. On the day of his departure for the west, Colonel Macleod led to the hymeneal altar at St. James Church one of Manitoba's own fairest and favorite daughters in the person of Miss Mary Isabella Drever. All who know either of the parties concerned will wish both long life and unalloyed happiness."**

Mary got the long life and some alloyed happiness. James got a shorter life; he was only 58 when he died in Calgary, by then a judge of the Supreme Court of the North West Territories. Just before he died, he was hoping to slow down, to finally stay home for awhile and enjoy some family life. But it was not to be. There were five children. They and Mary had a tough time of it after he died for, in spite of the fact that James was known and respected across Canada, he had never made much money. It is said there was $8 left after funeral expenses were paid. Mary had to depend, once again, on her self-reliance and strength, which she did. She did some dressmaking, friends helped out and eventually her daughters made good marriages. The Canadian government was reminded that they might at least offer Mary Macleod a pension, but they declined, so the Legislative Assembly of the North West Territories made her a one-time payment of $600 and that was the sum total paid for a lifetime of dedicated service to Canada.

One more related wedding story—after James Macleod died, daughter Nell went to work as an accountant at the Hudson's Bay Company store in Calgary. Suddenly, Ernest Cross, rancher, founder of Calgary Malting and Brewing, one of Calgary's Big Four backers of the Calgary Stampede, found reasons to go shopping at the Bay and one day, he walked upstairs to the accounting office and proposed marriage, just like that. Just like that, Nell left her desk and together they left the store to tell her mother the news. Mind you, she came back later and worked until shortly before the wedding date. Her mother needed the money, after all. On her last day, she made an error of one million dollars in adding up the day's receipts. The chief accountant corrected it later.

Her mother proposed a sensible wedding dress—a gray thing lined with pale rose satin, something that would last for years and work for many occasions. When Nell told Ernest of her disappointment, he ordered from Toronto an ivory satin gown that had such a long train that one cowboy in the church that afternoon of June 8, 1899, couldn't resist. He pitched his cowboy hat on the train as Nell went up the aisle. That's the story anyhow, and if he didn't, he should have.

1877...Local Boy Seeks Wife...

Cornelius O'Keefe had to go out to get a bride. He'd come to central BC in 1861 in search of gold—who wasn't in 1861—but when he found land, water, wild grass, ideal ranching land around Lake Okanagan, he decided to stay put and become a rancher. Sixteen years, a house, many cattle and good prospects for a good life later, O'Keefe returned to his hometown near Ottawa and married Mary Ann McKenna. O'Keefe's mother didn't even recognize her son when he turned up on his old doorstep and his dad had died in the interim, so the marriage wasn't likely arranged by his parents. Who did make the connection then? Were there always women waiting in the wings of these hometowns, waiting for local boy makes good to come home?

Mary Ann may have been willing and available, but she wasn't completely crazy. She talked Cornelius into bringing his cousin Elizabeth Coughlan with them—as company for her, as adventure for Elizabeth. That must have been the best kind of good news for O'Keefe's partner, Thomas Greenhow, for he and Elizabeth hit it off and were soon married. Father Pandosy, the Catholic priest who's well known for bringing fruit trees into the Kelowna area, conducted the marriage ceremony.

1878...Finally A Proper Wedding...

James Douglas didn't live to see his youngest daughter, Martha, married but he would surely have been pleased. Sighed a sigh of relief perhaps because hers was such a terribly proper wedding with all the accoutrements of a society wedding. Ten bridesmaids, a wedding dress designed by Victoria's most prominent designer, the Mendelssohn wedding march, a sumptuous wedding breakfast. Even a wedding photo. By 1878, Victoria had enough people to support a photographer; the Douglas family had enough money to employ him.

The Reformed Episcopal Church was densely crowded, the Victoria Colonist newspaper reported, **"by a brilliant assemblage of ladies and gentlemen to witness the nuptials of Dennis R. Harris of the C.P.R. survey with Miss Martha Douglas, youngest daughter of the late Sir James Douglas, K.C.B. "** (Notice that mama Douglas doesn't get a mention although she's very much alive and in the very front row right of the wedding picture.)

The ten bridesmaids were all dressed in white tarlatan, trimmed with ivy and wearing wreaths of orange blossoms. Martha **"looked charming in a rich white satin**

dress, made with the skill and taste of a Parisian modeste (sic), beautifully trimmed with white tulle and orange blossoms. A white tulle veil descended in graceful folds from the bride's head and the bridal crown was a wreath of orange blossoms."

Following the ceremony, the happy couple and party returned to the residence of the unmentionable mama, Lady James Douglas, **"where a sumptuous wedding breakfast was spread for the guests."** And last but not least, the paper reported that **"presents were numerous, costly and exceedingly handsome."**

Douglas would have liked all that because of his everlasting troubles with marriages—his own, his daughter Alice's, his wife's parents. No matter how important he got, no matter how many titles, there was always the fact that he and Amelia, a mixed blood 16 year old, had married **"in the custom of the country"** in 1828. They married again **"in the custom of the church"** in 1837 but that didn't matter. Nor did it matter that they were a loving pair, stayed faithful to one another, had 13 children together. Inevitably, eyebrows would be lifted when the subject of Amelia came up. Douglas himself was something of a snob about Amelia. When Martha was living and studying in England, her father wrote her and said it was, of course, fine to talk about certain Indian beliefs but don't mention Mama.

Interestingly, Douglas himself was some sort of racial mix but that didn't seem to matter as much.

Amelia's father, William Connolly, added to the marriage messes when he decided to retire from the Hudson's Bay Company and move to Montreal. At first, Suzanne came with him. She was the daughter of a Cree chief and Amelia's mother. Theirs had been a country marriage also. But it wasn't long before William decided Suzanne wouldn't do after all, so he packed her off to a convent in Winnipeg and married Julia Woolrich, who indeed was rich. That wouldn't have caused a great stir in society circles— HBC men abandoned their country wives fairly frequently. But what did set tongues wagging was the fact that Amelia's brother contested their father's will, claiming to be a legitimate heir which brought into question the legitimacy of all the children, Amelia included. The wife of the Governor of British Columbia. Lady Douglas, wife of Sir James Douglas. Tut tut.

Eventually, the suit was settled; the country marriage was recognized as a legal marriage and the children as legitimate. Amelia began to appear in public again.

But then there was Alice, another Douglas daughter. At 17, she ran away with Charles Good, an Englishman with good credentials but bad judgment. He had served for awhile as personal secretary to James Douglas, which brought him into contact with young Alice and ended in their slipping over the border to Port Townsend. There they were married by a Justice of the Peace. There wasn't much papa Douglas could do when they got back, but he did insist that they be married properly in the church. He'd had enough grief over weddings in his lifetime. So they made it official August 31, 1861.

It was all downhill from there. Good couldn't manage money nor make it; Alice couldn't manage him and eventually told her father she **"couldn't bear to even see him"** (her husband). Nine years and three children later, she did a flit to England **"to give the children a better education,"** she said, but everyone knew she was leaving Good. Not so fast, however. Good came and got her, brought her back to Victoria where her father and the bishop lectured her on the duties of a Christian wife. Eventually, Good took himself back to the old country and Alice took herself to California where she obtained a divorce, married somebody else and generally disappointed her parents.

Martha must have behaved herself. She disappears from newspaper accounts, which is what good Christian wives should do, and eventually the whole family— Dennis, Martha and children—moved into the Douglas mansion with Amelia.

1879...Choose One...

Maria was a Pruden. If you had lived in the 1860s and 1870s in western Canada, you would not have needed an introduction to the Pruden family for they were part of the Hudson's Bay Company (HBC) family. So were the Kennedys. Be connected to the HBC in those days and you were part of a select group. Have a daughter within that HBC group and you were very select indeed because there was a shortage of eligible women. Thus when young Maria Pruden visited Winnipeg with her father, news got around that here was an eligible and desirable woman. She was subsequently observed and upon arriving back home in Edmonton received five proposals in the mail. **"Since I'm bound to lose you anyway, you have to choose one,"** her father announced. So she chose George Kennedy.

On December 13, 1879, Mary and George were married in Hudson Bay headquarters, also known as the Big House in Edmonton. It was a cold dull day but Maria swept into the big hall in a dress that was a **"miracle to behold,"** according to the newspaper report. **"It swept the floor grandly with as large a train as any of the Paris gowns to be seen in the fashion books of the day."** Made by a dressmaker in Winnipeg, it was made of gray silk alpaca with fine satin frills around the high neck and sleeves that were high and long. The piece de resistance was the bonnet trimmed with ostrich plumes that alone cost $5.00.

For their honeymoon, George and Maria left the next morning for the Peace River country, the first part of the trip to be by horse and sleigh, the final miles by dog team. It was 60°F below when they left but they were a tough bunch, those early HBC people. Maria and George both had otter skin caps that helped protect them from the elements. Maria's had the added feature of a long and fashionable silk veil, which sounds like an utterly useless item for travelling in the north, but maybe she was able to use it to keep the mosquitoes off in the spring. For the next 20 years, they moved around the north with the HBC and then retired to Edmonton. George lived to be 80, Maria to be 98.

A hard life was often a long life.

THE 1880s

Settlers, scandals, the triumphant CPR
and a defeated Riel

The White/Russell wedding, 1889, Medicine Hat, AB

1880...The CPR and Slippery Annie...

The poets called it a ribbon of steel. Sir John A. Macdonald called it the tie that binds a country together. BC Premier Amor de Cosmos called for a compromise and lost his job. The natives called it an unwelcome nuisance. The Metis called it an infringement of their land rights. The settlers called it a lifesaver even if it was noisy, dirty and late.

Thus was the Canadian Pacific Railway on everybody's mind through the 1880s. It was promised to BC back in 1871 when they came on board Confederation but Sir John A. Macdonald must have had his fingers crossed when he promised that. Or else he had his numbers crossed. Whatever, that transcontinental train was nearly the undoing of Canada. It cost more than anyone dreamed, it was harder than anyone dreamed, it took more lives than anyone feared, it was a nightmare. But once the final spike was hammered into the rail at Craigellachie in 1885, it became the best thing that had ever happened to Canada...except if you were native or Metis. Then it became one more loss, one more change.

The train, you see, brought more people. Settlements grew up alongside the railway, surveyors pounded markers and piled piles of dirt to mark out sections of land, preachers arrived with Bibles and rules, farmers came with barbed wire and ranchers came with wire cutters. The place started filling up.

Slippery Annie Barclay arrived in Medicine Hat in the early 1880s and established a precarious existence as bootlegger, laundress and community character. Her rival in all these activities was Nigger Molly (she doesn't seem to have another name recorded for posterity) who dispensed her illicit wares from special leather paniers built into her bustle and brassiere. History does not record Annie's method of distribution, but if she deserved her nickname, then she probably had a variety of trading practices.

The pair of rivals made good news copy for the fledgling local paper but Annie eclipsed all news when she announced her forthcoming marriage to one of her best customers, a French Canadian man whose name seems to have disappeared into the mists of time. Just as he did. Anyway, Annie and her fiancé, both the worse for wear, arrived at the church at the appointed hour only to discover that the organist had not yet appeared. Can't have a wedding without music, Annie said, so she sat down and pumped out a few verses of *Comin' Thro' The Rye* and *Pop Goes the Weasel*. Come to think of it—Annie was simply ahead of her time. If only she'd known that 100 years later brides would often choose secular music over sacred, just as she had done. However, the organist was not amused when he arrived. In fact, he had a fit that his sacred organ was being used in such a loose fashion. Nor was the minister too thrilled. Maybe the two of you had better go home and sober up, he told Annie.

"The trouble, yer Riverence is, he won't come back when he's sober." Poor Annie. The good news is that they did marry eventually and return to Quebec. Molly, in the meantime, had the bootlegging business all sewed up.

1880s...The Basket Case Bride...

Over on the West Coast, a much more sedate wedding took place in 1882. Miss Nellie Irving was married to William Sutton Chandler, son of David Chandler, Esq. who was, as the newspaper baldly announced, a San Francisco millionaire. That fact may have accounted for the reception which went on for several days and included all the guests. First, there was the formal reception with food and music and dancing and such. Then at midnight, the bridal party and guests climbed onto the steamer Rithet and went upstream to Yale. There they got onto a train **"kindly placed at their disposal by the contractor"** and went as far as the suspension bridge in order to get a really good look at the Fraser Canyon. As if that weren't enough scenery to last a lifetime, they climbed back on the steamer, went back to New Westminster, freshened up, and then boarded another boat to take them on a leisurely cruise through Burrard Inlet to Victoria. Then— are you ready—the bride and groom left by ship bound for a year's tour of Europe.

The newspaper account concludes, **"While New Westminster grudges the loss of the fair bride, the best wishes of the whole community for their safety and future happiness will accompany her and her chosen life partner."**

Jessie Ann Smith, John Smith's new bride in 1884, also got a close up look at the Fraser Canyon but it was no picnic for her. The train trip from Yale to the end of steel scared the wits out of her. She was from Scotland where trains were pretty tame. Not this one. The tracks were just being laid; they were tippy, they were covered by rocks in places. Jessie Ann thought she'd never been so scared. Then she saw the Fraser River boiling away beneath her and was told she'd have to sit in a basket on a cable to cross this inferno. No problem, the river man said, the basket would dump her into a pile of straw on the other side. Maybe she should close her eyes. No way, she said, **"If that rope breaks, I would like to see where I am going."** So she kept her eyes open but she thought she'd never been so scared. But then they had to take a two seater buggy along a narrow mountain trail so high she couldn't see the bottom of the chasms and valleys on all sides. She thought she'd never been so scared. Actually, her new husband had never been so scarred because she kept grabbing his arm in such panic that he was black and blue.

Once home, she went to bed and more or less died. At least, that's what she thought when she was awakened by sweet mandolin music, that she must be in heaven, but it was just a neighbor arriving to chivaree the newlyweds. A chivaree was a surprise party held by neighbors and friends once newly wed couples got settled in their own home. Not all included mandolin music. In fact, most were rowdy, noisy, often embarrassing events.

To her credit, Jessie Ann got used to her new life. Bridges were built, roads got a bit wider, the railway got a bit closer. And Jessie started an apple orchard that became well known throughout BC.

1880s...Let Us Flea To Canada...

To entice settlers to western Canada, the two big landowners—the CPR and the government—put out a series of pamphlets with so-called first hand information about life in the boonies. **"The winter is cold, but not as hard to endure as the cold of poverty,"** Mrs. M. McKay of Wapella, NWT, said in one of the publications. Other writers mentioned the cold but put a positive spin on it by explaining that lots of long underwear could solve that problem. And for goodness sake, don't put on English airs and don't be too proud to ask for help, another pamphlet urged.

As for women who might come looking for husbands, Mrs. J.N. Davidson of Rapid City, MB, said, **"Bring sufficient good sense to avoid all romantic ideas of accepting the first offer of marriage on arriving here; also frivolous notions about dress, reading novels and the like."** In other words, you're going to have to work, girl. Better know it.

With any luck, the would-be bride read her words before John Pollock's. **"If you have any young girls in your country who would like to start housekeeping, this is the place to come. There are lots of young men who want housekeepers. I would like to give over the job of washing the dishes myself."**

Who wouldn't, John?

In spite of the occasional discouraging word here and there, settlers did come—mostly for the land. For opportunity. For fun. For their sons. For adventure. For freedom. Johann Sveinson was born in Iceland in 1858, came to Gimli with his folks 18 years later, tried North Dakota for awhile and finally settled near Red Deer, AB. Here was good land. Here, he and Steinum Thordarson, married in 1884, would raise 12 children, and those 12 children would eventually fill the Central Alberta phone book with the name Swainson.

In 1885, Douglas Gregson, a "green Englishman", arrived in Calgary and bought a team and wagon to get himself to a homestead in central Alberta. Trouble was he'd never harnessed or unharnessed a team before, so that first night, he undid every buckle in sight. Got the horses out of harness, alright, but was a terrible job the next day when it came time to harness up again. Gregson was a bachelor, like most male newcomers to the west, and he stayed that way. Could have had something to do with his hobby. He collected fleas and sent them to a collector in England. Made good money too.

Joshua Martell left his boyhood home in Cape Breton to seek his fortune and have some fun out west. By 1883, he was a manager at a coal mine in Nanaimo but it wasn't that much fun because he still yearned for his childhood sweetheart. One day, he heard she had been widowed so he promptly sent off a poetic proposal that ended with this verse:

> **If the cap does not fit you, just toss it away**
> **And say I'll have nothing to do with this sorry lad**

> **But if you should think you were fitted quite well**
> **Just drop a short note to Joshua Martell.**

Barbara didn't bother with a note. She came, they were married in Victoria.

1880s...Always A Mistress, Never A Bride...

Nicholas Flood Davin was for awhile The Voice of the Northwest. The Smartest Thing to Ever Hit Regina. The Man of the Moment. He loved it, wore plaid pants and a top hat just to be sure people remembered him. And he deserved all the attention at first.

He came to Canada in 1872 and began using his incredible ability with words and wit by writing for newspapers and occasionally practicing law. His most famous law case was the defense of the man who shot George Brown, editor of the Globe and prominent Liberal politician. Since there wasn't much to defend—the guy had obviously done it, Davin used the occasion to unfurl all the eloquence at his command. It made great copy and Davin had his fifteen minutes of fame.

That wasn't nearly enough. This guy ate fame for breakfast, so he headed west and started a newspaper, The Regina Leader, and managed to scoop all the other newspapers in Canada when he got an exclusive interview with Louis Riel just before his execution. His coup was a typical piece of Davin daring. Knowing that news reporters were not allowed into the jail, he dressed up as a priest and told the jailers he was there to hear Riel's confession. It worked. He got his story and more glory.

He also got elected as MP for Assiniboia West and had a fine time in the House of Commons. But under all his swagger and chutzpah was a private life that got pretty complicated. Soon after Davin established himself in Regina along came Kate Simpson Hayes, also a writer, also clever, witty and wise. Well, maybe not so wise. Separated from her husband and with two children in tow, she opened up a millinery shop, started writing for various publications in Canada, played the organ at the local Catholic Church and organized a literary club. On top of all that eminently respectable activity, she had two children by Davin. Regina was a small city in those days; you'd think people would have noticed the two pregnancies but apparently not. The first child, Henry Arthur, was cared for by a housekeeper somewhere and the little girl, no name, was left at a Catholic orphanage.

Davin was keen to marry Kate and have his children with them, but she refused, apparently because of the Catholic church's disapproval of divorce. Sounds a bit contradictory but there may have been other reasons. Davin was 15 years older than Kate and dipping into the sauce a bit much. Kate for her part had things she wanted to do with her life—write, travel, adventure. So Davin up and married another woman that nobody had heard of, but one that was willing to raise Davin's children. She was Eliza Jane Reid of Ottawa, a good sport, by all accounts. Not only did she take on

Davin's "nephew," Henry Arthur, but she joined all the right clubs in Regina, went on the campaign trail with him, kept his plaid pants pressed.

She would have taken on Davin's "niece" as well but she was nowhere to be found. Gone from the records of the orphanage. Lost without a trace. Even the private detective that Davin hired to locate her had no luck. It was as if she'd never been born.

The only clue to her whereabouts came from some nuns who remembered the day that Davin and Kate brought the baby to them. At that time, Davin had privately asked that the child NOT be baptized in accordance with Roman Catholic rites. He was not Catholic. But the baby was sickly and the nuns feared she wouldn't live. Rather than sentence her to eternity without proper baptism, they changed her name and baptised her. And no one could remember or would say what that name was.

That signalled the beginning of the end for Davin. He was so capable, so full of himself, but he couldn't even keep track of his own daughter. What's more, he lost the next election, he didn't have the paper anymore, and he wasn't invited to the most important party ever held in Regina. Then, he happened to run into Kate in Winnipeg, Kate who was now the heavy duty women's editor of the Winnipeg Free Press and a name in literary circles across Canada. They spoke only briefly on the street but in that moment Davin told her he'd like to acknowledge his two children in his will and name her as their mother. Kate didn't like the idea at all, gave him a dirty look and said, **"You go your way and I'll go mine."**

Two days later, he bought a gun and killed himself.

His wife did the right thing—honored him with a huge monument and many words in Ottawa's Beechwood Cemetery. Kate went her way, making a name for herself as the first woman journalist in Canada. The son, Henry Arthur Davin, went overseas in 1914 and was killed in the trenches in 1916. The official death notice stated the cause of his death was a rifle bullet through the heart.

And the daughter? She is still something of a mystery although there are letters in the SK Archives from Agnes Hammell who, by the sounds of things, had a perfectly awful life. She did grow up in a Catholic orphanage and for awhile believed she was the child of an errant priest. Not surprisingly, she was a troubled kid, cried a lot, was sick a lot. When she joined the Sisters of Sion at Prince Albert, the other sisters decided she was insane and nudged her out of the order. It was then that she began seeking answers about her origin.

Apparently, she started with the priest that she so hated because there's a letter from him dated April 27, 1925, that says, **"After well nigh 30 years holding back the truth from my dear Agnes, I now must tell all I know and I know enough."** He goes on to say that Davin was her father, he doesn't know the name of her mother, and she has a brother—Henry Arthur. In fact, he says, Henry Arthur came to see him about his sister but when he heard she was a nun decided not to disturb her religious life.

Speaking of disturbed, Agnes was really upset when she realized she might have met her brother, might have known something about her family, but the powers-that-be had discouraged it. As well, she wanted to know if he'd had a will. Was she mentioned? **"But that is not the important point now,"** she wrote in a letter dated June 26, 1925. **"It is this—who was my real mother? Where is she? There is a woman who claims to know and of course I am willing to work for the money she wants in order to find my own mother, but I could be fooled and I don't want to be."**

She ended the letter thus: **"I go by the name I sign not knowing sooner that my father was Nicholas Flood Davin. Please help me Sister. Pray to remember what Arthur said. Send me every detail. I will be so grateful."** Signed…Agnes Hammell.

What a tragedy. There is no record that Agnes ever hooked up with Kate. A teacher for awhile, an artist and finally a housekeeper, she sounds throughout her file of correspondence like a very troubled woman. She never married.

1880s…Evelina's Curse Upon Riel…

While the government and the CPR thought the railway was the most important thing happening in Canada in the 1880's, the Indians and Metis thought Louis Riel was. He was, after all, protesting that blasted railway. He was sticking up for the natives who were losing their land, their livelihood, their very being. He may have been a bit hard to figure out but at least he spoke up. He spoke out.

When he decided to form his own government and base it in Batoche in what is now northern Saskatchewan, his countrymen thought that was just fine. If the suits in Ottawa could make a government, why couldn't they? They'd been in the west longer; they shouldn't be pushed out without a by-your-leave. And Riel was willing to take that message to Ottawa. He was their man.

Even when the words turned into armed conflict in the spring of 1885, he was still their man although they rather wished that Gabriel Dumont could be in charge of military affairs while Riel looked after governmental affairs. Dumont was a much better tactician, a natural military leader. However, neither Dumont nor Riel could hold out against government troops armed with cannons and NWMP armed with authority. The North West Rebellion was more or less over by summer 1885, and Louis Riel was hanged for his part in it by November, 1885. It might have ended there.

But Riel became an even larger hero. Today he's known as the Father of Manitoba, and is celebrated in song and literature. He even has two statues in his honor in Winnipeg. One of the statues is a fearsome looking black thing that looks vaguely like a man wrapped in a cloak; the other is your basic bronze statue of a man larger than life. Together, they're something like Riel himself. A puzzle. A hero. A traitor. A martyr. A flawed human being.

What doesn't make it into the history books and the headlines is anything about Riel, the husband and father.

Riel's family lived in the French part of the Red River settlement, and young Louis did well in school, so well in fact that Bishop Tache arranged for him to take religious training at a college in Montreal. There, he fell in love with a young woman and left college to marry her, only to be rejected by his beloved's family. It was a life of wandering from then on—to the US for awhile, back to the Red River and a major part in the 1870 uprising, back to the US to escape prison, back to Quebec for a spell in an insane asylum, back to the US where finally he met Evelina and decided to settle down. Enough of this rootless life, except that he had no money and no prospects and soon no Evelina. He was 35 years old.

So, he wandered west to Montana and somewhere along the way married Marguerite Monette, a young Metis woman 16 years his junior. Their first wedding ceremony was likely conducted by her father but Riel was too religious to let it go at that. He had a Jesuit missionary bless their union just in time for the birth of their first child—a son, Jean, born in spring of 1882.

A year later, Evelina caught up with him. Theirs was a misunderstanding a mile wide. Riel thought she had told him to go away because he'd never be able to support her. She thought he was going away to make enough money to support her. Tell me it isn't so, she wrote to Louis when she heard about his marriage. **"If you do not do so, you will bring on yourself the greatest curses God can utter, for having destroyed forever the future of one who, if this is the case, has a single regret, having known and loved you."**

She was a scorned woman and mad as hell but what could Riel do? He was married, his wife was about to have their second child. What's more, there was talk of rebellion on the prairies again. Riel was being courted to take on leadership once more. So, Evelina 's anger was never dealt with, but her curse hurt. Riel had visions, he wrote and thought constantly about God and the saints, he prayed all the time. The last thing he wanted was a bad luck curse.

The North West Rebellion was one of the most confusing, one-sided battles ever fought. It wasn't planned, it wasn't organized, it wasn't fair, but Riel's men did shoot at soldiers and NWMP, and vice versa. In the end, the guns won, as guns do, and Riel was rounded up and put in jail for treason. His trial was quick, the verdict harsh— execution by hanging.

All through his grown life, he had been a prolific writer of poetry and philosophy, some of which is mad, some of which is brilliant. If only he could have been an ordinary man so that people could have understood him, but he was so complex and so crazy at times, there was no understanding him. Anyway, this is what he wrote about his family while in jail: **"My God! Through the divine grace of Jesus Christ, guide and mercifully show my wife how to raise our little children, the precious little children You have given us. Let her make them behave at meals; let her make them understand at an early age the advantages of temperance in eating and drinking. Saint Joseph,** bless my wife that she may be a Christian mother most pleasing to God in everything, always and everywhere, but particularly in seeing to the education of her children."

Those poor children. A third child was born shortly before Riel's execution but lived two hours only. Riel never saw him and said later that the child had had **"an hour to be born and an hour to die."** The middle child, Marie-Angelique, a blonde beauty in whom Riel took great pride, died of diphtheria just before her 14th birthday. And Jean, the oldest, died at age 26 from a seemingly minor fracture. He had no descendants so Riel has no direct descendants.

Six months after Riel's death, Marguerite died too. There's not one happy thing about this story—the land rights of natives and Metis have never been entirely settled, the North West Rebellion was a civil war—Canadians vs Canadians—in a nation that thinks of itself as peaceful, and Riel still doesn't rest in peace in the minds of Canadians. Witness the arguments within government over the possibility of granting Riel a posthumous pardon.

Still, life goes on and it did in 1885 also. Annie Brown had the bad luck to arrive in Regina in the midst of North West Rebellion fever. First, she tells her sister about the wedding itself on May 27, 1885: **"This is only a hurried line to tell you Tom and I were married this morning at 11 o'clock but at Regina instead of as hoped at Qu'Appelle. All the ministers of this district are here attending a convention and though Tom would have even come as far as Winnipeg if it could have been done, there was nothing for it …but to come on here. …I almost forgot to tell you that a little girl friend of Tom's presented me with a bunch of lovely prairie flowers in church."**

A few weeks later, she quotes her husband saying, **"I saw McGir from the Indian office tonight. He tells me they are greatly strengthening the Indian reserves at Battleford, Fort Pitt and other places of the rebellion. I only hope I shall not be elected for I should dread taking you among those beasts."** Needless to say, Annie stays awake the rest of the night thinking about the two women who were taken hostage by the Indians at Frog Lake when nine men were killed there in one of the first battles of the rebellion.

Still, Annie, as lonesome as she is and as frightened, learns to like the place. **"I unpacked my boxes and fitted up my kitchen shelves and draped my bed and windows, baked and cooked to my heart's content and was very happy as I looked from my doors for though it was but the weary weary prairie, yet as far as my eye could reach the rich land with its teeming pastures was my very own, for English people can hardly comprehend an estate of 320 acres."**

There it is—the eternal conundrum of the west. Louis Riel was right—the Indian and Metis had been there first. The land was theirs. But Annie comes from England on the invitation of the Canadian government. In good faith, she and husband claim 320 acres, work them, love them. By their efforts and their love, they claim the land.

Who's on first and what's on second?

1884...Horse Thief or Bridegroom?

Annie Hislop's wedding was just about the most exciting thing that happened in the summer of 1884 in the district of Arcola, NWT. It was the first formal wedding in the area for one thing and for another, it was a chance to socialize, to meet some neighbors and think about something besides work. So people came from all over, making their way through prairies grass and flowers to the Hislop homestead.

There, they made their way to the back bedroom where the actual marriage ceremony was to take place. The kitchen and living room parts of the house were full of tables covered with food, so the back bedroom got the nod. Decorated with a bridal arch made of prairie flowers with more prairie flowers in bowls around the room, it looked downright festive, not at all like a bedroom. And there, Annie and Dougald Strachan said their vows.

Annie didn't come from a good Scottish family for nothing. Her dress was a practical brick red color, designed with a bustle and tight bodice, high neck and fitted sleeves. She'd be able to get lots of wear out of it after the ceremony. Dougald was almost more splendid than his bride in that he wore a black broadcloth suit, white starched stiff shirt and stiff collar. In fact, he had been detained in Moosimin when he got off the train there enroute to Arcola. He looked too good to be true so the local NWMP checked him out to be sure he wasn't the horse thief they'd been looking for.

During the signing of the register, J.M. White sang, *O Love That Will Not Let Me Go*, a hymn that still finds its place in wedding ceremonies. And then it was party time. First the food—sliced ham and mutton, vegetables, pickles and salads, as much butter as you could pile on fresh bread and cakes of every description. Last but not least, wild strawberries and cream.

No wine or spirits. The Hislops were teetotallers and so was the territory at the time. So it was tea with all the cream and sugar that you could want. **"It's a fine spread you've put on,"** neighbor Mrs. Robert Kerr said to Annie's mother as she left to walk the two miles to her home where the cows and babies awaited her attention.

She was the only one to leave for there was dancing to be had. Dan McDougall tuned his fiddle and then played *Inverness Gathering* for the bride and groom. Guests whispered that they'd heard Annie had fallen for Dougald because of his splendid dancing and now they knew it was true. There was such feeling in that little crowd, appreciation for love and community and homeland.

At dawn, Annie's father strapped trunks and parcels to his buckboard and took the newly weds 75 miles across the prairies to Moosimin where they boarded the train for their new home.

1886...Around the World in 103 Days...

Alfred Garrioch, a missionary with the Anglican Church, worked among the Beaver Indians in northern Alberta and eventually developed a Beaver alphabet with which he translated some of the Scriptures. In London, England, in 1886, to get this material printed, he met Agnes and married her. Agnes was a city girl. Imagine her reaction when, 103 days after leaving London, she stood on top of the Dunvegan hill looking down at the Peace River, and saw exactly three buildings. One was theirs, one was the Hudson's Bay trader and one belonged to the Catholic priest. Beyond them stretched hills, bush, sky—not a road to be seen, not a store or doctor or hospital.

Their first child survived but only because a native woman wet nursed him. The second baby was not so lucky. A day after Caroline was born, Garrioch wrote in his diary for April 26, 1888: **"Our dear little daughter passed away at 6 o'clock this evening. Its autograph text in Mrs. Garrioch's book of birthdays is 'Blessed be the name of the Lord.' And while our tears flow, we are endeavoring to be resigned."**

Baby Caroline was buried behind their wilderness mission center. The fence that her father built around her to protect her from the animals is still there, next to a grove of maples that he started as well.

It wasn't easy, this business of pioneering in a new country. It wasn't easy being an Indian or Metis either, the people who thought their home was on the range, any range. In 1881, the natives outnumbered Europeans by eight to one; twenty years later, they were outnumbered five to one.

1889...Bridegroom on the Ropes

Nobody knows for sure but family lore has it that Dave White was in his cups one night at the NWMP barracks in Medicine Hat, AB, when who should appear but a bonny Scottish lass singing an old country ballad and dancing the Highland Fling? Of course, Dave proposed. How could he not? He was far from his home in Ireland, she was young and lovely and far from her home in Scotland. The fact that the Scottish and Irish weren't always pals in the old country didn't matter anymore; they were in Canada now.

 Maybe he got cold feet the next day; there are those who say so. Maybe Elizabeth got so upset she went to Regina to stay with her brother for awhile; that too is said. Maybe that brother did mention certain broken promises to the NWMP brass, but never mind all the premarital jitters. They were married August 7, 1889, and to all intents and purposes, they lived happily ever after. In fact, the newspaper account of their 50th anniversary party reported that **"the happiness reflected on their faces did much to convince one, if any convincing was needed, that the married state is the ideal one for normal human beings."** That's from the Maple Creek News, August 17, 1839.

Dave White came to Canada in 1884 and promptly hooked up with the most exciting game in town—the North West Mounted Police. On November 16, 1885, in Regina, he was one of the guards assigned to keep the crowds in order at the hanging of Louis Riel. In fact, there's another rumour about Dave White that's irresistible. It is said that he kept the rope that hanged Riel and sold pieces of it later…when he was in his cups. He was, as they say, a convivial man.

Elizabeth Russell came from Scotland to visit her brother in the Cypress Hills area and ended up working as a home nurse and midwife at the NWMP barracks in Medicine Hat. That's where she met the smooth talking Irishman, and that's where this story started. A year after they were married, Dave and Elizabeth moved to a ranch in the Cypress Hills near Maple Creek, SK, and that's where the White family dynasty started. There were eight children. They had children and so on. The White ranch is still in

White hands, and the present generation is rather proud of the interesting stories about the first Canadian Whites. Donny White, curator at the Medicine Hat Museum, says loyally of them, **"I like to think their marriage turned out just as Elizabeth and Dave imagined on that first night they met at the Police Barracks."**

1889...Spittoons at the Altar...

Anna Scott Harvey could certainly have been forgiven for having second thoughts about her marriage. In fact, she could have been forgiven for turning right around and going back to Ireland. Trouble was she didn't have the money so she had to try to find her intended somewhere in the Chilcotin region of northern BC. It was like looking for a needle in a haystack, the Chilcotin being in 1889 one big mostly empty area without telephones, mail service or roads.

In the meantime, Alexander Graham was toiling away on an isolated ranch, knowing that he had sent money for Anna's trip but not knowing just when she might arrive.

Anna had already travelled halfway around the world—by boat to New York and then by railway to Ashcroft, BC. No sign of Alexander, so she climbed on the stage to Soda Creek, a bumpy dusty ride that took three days. Still no Alexander. By now, she figured she'd been jilted, abandoned, forgotten, but since she still had the problem of insufficient funds, she decided to stay in the hotel at Soda Creek for a few days to think about her options. That too was an eye opener—literally. The hotel had been built with green lumber so that as the boards dried, they left inch wide cracks in the walls. With no privacy at all, Anna found it hard to sleep. Mind you, the bedbugs didn't help either. They kept dropping from the ceiling onto her bed so that she had to stay awake to beat them off. After a sleepless night, she was a wreck.

That was when, wouldn't you know it, Alexander finally found her. Her letter had been lost in the mail. Actually, it wasn't lost; it was just slow. When you live 150 miles from the nearest post office, it can take awhile for a letter to arrive courtesy passing neighbors or passing strangers.

It still wasn't happy-ever-after time. Anna and Alexander now had to find a minister. Back onto the bumpy stage coach until finally in Clinton, they found a minister who just happened to be travelling from Barkerville back to England. Sure, he'd take time to marry them. So that was done in the Clinton Hotel, no flowers or decorations except for the row of well used brass spittoons which decorated the foyer of the famous old hotel.

Now came the honeymoon trip. If Anna had signed up for an adventure tour, she couldn't have asked for more, but as it was, she had just signed up for a marriage. She didn't know about the Fraser River and the fact she'd have to cross it in a dugout canoe that also ferried a sheep. She didn't cross that river again until a bridge was built 23 years later. She didn't know that women were expected to put their legs around a horse and therefore had to let ankles and sometimes even shins show. Nor did she know that riding a horse left a body so sore and tired. She was one tired camper when they finally got to the Withrow ranch days later. At least she could rest for a little while on the straw filled mattresses next to the cast iron stove in the log shack with the wash tub hanging on the wall right outside the door. Then she realized these things were her responsibility. There was no going back.

Year later, after the Grahams built up their own considerable ranch, Anna became the local postmistress. She was one who knew how important a good mail service could be.

1889...Fire, Brimstone and Racket...

Charles Wagstaff and Sarah Cotton had a different kind of problem with transportation when they were married in Medicine Hat in 1889. Theirs was the first recorded wedding in Medicine Hat and because it was such a big deal, Wagstaff's fellow workers on the CPR decided to make a joyful noise and then some. Thus, they turned on every whistle that would whistle, every horn that would blow, as soon as the young couple stood before the minister in a house near the train station. The noise deafened everyone except the minister who, because he was deaf already, just kept right on saying the words that would make them husband and wife.

It's a scene that Hollywood could use, especially the part about the selfsame jokers holding burning torches to light the way for the newly weds after they left the church. A torchlight parade except that the torches were brooms dipped in oil and set alight. A hot time in the old town that night!

THE 1890s

New Canadians by the boatload, gold diggers by Bonanza, wives for sale, and Hallelujah!

The Bomford/Small wedding, 1892, Medicine Hat, AB

53

1890...No Mush Allowed...

The 1880s in western Canada had been so action packed what with railways, rebellions and cultural revolutions that it's no wonder the 1890s started out on the slow side. The west paused to yawn for a year or two. Also to mourn. Chief Crowfoot of the Blackfoot nation in southern Alberta died in 1890 and Sir John A. Macdonald in 1891. Both deaths signaled change for the west. Crowfoot's death meant there was one less wise person making sense of all the unhappy changes being forced upon his people, and Macdonald's ditto.

Macdonald may have got himself into the glue about money for the railroad, but he did force the original four provinces of Canada—Ontario, Quebec, Nova Scotia and New Brunswick—to understand there was a west and we could belong to the same country even if it would have been easier and more logical to make north/south connections. That's what he did—he put the west into the map of Canada.

In contrast, Crowfoot's nation was losing its place on the map when he died. The Indians of western Canada were mostly on reserves by then, under the control of government agents and government money. They barely knew if they were coming or going, but it mostly felt like they were going. To have Crowfoot die in the midst of such anguish was too much.

So it was time on all western fronts to take a breather. To slow down and add up.

Even romances were pretty restrained. Rev. David McQueen in Edmonton wrote this matter-of-fact letter to his sister: **"They all tell me I would be better if I were married to the right kind of woman. But that is just where the trouble comes in, and besides, at present, I see no way of keeping anymore than myself. Furniture here is very dear. The common chair on which I am sitting at present cost $4.00 and I had to put it together myself. I paid $2.50 for a granite water pitcher and $8.50 for a mattress, and everything else in proportion. It would take a fortune to furnish a house in good style in this part of the world."**

However, a few years later, he met a woman for whom he felt some "attraction," he said. In fact, he thought perhaps there was "mutual attraction." That was as mushy as he was going to get—in print anyway. When he and Catherine Robertson were married in Ontario in 1890, they left immediately by train for Calgary where they changed to horse and buggy for the remainder of the trip to Edmonton. Whether he had more furniture by that time is never mentioned, but apparently Catherine made a splendid minister's wife.

1890...No Arguments Over Religion...

Henry Moffat didn't waste any mushy words either. This is what he wrote about his wedding day in his diary: **"I, Henry Moffat, and Jennie Roddie got united in**

matrimony at A.D. McInnis's at 11 am by the Holy Father Martiat. Had a good dinner and then drove home, arriving here at 7 pm."

He does not record the wedding gifts received but maybe they were given the chicken that ran across the yard just as the picture was taken. After all, they planned to run Lansdowne House, a stopping place for teamsters and travellers going north to Barkerville. They would need one chicken in the pot at all times, one ready for the pot and others near the door at all times. That's how you ran a combination hotel, restaurant and stable in the 1890s.

And speaking of pictures, it's the only one in the book that includes a shotgun in the hands of a wedding guest. It must have been a source of pride for the young man who's holding it, that and nothing more, for the wedding was not a shotgun wedding. That's the term for a wedding that is forced upon a groom by an angry father who fears the wedding will be followed in less than nine months by the birth of a baby. Henry and Jennie were married August 15, 1890. Nine months and two weeks later, safely past the limit, Henry recorded in his diary, **"Born this day at 6 o'clock in the evening in Lansdowne House by my wife a fine son weighing about 10 pounds and all well, thank God."**

As well as running the very busy stopping place, Henry operated his own freighting outfit up and down the road to Barkerville. When he was away, Jennie took on the diary responsibilities. On June 7, 1892, she said, **"Very heavy rain here tonight….Alexander Bohanon Moffat started to creep tonight for the first time at 6 o'clock."** (Alexander was the fine son mentioned above.)

On June 30, 1892, she wrote, **"No one passed today."**

On January 2, 1894, she wrote, **"Mr. Middleton, Mr. Craig, Mr. Olson, Mr. McLeod, John McInnes. All came here this morning and drunk wisky (sic) and ate cake so they could not see straight."**

The diary entries also serve to measure Jennie's moods. If she refers to her husband as Mr. Moffat, the winds blow cold. If he's Henry Moffat, the weather's a bit warmer, but if he appears as Harry, then Harry can come in out of the cold.

There was no arguing about religion, however. Early in their marriage, they agreed that any Moffat boys would be raised Protestant like their father, the girls Catholic. There were five boys, four girls. Mind you, there is a rumour that Jennie secretly baptised the boys when she was mad at Mr. Moffat, but the present day relatives doubt the rumour. Seems that most of the cousins on the male Moffat side are Presbyterians while the female side are Catholic.

So Canada in the early 1890s snoozed along. Some settlers came into the west and took up homesteads. Some left once they discovered their grain froze before it ripened. Some ranchers tried ranching, then lost their cattle in terrible blizzards. Many moved on. Here and there a store opened, here and there a school bell rang. But there was no stampede, no great rush to take up the land that waited under the big skies. Until Clifford Sifton, that is.

Without Sir John A. Macdonald at the helm, the Conservatives lost the federal election in 1886, and Liberal Sir Wilfred Laurier won. He, in turn, put Sifton on the throne of the west. He made him Minister of the Interior; his job to fill up all that land out there. That's when Sifton made his famous speech about immigration. **"I think a stalwart peasant in a sheepskin coat, born on the soil, whose forefathers have been farmers for ten generations, with a stout wife and a half dozen children, is good quality."**

Sounds pretty patronizing in today's terms but in 1890s Canada with its largely British population, those were fighting words. Russians, Poles, Ukrainians, Eastern Europeans, were not held in high regard. They couldn't speak the language. Their churches had onion shaped domes on them. They smelled of garlic. They didn't know Queen Victoria from a hole in the ground, etc. But Sifton paid no attention, sent agents and information all over Europe and in 10 years brought 250,000 people to the prairies. An amazing feat of human migration.

Then, just so BC wouldn't feel left out, gold was discovered in the Yukon. Guess where the gold seekers came to first? Guess where a whole lot of them stayed?

1891...The Cowboy Poet...

Oh, to be in 1891 when romance was considered manly, when even hard ridin', hard livin' cowboys took time out to write a passionate proposal like this:

"Dear, I don't know what you will think of me, but I must tell you I can't keep it any longer I love you, do you think that you can take me, if you only know how dearly I love you, I am sure you would. Miss, it is time to get married we'll soon be getting old we are made to get married why should not get married, I never could think of no one else but you and you are the first one and the only one. Goodbye miss I will see you some day. Yours respectfully, Wm. Kane. PS...you will find a silk handkerchief."

How any woman could resist such a heartfelt appeal is hard to imagine, and Susan Watkinson didn't. A poem then followed from her suitor:

> **"O let the love that I have shown, by you remembered be,**
> **and let it be known that you belong to me.**
> **But while we wait for that sweet day,**
> **we'll wipe our bitter tears away,**
> **since we are not alone."**

They were married December 15, 1891.

Billy Kane was a handsome devil, a rancher on the Cariboo Trail in northern BC. A horse whisperer before that term became popular, he was very knowledgeable about the ways of his horses and consequently was able to increase his herds and do a lively business with horses, cattle and grains. Susan Watkinson lived with her family on a neighboring ranch cum stopping place, and that's how they met. She too was a thoroughly capable woman, raised on a remote ranch, used to frontier conditions. When Billy proposed, she got busy and made her own wedding dress, a rust colored brocaded silk with a bustle, peplum and 18 handmade buttonholes that would do any modern machine proud. The dress is still worn by family members but they have to be very small to get into it. The last time it appeared it was on a 13 year old great great granddaughter.

Billy and Susan ended up with three farms, seven sons and one daughter.

1891...Gifts Fell Like Rain...

O to be in Victoria when the Cridge/Laundy wedding took place, a most splendid affair made even more splendid by the presence of the bride's father, Bishop Cridge of the Reformed Episcopalian Church. His was a household name in Victoria, the man who had spurned the Anglican Church to become a minister in the Episcopalian Church.

An unheard-of switch but Cridge did it and took most of the Anglican congregation with him. It was a huge story in Victoria so naturally the wedding of his daughter Ellen had extra appeal. She was marrying Thomas Laundy, a Bank of BC employee. He gets short shrift in the descriptions of the wedding but then bridegrooms often do. The bride—and in this case, her father—are the stars of the event.

This is how the newspaper described her entrance. **"Every eye was fixed upon the main door as it opened to admit the bride, leaning upon her father's arm. She wore white surah silk, Princess style, with court train and lace flouncing. A white girdle and full veil completed the costume, 'and never did a bride appear more fair.' Her wreath was of real orange blossoms and the same sweet flowers were prominent in her hand bouquet...which was decorated with delicate hand-painted streamers."**

She had four bridesmaids—Miss Cridge attired in salmon pink Bengaline silk, Miss E. Pemberton in Nile green, Miss S. Pemberton in pale blue and Miss Green in heliotrope. Master Edward Cridge, nephew of the bride, was dressed *á la* Little Lord Fauntleroy in blue velvet and white lace. Her niece wore white nun's veiling and lace.

And so on. There was no stone unturned for this occasion. The entire church choir sang, a party of children strewed flowers before the newly weds, and the gifts—the gifts were so numerous that the newspaper reported, **"they may be said to have fallen in a silver shower, so many were they and so valuable."** Among the numerous gifts, every one of which was listed in the newspaper, were six silver salt cellars.

How could any wedding be more splendid?

1891...Twenty Maids All in a Row...

A week later in Victoria, the Cridge/Laundy wedding was completely eclipsed, wiped off the map, by the Dunsmuir/Musgrave wedding. The difference? Money, pure and simple.

Jessie Sophia Dunsmuir was the daughter of Sir Robert Dunsmuir, the millionaire coal king of BC. He wasn't terribly popular with the thousands of men who worked in his mines—he outlawed unions and worked his men ruthlessly—but he had money. Money bestows status, no matter how it's earned, so the Dunsmuir's were Society with a capital S. And when they built the biggest most expensive house in Victoria, also known as Craigdarroch Castle, they ruled by the divine right of money.

Jessie, daughter #6, very cleverly added to the laurels of the Dunsmuir family by finding herself a husband with a title. He was Sir Richard John Musgrave, Baronet, of Waterford County, Ireland. Actually, he was the clever one. His family had a title, land, entry to British royal circles and all that, but they didn't have a whole lot of money. It was a match made in heaven or the nearest bank, whichever.

The **"most fashionable and brilliant wedding witnessed in Victoria for many months"** took place in Christ Church Cathedral, of course. Even if Rev. Cridge had taken away most of the congregation, it still had the reputation and size required for a wedding like this. Size mattered for a whole lot of reasons. Take the decorations, for example. **"Many a time has the old cathedral been decked with bright flowers for some festive event, but never more artistically or more effectively than yesterday. Palms predominated the decorations, forming a wall of green between the chancel screen and the interested congregation. The choir rails were hidden in a wealth of white roses, asters and verbena; the pulpit was festooned with ivy, relieved with hydrangea, and the altar was embedded in roses,"** the Victoria Daily Colonist reported. They did not report where Rev. Canon Beanlands stood among the embedded roses.

The invited guests were the cream of Victoria society. Again the newspaper sorted out the haves and have nots of the situation. **"Two o'clock was the hour set for the ceremony and at that time the body of the Cathedral was filled with invited guests while hundreds of ladies and dozens of gentlemen not so highly honored, crowded the side seats in the church, the aisles, the churchyard and the streets. Those fortunate in securing outside standing room were forced to content themselves with one short look at the bride as she entered the church."**

It was as close to a royal wedding as BC ever got, including the fact that Jessie was attended by six young bridesmaids, two trainbearers, two flower girls and 20 maids of honor.

And the dress? How did it rate among the embedded roses and the 30 beautiful attendants, most of whom were also in white? It tried. It really tried, but in a picture taken after the wedding of Jessie with her 20 maids of honor, it looks like just another expensive dress. It was brocaded in silver in the pattern of the Prince of Wales crest and the veil and trimmings were of Honiton lace, both features being the most expensive options available.

Once again, the gifts were listed in the newspaper, everything from the bride's mother's gift of an emerald and diamond ring and cheque to a silver salt cellar from Mr. and Mrs. Tye. (Only one salt cellar for this couple.) These lists must have made very interesting reading for rich and poor alike—the rich could compare notes on who gave what and how much it cost; the poor could only shake their heads and wish.

Money didn't, in the end, buy the Dunsmuirs happiness. Jessie kept her end of the bargain. Lived in Ireland and mixed with high society, paid for much of it with Dunsmuir money but lived a rather lonesome life so far from home. Her two brothers who might have been expected to take over their father's coal and railway empire after he died were foiled by their mother who held the purse strings and control. One of them died young; the other tackled politics for awhile—premier of BC for a few years, the lieutenant governor for a few more, but he didn't like politics. After a messy court case about control of the Dunsmuir fortunes, he retreated into a private life.

The daughters, all eight of them, got married and with the help of Dunsmuir money had big houses and a place in society. Some enjoyed it.

1892...Made Happy For Life...

There was a wedding in Medicine Hat, AB, on December 27, 1892, and this is how the Medicine Hat Times reported the event: **"The Christmas season has brought more than its usual number of weddings this year, a sure indication of the ever increasing prosperity of the Territories. The last one, which made happy for life Mr. Seymour Bomford and Miss Mary Small, was a very pleasant affair. Misses Calder and Davis acted as bridesmaids and Mr. Sherman supported the bridegroom through the trying ordeal. The knot was tied by Rev. C. Stephen after which the numerous guests were treated to a sumptuous supper and a dance by the bride's parents."**

Also in the local news that week were these pieces of Medicine Hat life:

"Mr. James Sanderson commences next week to harvest ice on the river. The ice this year is said to excel that of any previous year."

"Mr. E. Pearson returned from Brandon, MB, last week. He reports business bright and active in the wheat city."

"Owing to the number of other dances in town this week, the committee of management of the Quadrille Club have decided to hold no meeting this week."

Obviously Medicine Hat is pleased with itself in the last week of 1892, and why not? The town is growing slowly but surely, the CPR roars through regularly, some locals have actually managed to make trees grow, there's a hospital in the community now and more dances than dancers.

As for the couple "made happy for life," it seems as if they were. The groom may have needed help through the trying ordeal in 1892 but in 1952 when they celebrated their 60th wedding anniversary, he held his own nicely. **"Life has been good to us,"** he told the assembled guests and gave his bride a diamond ring. It was their diamond wedding anniversary, after all.

The couple met on a ferry going to a community picnic. She was 15, he 23. She bought an ice cream cone from him and he said, **"You're going to be my girl."** How could any girl resist that dashing mustache and so they were married several years later. Her wedding dress was the latest in fashion—wasp waisted with puff sleeves and fine detailing on the bodice. He wore a three-piece suit, a high collar, silk tie with jeweled pin and a watch chain.

He didn't get a new watch to go with the chain when he left the CPR after 43 years of service, but he did cherish the memory of being part of the train crew for the royal visit in 1901. When King George V decided he'd get off the train at Banff and go fishing for awhile, the crew, including Bomford, had to stay at their posts—no food, no rest—until the King returned some 12 hours later. In those days, it was an honor to be held up indefinitely—even without food—by royalty.

Seymour and Mary Bomford, 1892, Medicine Hat, AB

1892...Struck By Love and Lightning...

John Ware and Mildred Lewis were also married in 1892 but they were not typical pioneers. They were black, and to be black in western Canada in the 1890s was to be different. On top of that, John Ware chose to be a cowboy and nobody had ever heard of a black cowboy. Known as "Nigger John", a name that may have started out as a thoughtless or pejorative term but soon took on shades of admiration, he was such a good horseman. There wasn't a horse that he couldn't ride, or so the legend grew.

During their courtship, John and Mildred were struck by lightning. That's not a poetic way of saying they fell in love suddenly. That's a fact. John had agreed to drive Mildred and her mother home from Calgary one fine summer day when a storm blew up suddenly and fiercely. There was nowhere to hide on the open prairie so John just urged his team faster and faster, trying to outrun the storm. Suddenly, lightning struck right in front of them and killed, on the spot, the two horses pulling the open wagon. A second faster and the passengers in the wagon would have been victims. Still shaken by the near miss, John had to wrestle the bodies of the dead horses out of the harness and out of the way, and, since there were no other horses around, what could he do? He picked up the traces and pulled the democrat himself.

If that wouldn't impress a girl, what would! They were married the next year. The Calgary Tribune reported: **"Very many of our readers will join with us in wishing Mr. John Ware and bride who were married Tuesday morning all happiness and prosperity in their new sphere of life. The ceremony was performed by the Rev. Mr. Cross, pastor of the Baptist Church, at the residence of the bride's parents in Calgary. The bride is of a happy disposition, well cultured and accomplished, and probably no man in the district has a greater number of warm personal friends than the groom. The Tribune extends heartiest congratulations."**

It was happy-ever-after for awhile. They ranched successfully east of Calgary, John continued to impress the countryside with his horse skills, but when baby #5 came along, neither Mildred nor the baby lived for long. Then, irony of ironies, John was out riding one day checking on his herds when his horse stepped in a gopher hole. John, the man who could ride any horse, was thrown in such a way that he broke his back and died soon after.

Only one of the four surviving children married but he had no children, so there are no direct descendants of the famous black cowboy and his wife Mildred.

1895...Married Life on the Edge of Nowhere...

Anna Gaudin's eyes are heavy with tears in her wedding picture but it's not because of her husband. It's because of their son. It's a long story.

Anna Young and Samuel Gaudin were married on June 22, 1895, in Norway House

Anna and Samuel Gaudin, 1895, Norway House, MB

in northern Manitoba. She was 30, a trained nurse with experience in major US hospitals. He was 34, a missionary teacher at Norway House Indian residential school. Because there were no photographers or cameras in such an isolated area, a wedding picture was postponed until they were able to "go out." That didn't happen until 1901, after a lot of water had passed under the bridge, but Samuel still wanted a picture. He was very proud of Anna's dress, very proud of Anna, for that matter. So Anna agreed, but her heart wasn't in it.

Anna's wedding dress was a beautiful cream colored brocade trimmed with ivory colored lace. She had it in her trunk when she arrived in 1895 at the edge of nowhere in northern Manitoba. She might be far from friends and family on her wedding day but she would have a proper wedding dress. And it made a great impression, first at Norway House where the ceremony took place and then two weeks later when she and Samuel finally arrived at their mission in Nelson House. Mrs. Stout, the wife of the Hudson's Bay manager there, asked her to wear it one more time, at church, perhaps. So Anna hauled it out of her trunks, shook out the wrinkles and wore it. The congregation lined up after the service to greet her; some kissed her shyly and some came back for seconds until Samuel said Enough.

As for flowers and all those other trappings of a wedding, Anna and Samuel had the northern version. The minister who had come to Norway House on the same York boat as Anna picked a bouquet of wild flowers, tied them with a printed ribbon, and presented them to her at the church. An elderly native served as an usher in that he kept the community dogs out of the church while the service was on, and the cook from the boat surprised them all with a cake. It was a happy day.

The honeymoon consisted of a 200-mile canoe and portage trip from Norway House to Nelson House, site of Samuel's mission in northern Manitoba. The canoe part wasn't bad. In fact, Anna was delighted with the countryside—so vast, so beautiful, and since she wasn't yet expected to paddle her own canoe, she had plenty of time to enjoy the scenery. But the portages were quite another matter, often swampy and hot, filled with muck and mosquitoes. Her long skirts got heavier and hotter. By the end of some days, they could stand by themselves. But this was not a woman to complain. She could see that the native oarsmen who had to carry the canoes and the supplies through the portages had a much tougher time.

Maybe Samuel was nervous. What do you talk about on a honeymoon anyway, especially when you are surrounded by other people? Maybe Samuel was simply anxious that his new wife should understand this country. Whatever the reason, he spent a fair amount of time on that two-week trip telling her about the various disasters that had taken place along the way. Here lies Rev. Edward Eves who drowned in the Pelican Rapids, he explained one day and stopped the boats to get a better look at the lonely grave. Another day, after a particularly dangerous bit of canoeing, he pointed out Sea Falls where Chief Factor Boulanger overbalanced his canoe and went under, never to be seen again. And so on.

If Anna wasn't fearless before she came north, she soon was—at least as far as travel was concerned. For the rest of her time in the north, she walked, paddled, snowshoed, dog teamed wherever she was needed and never had an accident. If only she'd had the same luck with the children.

Anna gave her heart and soul to the people of the North for the next 39 years, Samuel likewise for 44. Anna was the nurse, the doctor, the caregiver; Samuel the teacher, the Christian missionary, the builder. Together, they were the parents to their own seven children and countless others who needed their help. But it was those children that gave them the greatest heartache. Baby David died suddenly when they went out to Winnipeg in 1901. They were never sure what caused his death. That's when the wedding picture was taken. That's why Anna looks so sad. Then back in the north, May died of diphtheria. It would have taken three weeks to go out for the antitoxin serum, three weeks to come back. May didn't have that kind of time. Ida died of what seemed like a mild croup. So did Edith. The modern guess is that they too died of diphtheria but there were no characteristic signs of diphtheria. Anna checked for that, but no matter what she did, she couldn't save them. Her grief was unending. How could she not have the knowledge, the strength to save her own children?

The good news is that Irene, Betty and Nelson survived and before Anna and Samuel left the north, the airplane had made its magical appearance, changing forever conditions of life and death in the North.

1895...A Disastrous Wedding Feast...

The next 1895 wedding story is about as different from the Gaudin story as anything could be. It seems there was a Cree Indian known as Almighty Voice who took a fourth wife and decided to celebrate the event. In order to do justice to the party, he needed a big roast so he killed a neighbor's cow. The neighbor complained to the NWMP at Duck Lake in what was then the North West Territories, and that set in motion the most incredible manhunt in Canada's history. In the end, the score was seven men dead for one cow.

The first man to die was Sergeant Colin Colebrook who rode out on what he thought was a routine investigation into a missing cow. For some reason or other, Almighty Voice shot and killed him, and then headed for the hills where he outwitted and outran the police and volunteer lawmen for 19 months. He would have escaped then too except that the law brought in cannons and literally tore up the forest surrounding him. Two of his buddies died, three more lawmen died, Almighty Voice died.

What a waste. Hollywood was the only winner, if winner is the right word. They made two movies out of the nasty story. No movies have been made of the Gaudin story.

1896...Sarah Brock Marries A Brick...

1896 was the calm before the storm in western Canada. Clifford Sifton hadn't had time to fill the prairies with sturdy peasant farmers yet. The Carmacks and Skookum Jim had not yet told the world about the gold in Bonanza Creek, which meant that BC residents had no idea of the stampede that was about to come their way. They were still pleased to be a clone of England, a center of civility where wedding guests gave gifts like old English silver scallop shells and old Scotch silver toddy ladles, whatever they were. As for Alberta and Saskatchewan, they weren't anything but the North West Territories, still a land where fur traders made incredible journeys into incredibly distant lonely outposts.

Just ask Sarah Brock who became Sarah Brick in 1896 and for her honeymoon trip traveled with her new husband from Edmonton to Fort Vermilion, NWT. That's 700 miles as the crow flies. Too bad they weren't crows. Their trip proceeded thus:

— Order and assemble food, household equipment, medicines, tools, clothing, etc. that might be needed in a remote outpost in the next year.
— Pile all that stuff onto wagons, hitch up the horses and head overland to Athabasca Landing. Trip could take five days or fifteen. Depended on the weather, horses, drivers, roads.
— Unload and reload everything onto York boats to go up the Athabasca and Slave Rivers until the rapids are reached. Unload and haul everything in a portage around the rapids.
— Pull the boats up the channel formed by the rapids. Load again.
— Cross Lesser Slave Lake by means of sails on the boats, a hairy experience in storms. There were a lot of storms on that lake.
— Once across, load everything onto wagons again, find the horses, travel overland to Peace River Crossing (now the town of Peace River.)
— On the banks of the river, build a log raft some 100'x150'. Fence off one end for the horses and the hay, pile the other stuff at the other end, put 19 year old, tender new bride Sarah in the middle. Push off into the mighty Peace River and hope you can stop when you spot Fred's cabin alongside the river near Fort Vermilion.
— Once you get there, enjoy the beaver tail and moose nose dishes which the natives have made especially for you. Figure out how to say no thank you for such delicacies.

People would pay big money for that sort of high adventure tour nowadays but for Sarah and Fred, it was the only way to go. He was an independent fur trader. If he wanted to beat the Hudson's Bay Company to furs that the natives had, he had to be nearby. For the next 11 years, they did this trip twice a year, taking furs out to sell, bringing back supplies. Once, Sarah lost her wedding and engagement rings enroute.

She was washing her hands in a basin of soap and water when she heard the baby cry. Her rings were in the wash basin, she knew that, but couldn't stop right then to fish them out. Along came Fred who in the process of cleaning up camp threw out the dirty water. Sarah tended the baby, got back in the boat and some five miles further up the river remembered her rings. Too late. They couldn't turn back. **"I had always heard it was bad luck to lose your wedding ring,"** she wrote in a memoir years later. But Fred hadn't been going up and down that route for years for nothing. Next time they went by, he remembered the spot and found the rings.

Sarah was a brick in more ways than one. Three of their four children were delivered in their home 700 miles from hospital / doctor / mother, but she did have the services of an old native woman who delivered most of the babies in the area. **"She was a dear old lady, and one I shall never forget as she helped and comforted me."** Sarah wrote. Baby #4 came on New Years Eve. The following day was Kissing Day among the natives in the north so young baby boy Brick was a "mighty kissed baby" who in spite of a less than sterile beginning grew to be a good strong Brick.

Fred Brick's father was the first to venture into the north country. An Anglican missionary on the banks of the Peace River at Dunvegan, he decided to plant a garden to stretch his food supplies and discovered that vegetables grew very well indeed. So he tried wheat one year. The gods were with him. The wheat grew wonderfully and biggest miracle of all—the frost stayed away until it was fully ripe. So, just for the heck of it, Rev. Gough Brick sent a sample to the Chicago World's Fair. It didn't win prizes but it put the Peace River country on the map.

1896...The Bride of the Klondike...

Ethel Bush decided the north was just the ticket for her too. When her fiancé Clarence Berry murmured that he thought they should put the wedding off for a year or two, just until he could find the gold that he knew was in the Yukon somewhere, Ethel murmured, **"I'm coming with you."** Her folks had a fit, Clarence wasn't too sure, but she brought it off. Put together a trousseau of warm heavy duty clothing, then married Clarence on March 10, 1896, in Seattle and left immediately for the north. The trip was no sweat at all; Ethel was the only woman in the party so she got to ride in a sled up over the dreaded Chilkoot Pass and beyond to Forty Mile. It wasn't until she was left alone at their camp while the men went prospecting that she realized this might not be the biggest picnic ever. **"Just imagine sitting for hours in one's home doing nothing, looking out a scrap of a window and seeing nothing, searching for work and finding nothing."**

Clarence, however, found something. He was nearby when gold was found in Bonanza Creek so he was able to stake a claim before the outside world heard about the find. When he and Ethel got off the steamer in Seattle a year later, they were rich. One newspaper writer asked Ethel why she had ever agreed to go into the dangerous north and she replied, **"I went because my husband went and I wanted to be with him."** With that answer, she became known as the Bride of the Klondike.

Clarence had a brother working in the gold mines in the Yukon; Ethel had a sister who wanted to go north with them on their next trip. Eventually, Henry married Tot, and the two Berry families became very rich indeed, partly because they left the north with their money and invested it in black gold, in the oil industry in other words.

1896... Her Mother-in-law Made Her Do It...

Life wasn't nearly as dramatic for Nellie Mooney, a young schoolteacher in Manitoba in 1896. Mind you, she thought it was pretty dramatic because she decided she would get married after all. Marriage had never been in her plans. A writer was what she wanted to be, one who traveled the world and met fascinating people. But along came Mrs. McClung and she changed her mind.

Mrs. McClung was Wes McClung's mother. Wes was a nice guy, Nellie was attracted to him especially since he agreed she could have a mind of her own, but what clinched the deal was his mother. **"I felt sure Mrs. McClung's son must be the sort of man I would like. She had all the sweetness, charm and beauty of the old-fashioned woman, and in addition to this had a fearless and even radical mind."**

So Nellie took the plunge, married Wes McClung at 8 am August 25, 1896. It was an awful day—dark with rain and so much wind that grain was flattened in nearby fields. Poor omens, Nellie admitted later. But the Presbyterian Church was decorated with sheaves of wheat and fall flowers, and neighbors and friends brought so much goodwill that Nellie couldn't be downcast. And by the time she and Wes caught the 4:00 pm train, the rain was letting up, there was clearing in the west. That's the name she used for the first volume of her autobiography, *Clearing in the West*.

Nellie doesn't mention her wedding dress or any domestic details about the wedding in her books, but she wouldn't, would she, if she were determined not to let domesticity run her life? Her daughter donated the dress many years later to the Western Development Museum in Saskatoon. There it is in all its glory, and it is quite lovely. Nellie should have told us a bit more about it in spite of her determination to take the high road. It's a gold velvet two piece, the skirt flared from a very small waist, the tight fitting bodice finished with a high neck, full sleeves and seed embroidery across the yoke.

The McClungs moved from Manitou to Winnipeg to Edmonton to Calgary to Victoria. Maybe that's why the dress is in Saskatchewan; it was the only western province that they didn't live in for awhile. Everywhere they went, Nellie made a difference—worked for the vote for women, spoke out against the sale of liquor, taught Sunday School and scolded church officials for keeping women out of the pulpit, joined four other Alberta women to have Canadian women declared persons, and so on. It's hard to figure how one woman had time to do all that and raise five children, write 15 novels, one powerful social critique, and numerous newspaper articles. She was a powerhouse and she was right in her choice of husband. He supported her always and never said boo when she used her own mind.

1896...Who Needs Horses?

The Macdonald/Fleet wedding took place in Victoria in the fall of 1896. It too had to put up with less than ideal weather but the newspaper account is not nearly as accepting of the vicissitudes of life as Nellie was. **"A wedding under cloudy skies and with the rain descending in a veritable deluge is not usually an over-joyous ceremony. Yesterday it rained despite the fact that bright weather was in demand, and under ordinary circumstances everyone would have felt vexed at the contrariness of things generally and at the weather clerk in particular, for it was the day of the Fleet/Macdonald nuptials."** In other words, even the weather should have behaved for this high society wedding.

That it didn't was rationalized further: **"Remembering that it was a naval wedding and that water was therefore a very necessary adjunct, everyone interested became philosophical and while the sun could not be compelled to shine, it was clearly demonstrated that his presence was not essential by any means to make the wedding of Commander Ernest J. Fleet, RN of HMCS Icarus, and Miss Edythe Mary, daughter of Senator and Mrs. W.J. Macdonald of Armadale—the merriest marriage of many months."**

One can only hope that the principals of this wedding had as much fun as the newspaper reporter who went on for four long columns to describe this merry wedding. The jolly jack tars (the sailors from the Icarus) figured big in this event. They put up a canopy so the wedding party might **"enter the sacred edifice dryshod from their carriages."** They formed a guard of honor—cutlasses drawn—outside the church, and for the crowning touch pulled the coach from the church to the bride's home for the reception. **"When Commander and Mrs. Fleet reached the waiting carriage, they found that the horses had been removed and in their places stood thirty bluejackets under petty officer Dunlop, G.I., manning red, white and blue running lines. Not content with hauling their commander and his bride direct to Armadale, the jack tars with great enthusiasm took the carriage round by Douglas, Yates and Government Streets, across the bridge and so to Senator Macdonald's beautiful residence where the sailors were given a lunch."**

It was the least they could do.

The bride wore white—white satin brocade, white chiffon, white tulle veil, white heather and stag's horn moss worn in her white orange blossoms—but she pales beside the description of the bridesmaids. The Misses Macdonald, Pearse, Cridge, Pemberton, Devereux and Finlayson wore white dresses with black velvet picture hats trimmed with white plumes and scarlet geraniums. Each bridesmaid carried a bouquet of yellow and white chrysanthemums tied with steamers of red, white and blue satin ribbons, and each wore a gold brooch—both bouquets and brooches being a gift of the groom.

And speaking of gifts, that's what the newspaper account does for two long columns of fine printing. There are 148 gifts listed with more to come, the paper assures us. Modern newspapers don't cover weddings anymore unless they be royalty or Hollywood but maybe they should. The list of gifts for the Fleet wedding is a textbook of who's who and what's what in Victoria in 1896. Here's a partial list: Lord and Lady Aberdeen, handsome clock with chimes; Mr. and Mrs. Macdonald, checks; Admiral Palliser, check; Mrs. and Miss Dunsmuir, check; Mr. and Mrs. Pearse, checks; Mrs. Munro, check; Miss Beatrice Pearse, silver glove stretcher; Mr. John Warburg, cut glass ink stand; Bishop and Mrs. Cridge, handsome illustrated Bible; Mr. Duncan of Metlakatla, silver spoons carved by Indians; Mr. and Mrs. Oliver, silver mustard pot; Mr. and Mrs. Laundy, silver card case with initials; Mr. and Mrs. M.T. Johnson, Japanese gong; Mr. and Mrs. William Wilson, Honiton lace handkerchief; Sir Charles H. Tupper, pair silver and crystal vases; Mrs. Powell, silver bonbon dishes; the Mayor and Mrs. Beaven, silver salver; Lieutenant Governor and Mrs. Dewdney, silver mounted tortoiseshell pin box, and so on.

The new bride could spend the rest of her life polishing silver, but she will not. The servants will.

1897...Praise the Lord and Pass the Wedding Cake...

You might think that all weddings are "hallelujah" occasions but it's only in the Salvation Army that weddings are officially termed "Hallelujah" weddings. In 1897, there was extra reason for hallelujah because the Federal government amended the Marriage Act to give Salvation Army officers equal rights with ordained clergymen to perform weddings.

So, on the night of March 25, 1897, Jabez Townsend and Annie Elizabeth Reilly donned their uniforms and as usual stood on a downtown street corner in Victoria, BC, singing hymns and saying prayers for the salvation of the souls around them. Then Jabez put his trombone under his arm, Annie put her hymn book away, and they proceeded together to the Salvation Army barracks where they would be the first Salvationist couple in Canada to be married by one of their own.

History was in the making, but you'd never know it. There were no flowers, no fancy dresses, no fuss. Just Jabez and Annie in front of a large audience composed mainly of their fellow workers in God. They listened and agreed to the conditions that Salvation Army requires of its members, and then listened and agreed to the marriage vows required by law. Once the pact was sealed, the audience let loose a volley of cheers accompanied in this case by the booming of a big brass band. Jabez was, after all, the bandmaster.

Saints and sinners alike were invited to the reception in the barracks, and those who had 15¢ were asked to contribute that much. Water was used for the toasts, the pieces of wedding cake that Annie passed around were pretty small, but money was scarce. Money was to be used for the salvation of souls and the nurturing of bodies. Waste not, want not, glorify God. And the band played on.

Annie continued to serve with the Salvation Army family even after they had a family of eight children. For years, her alarm clock was the sound of the first streetcar passing their house at 6 am. She'd be up and doing for the rest of a long day—writing for the War Cry, working for the Women's Christian Temperance Union, visiting old folks in nursing homes, playing piano at the Harbor Lights Center, helping whoever, whenever. One day just past her 70th birthday in 1947, she had a heart attack and died the next morning at 6 am. Jabez, also a lifelong worker for the army, had predeceased her by seven years.

1897...Love At First Sight...

Irene and Walter Parlby had intended to have a church wedding but the Ides of March decreed otherwise. In other words, a spring blizzard appeared out of nowhere and blocked the roads to the church. Since the bishop was already staying with Irene's relatives, the decision was made to have it at their house and be done with it. It was still a gala affair.

The Parlby story is one of great romance although they would never have talked like that being of stiff upper lip, mind your own business, British background. Irene Marryat, being of sound body and rich family, decided to visit relatives in far off Canada, the land of ice and snow. Why not? She had been all over the world. This would just be one more adventure. But soon after arriving in the Lacombe area, she was out one day driving around the countryside. There, beside a tidy log house on the banks of a picturesque lake was Walter Parlby, an Oxford educated Brit who had come to Canada looking for adventure and challenge. He took one look at the attractive newcomer; she likewise, and they were smitten. That was the summer of 1896. The wedding was set for March 15, 1897.

Irene had first to figure out housekeeping. It had never been part of her education at English and Swiss schools, but she studied Mrs. Beeton's book of Cookery and Household Management. She watched the women around her—how they gardened, canned, cooked, managed. She wrote away to England for dishes and linen and books. And last but not least, she planned the wedding. A white wedding dress, she could see, would not make much sense in this land of dirt, mud and snow so she ordered a navy blue velvet trimmed with fur. Meanwhile, Walter added another room to his cabin, so that after the wedding ceremony, after cutting the wedding cake that had been sent from London's famous Fortnum's and Mason department store, the couple drove through the snowdrifts to their cozy three room house.

There, Irene put her studies to work and produced her first meal as a married woman. What did she serve? **"Fish, nothing but fish,"** she explained at their 50th anniversary party. **"That was all that was available until the road cleared. But it tasted wonderful."**

Years later after Irene had become an Alberta MLA and Minister Without Portfolio, she was asked to be a Canadian representative to the League of Nations meeting in Geneva. In a letter that she wrote to Walter, she described the important issues that were being discussed plus the glittering social events that accompanied the business sessions. **"Do you know what the best part of all this is?"** Walter asked their son. **"It's that she's my wife."** He was always so proud of her, and she was always so anxious to get back to him and home.

1897...Wives For Sale, Cheap

It was in 1897 that the news of Klondike gold hit the outside world. George Carmack, Dawson Charlie and Skookum Jim found the stuff in 1896 but it took a year before newspapers caught on, before the likes of Ethel and Clarence Berry disembarked in Seattle with pots of gold in their suitcases. Once that happened, the rush was on.

For thousands of men, visions of nuggets danced in their heads and they were off to the Klondike. Never mind that the Chilkoot Pass was a killer and the good spots along the Bonanza Creek were all gone. Never mind any of it, including the fact that there were no women to warm the hearts and feet. Mind you, women had their own dreams about gold, so when a San Francisco reporter decided to test the waters with a fake ad for **"a young lady or widow, not over 30, unencumbered and matrimonially inclined"** to accompany an unnamed Klondike prospector, there were 34 applications within the week. One woman said she'd marry, sight unseen, because **"I have read everything in the papers about the gold up there and I am free to confess I want some of it."**

There were even some schemes that sounded a great deal like the brideships of the 1860s. There were more women than men in parts of the US, a result of the Civil War, so why not send off a few thousand to the north? The idea never actually got off the ground, partly because the rush was over in a few years, but there were takers on both sides!

And finally there was the American entrepreneur who decided there was more than one way to get some of that gold. He'd find women who were willing to go north and be auctioned off. According to a newspaper report, **"The girls will then be put on the auction block and sold to the highest bidder for nuggets. He (the guy who came up with this idea) expects some of the girls will be worth almost their weight in gold. They will have nothing to say as to whom their husbands will be. His disposition, color of hair and eyes, nationality, age, etc.will not be taken into consideration. The gold goes to Carrington and the girl owns the Klondiker."**

Again, it was said that there were takers for Carrington's scheme but maybe there were rules about slave auctions by that time, or maybe the gold rush was over. At any rate, the idea faltered before it got to the altar.

1898...First Comes Love, Then Comes Politics...

Such a pretty young woman—chin up, eyes straight ahead, comfortable in a beautiful dress in a beautiful setting. She'll live a life of privilege with servants in the back bedrooms and a chauffeur in the gatehouse, right?

Right, except that Edith McTavish complicated her nice life with politics. But that came later. First her wedding to Arthur Rogers of Winnipeg on June 1, 1898.

The Manitoba Free Press was restrained in its coverage of what they patronizingly called **"a very pretty matrimonial event. The bride wore a handsome gown of white Duchess satin trimmed with chiffon and pearl passementerie with a bridal veil and orange blossoms, and carried a large bouquet of white roses. Her cousin, Miss Maud McTavish, was maid of honor, and Miss Grace McTavish and Miss Maude Campbell acted as bridesmaids. They were costumed alike in pretty silk gowns trimmed with chiffon and wore white picture hats and carried large shower bouquets of pink roses."**

For the first few years, their life was a bowl of cherries—hunt club balls, private parties, summer cottages, sailing races, croquet on the lawn and by the way four children. Edith turned into one heck of an organizer. You want a social event? Edith could do it with one hand behind her back and several servants behind that. But when the war came in 1914, things changed. Suddenly, there were more poor people, families with fathers overseas, women who needed maternity care, children in need. Edith gradually shifted her organizational talents beyond her own family and class and ended up in 1920 as a Liberal MLA, Manitoba's first female MLA. Mind you, she had to help get the vote for women before she could be elected as a woman, but she did that too along with Nellie McClung, Cora Hind and Lillian Beynon Thomas. Thanks to them and others, Manitoba became the first province in Canada to extend the franchise to women. That was 1916.

Her ancestors, male and female, would have been proud of her. Most of them were related to the fur trade in one way or another…which is how Edith came to be part of the elite in Manitoba in the first place. In some places, money and position put one into society. In Manitoba, it was Hudson's Bay Company connections that did it.

And how did she and Arthur meet? Well, it was her Uncle Archie in Winnipeg who brought them together. He asked Edith to visit, and while she was there, she met his friend Arthur Rogers and that was that. Arthur was the quiet one of the pair. He quietly made lots of money and quietly managed it so well that he sold his portfolio of stocks and bonds in March, 1929, just months before the stock market crash, and just one month before his own death. Edith died eight years later.

1898…How To Tell Sex From Shoes…

Contrast the story of the Rogers—a life of privilege mixed with social responsibility—with the Rattenbury story that even now is hard to believe.

Francis Rattenbury burst onto the scene in Victoria just as politicians had decided there should be a new Parliament building in Victoria. A good-looking charmer from Britain, the ink barely dry on his architectural papers, he entered the competition for the huge government project and won it. More established architects were stunned, but Ratz had the vision that the planners wanted—big, showy, British, so grand that

Edith Rogers, 1898, Winnipeg, MB

Vancouver could never take away Victoria's right to be capital city. Victoria was very pleased with herself the day it opened Feb. 10, 1898.

Ratz was the talk of the town and was wined and dined generously, especially by those who had eligible daughters. He was a catch and then some. But he stunned Victoria again when he married Florence Nunn, a nobody who, it was said, was neither rich nor pretty. In her wedding picture, however, she looks pretty enough—dark curly hair, a slight figure, a dress that Rattenbury might have picked in that it was quite grand like one of his buildings—a long white two piece with tucks, ruffles, rows of buttons, lace above and below. It's true that her nose is a bit big and her eyes do seem to bug out, but it's not as if she'd scare the horses in the street. Nevertheless, Victoria whispered about his choice and continued to whisper when a son appeared fairly quickly.

Ratz and Florrie settled down to what seemed a fairly normal life—first the son, then a daughter and then a nice house in Oak Bay. Ratz kept building grand buildings— the Empress Hotel, courthouses in Nelson, Vancouver and Nanaimo, hotels in the national parks. He was having a fine time professionally but losing it personally. Florrie gave up trying to fit into Victoria society, got fat, never went anywhere, with the result that Ratz withdrew more and more from her. Eventually, the only contact between the two of them was made by daughter Mary who carried messages back and forth.

Enter Alma. Thirty years younger than the 56 year old Rattenbury, a twice-married beauty that would now be called a ditzy blonde, a musician and pianist who could charm the birds out of the trees, she bowled him over. Made him feel young. Made him feel his career could go on forever. He was hooked. At first, it was a discreet affair but Rattenbury wanted more so asked Florrie for a divorce. That's when quiet little Florrie roared. No way, she said. No matter how hard Rattenbury argued, no matter how much money or how many houses he promised her, she would not grant him a divorce. So Rattenbury turned off the heat and the lights in the house, removed much of the furniture. Florrie stayed put. Rattenbury went out in public with Alma. Florrie stayed put. It was only when her husband brought his mistress to their home and installed her in his bedroom that Florrie finally gave in.

So Alma and Francis were married and had a perfectly miserable time from then on. Florrie could have said, It serves you right.

They had a son, that was good, but Rattenbury discovered Victoria was hard on those who play footlooose and fancy free with their wives. He didn't get as many commissions, he and Alma weren't invited to sit at the tables of society, and Alma's charms wore thin very quickly. In 1930, they moved to England, and settled in a nice place in the countryside around Bournemouth. Because it was somewhat isolated and because Alma was such a ditz, they had to have a chauffeur. And therein lies the end of this sorry tale.

The chauffeur was a 17-year-old boy, George Stoner, a slow naïve lad who didn't know sex from shoes. But he learned, thanks to Alma, and the two of them had a flaming affair right under Rattenbury's nose. Speak of history repeating itself. Booze and drugs complicated the story but somehow Rattenbury ended up dead in his own living room, killed by several hard blows of a mallet. Alma babbled on about possible suicide, her own depression, George's innocence, etc. until they were both jailed and charged with murder.

It was a spectacular trial, covered word for word as it ground through the Old Bailey in London. Alma did well on the stand; she was so frank and/or stupid that it didn't seem she could possibly be guilty of thumping her husband over the head with a mallet. George, on the other hand, wasn't put on the stand; his lawyer argued on his behalf but it wasn't good enough. George was found guilty and sentenced to hang, Alma was sent home.

Four days later, Alma stabbed herself to death. Newspapers figured she must really have loved George, that she killed herself out of despair over his imminent execution. But it doesn't compute; Alma didn't seem the type. Still, who can tell what's in the human heart, especially one that never stayed put anyway? If she'd just waited awhile, she would have seen George's sentence changed to life imprisonment. In fact, he was released early to fight in WW11, then came home and lived a quiet life.

1898...I Do on the Chilkoot Pass...

Meanwhile up in the Klondike, men and women continued to fight their way through thick and thin to get themselves to the gold fields. They couldn't have cared less about society weddings in Winnipeg and Victoria; all they could do was stay alive long enough to get to the gold. The crazy making gold. However, here and there in the craziness was a reminder of lovelier times. In Melanie Mayer's book, *Klondike Women* is the story of Marie Isharov, a 20 year old woman from Poland going into the north with her father, and Frank Brady, a Montana prospector. The two fell in love on the trail and decided to be married on top of the Chilkoot Pass. Friends agreed to arrange some sort of ceremony.

Thus, within sight of the top, a man who just happened to have his accordion with him stepped into the line and began playing Lohengrin's *Wedding March*. Friends followed the musician up the Golden Stairs, then came Marie dressed sensibly in her hiking ensemble, then Marie's father and finally interested onlookers who couldn't resist the sound of home and happier occasions. At the top waited the groom and the minister. A Seattle newspaper reported: **"Resting their heavy packs on the snow, this gathering of gold seekers from all parts of the earth stood with uncovered heads and reverently watched the minister of God join in Holy wedlock the handsome Montana Miner and the beautiful Polish girl."**

Let's hope they got gold in more ways than one!

1899...The Music Man...

Where, do you suppose, Hugo is pointing? North? Is he already telling his new wife about Canada and sharing his secret desire to go there? She doesn't look entirely convinced but then she might also be wondering just how to ride this beast of a bicycle.

Hugo and Marie Gottschlich are on their honeymoon. They've just been married in the Mormon Temple at Salt Lake City and are on their way back to Hugo's business in Oakley, Idaho. The bike riding is just a diversion; they're actually travelling by covered wagon. He's a blacksmith but he wants to be a farmer. He wants his own land. That's why Canada is much on his mind. That's why he's pointing north.

Hugo came to the new world of the US first. Many did. An immigrant from Germany in 1896, he settled first in Idaho, met Marie Gunther, also a German immigrant, and married her in October, 1899. A year and a half later, he followed his dream and headed north to scout out the area around what is now Lacombe, AB. Then, it was just an inviting piece of the North West Territories. He couldn't resist. The town needed a blacksmith, and he needed/wanted land. So that's how the Gottschlich family was established in Canada. There's five generations of them now, and the original farm site is still owned and lived upon by a Gottschlich connection.

By 1905, the North West Territories had given birth to so many new homes that the Canadian government decided to divide the territory into two separate provinces and make them equal partners in Confederation, although that word "equal" still sticks in the craw of many westerners. It's hard to be Johnny-come-lately provinces. But Hugo wasn't worrying about equality on September 1, 1905. He was worrying about his band. They were in Edmonton to take part in the official ceremonies marking Alberta's new status as a province. That was Hugo's other contribution to his new country. He could play almost any musical instrument and he could lead a band. Thanks to him, Lacombe had such a good band that they were invited to be part of the official ceremonies. He taught music too, and daughter Erma was so proficient on the piano by the time she was 13 that the local movie house hired her to play background music for silent movies. Last but not least—for country dances were the glue and glitter of isolated rural areas—the Gottschlich family provided the music for countless country dances and wedding dances. It was Lacombe's lucky day when Hugo paused to point north.

1899...Mother's Advice About Marriage...

Even though women shared equally with men the work and worry of a new home in a new country, there were still the most incredible social expectations of the two sexes. Men were to lead, women follow. Men had control of the land and money, women didn't ask. Women had the babies, men didn't ask. Men inherited land and position,

Hugo and Marie Gottschlich, 1899, Utah

women had to marry it. And so on. Here's part of a letter written at the turn of the century. It's advice from a mother to a daughter:

"My dear daughter, You have just entered into that state which is replete with happiness or misery….You are allied to a man of honor, of talents, and of an open generous disposition. You have therefore, in your power, all the essential ingredients of domestic happiness—it cannot be marred if you now reflect upon that system of conduct which you ought invariably to pursue; if you now see clearly the path from which you will resolve never to deviate…

The first maxim which you should impress deeply upon your mind is, never attempt to control your husband by opposition, by displeasure of any kind which is attended with an angry look or expression. The cement of his affection is suddenly stopped, his attachment is weakened, he begins to feel a mortification the most pungent, he is belittled even in his own eyes, and be assured the wife who once excites those sentiments in the breast of a husband will never regain the high ground which she might and ought to have retained…..

Has your husband staid (sic) out longer than you expected? When he returns, receive him as the partner of your heart. Has he disappointed you in something you expected, whether of ornament or furniture, or of any convenience? Never evince discontent, receive his apology with cheerfulness. Does he, when you are housekeeper, invite company without informing you of it, or bring home with him a friend? Whatever may be your repast, however scanty it may be, however impossible it may be to add to it, receive them with a pleasing countenance, adorn your table with cheerfulness, give to your husband and to your company a hearty welcome. It will compensate for every other deficiency. It will evince love for your husband, good sense in yourself and that politeness of manner which acts as the most powerful choice. Never be discontented on any occasion of this nature.

In the next place as your husband's success in his profession will depend upon his popularity, and as the manners of a wife have an influence in extending or lessening the respect and esteem of others for her husband, you should take care to be affable to the poorest as well as to the richest. A reserved haughtiness is a sure indication of a weak mind and an unfeeling heart…

Do not devote much of your time to novels. There are a few which may be useful and improving and in giving a higher tone to our moral sensibility, but they tend to vitiate the taste, and to produce a disrelish for substantial intellectual food. Most plays are of the same cast."

She was right. Somewhere along the line we lost our taste for substantial intellectual food. We watch television instead.

This letter is in the Provincial Archives of Alberta. It is not signed. There's no way to find out whether the daughter took her mother's advice, whether she lived happily ever after. But it's a powerful example of the way we were.

THE 1900s

**Sister Mary's husband, two new provinces,
a secret wife, rubber boots and bread**

The Sacret/Allen wedding, 1905, Vancouver, BC

1900...The Veil of Tears...

The first time Mary Elizabeth Martin got married, she married the church and became Sister Mary of the Cross, a member of the Catholic order of the Sisters of St. Ann. A picture was taken.

The second time she got married, she became Mrs. Joseph Bettinger, an outcast of the Catholic order of nuns and the community generally. No pictures were taken.

The third time she married, she became Mrs. W.W. Barton. Nobody cared anymore. No pictures.

Mary Elizabeth's life was a tough one right from the beginning. Her mother came from England in 1863 on the brideship Robert Lowe. As proof, if proof were needed, that not all marriages/connections made by single women when they landed in the land of single men turned out well, her mother had a tough time. Two girls were born, given the last name Martin, but Martin seems to have disappeared from the scene fairly promptly which probably accounts for the fact that Mary Elizabeth at age five ends up in a convent. There she stays until she's old enough to take religious training herself and join the Sisters of St. Ann. In 1885, Mary Elizabeth put her red hair beneath a wimple and became Sister Mary of the Cross.

The Sisters of St. Ann were a teaching order who early on declared their intention to **"teach the poor children of the forest"** on the Pacific coast. They set up the first school in Fort Victoria and by the time Sister Mary of the Cross was part of their organization, they had schools up and down remote areas of BC, Alaska and the Yukon. In 1898, when Dawson City was the craziest place on earth, and Father Judge was the busiest man on earth, Sister Mary and three other nuns were sent there to help. Mostly, they worked in the hospital; typhoid and scurvy had hit hard through the long winter and there was no end to the help needed. However, the nuns watched for an opportunity to establish a school; they still kept their focus in mind. And it was that teaching focus that got Sister Mary into trouble.

One of the doctors at the hospital expressed an interest in the Catholic religion. Sister Mary was given the job of instructing him. One thing led to another and they fell in love.

It just wasn't done in those days, that a nun should consider leaving her order. The Mother Superior came out from Victoria, Mother Mary Angel Guardian, but neither her persuasion nor her name—which should have straightened out any religious problem—would change Sister Mary's mind. She was leaving so that she could marry. By December, 1899, she was back to plain Mary Elizabeth Martin.

The community was so scandalized by this unheard of defection that Mary Elizabeth went out to Tacoma and renewed acquaintance with her long lost mother who, by this time, had a fourth husband and eight more children. It was in Tacoma that she and Dr. Joseph Bettinger were married July 16, 1900. The marriage certificate lists their ages as

Sister Mary of the Cross, Dawson City, YT

32 and 34 respectively.

It should have been happy ever after from then on but life doesn't always work that way. Joseph and Mary honeymooned in Detroit where his folks lived, and then returned to Dawson City. Maybe they thought the scandal would have died down by then, but it hadn't. Dr. Bettinger wasn't allowed back in the Catholic hospital and when he tried to make a living as a pharmacist, he was turned down for that as well. They struggled along but by December had decided they'd have to go out. The north wouldn't forgive and forget. So they made a deal. In order to save money, he would walk out to Whitehorse and she could take the stage a few days later and meet him there. Once in Whitehorse, they'd travel together to Skagway and then to Vancouver.

He never arrived. Mary got there as scheduled but day after day he failed to show up. It was December, it was 50 below, it was a crazy idea in the first place. The police searched for him, but there was no sign of him. On January 28, 1901, Mary wrote officials in Skagway: **"I have concluded and indeed I am almost positive that my dear lost husband is no longer capable of succoring me, as far as temporal wants are concerned, for I now believe him in a far and happier land where I hope to be reunited to him when it will please our Heavenly Father to call me from the vale of tears."**

That's how an ex-nun talks, and she was right. He was no longer capable of succoring her. In April when the snow melted along the trail, his body was found, frozen where he fell, half eaten by animals.

Remember that Mary had been in a convent from the age of five. She hadn't had to deal with secular things like money and lawyers and police, but she had to now. The police finally decided that Joseph died of natural causes, no foul play involved, so his body was released for burial. By this time, Mary was back in Tacoma. Could they send the body to Tacoma? Yes, but it would cost $390.00. Where would she get that kind of money? There were lawyers' fees to pay as well. In the end, she had to agree to have Joseph's body buried near Stewart River where he died. Then she had to get a job. Even far from the north, she had a hard time, ended up working as a waitress in a Seattle restaurant.

Apparently, Joseph's family didn't help her out. In the obituary of his mother years later in a Detroit paper, reference was made to Joseph thus: **"Mrs. Bettinger's only son, Dr Joseph Bettinger, died in a storm in the Klondike 25 years ago while doing medical research work."**

Mary's third husband was a regular at the restaurant where she worked. She and W.W. Barton had two children. One of those children had a daughter Barbara and it's Barbara who took up the story of her grandmother. Mary never really told her kids about the north or her life as a nun. It was only after her death in 1959 at the age of 96, that Mary's other life began to unfold.

1900...The Color Of Wallpaper...

The gold rush in the Yukon was beginning to slow down by 1900, but the land rush on the prairies continued. Ella Sykes was a British journalist who came to Canada to investigate the lives of her fellow countrymen and women. Did they succeed in this new land, were they happy, etc? On the boat over, she heard again and again that life was "bigger" in the Dominion. That's what we were called then—the Dominion. It was bigger alright, one of the women told Sykes. She had been in the Dominion for ten years or so and didn't regret it, she said, but it was more than she had ever bargained for.

"My husband (we weren't married then) wrote to me to come out to him at Winnipeg, as he had got a home for me at last, and I left my own people with any amount of things for our new house, as Fred had told me how dear everything was across the Atlantic. Well, he met me all right and we were married, but before we went off to the prairie I had to do some shopping in Winnipeg, and I remember asking him what was the color of our bedroom paper, as I wanted to get a toilet set to match it. He didn't say much then, but I shall never forget my feelings when I found our new home was just a one-roomed wooden shack divided in two with a curtain and not papered at all. It was an awful shock to me, I can tell you. Of course, I couldn't unpack my boxes, and I found that I had to do the cooking and washing for three men besides my husband and was left alone all day long. How I got through that first year, I hardly know."

There were lots of these stories. By 1900 one Canadian in ten was a westerner.

1901...Sam McGee Uncremated...

There are strange things done in the midnight sun but Sam McGee didn't do any of them. Oh, he may have howled at the moon occasionally when he couldn't find gold, or he may have muttered under his breath when his bank account got low. But for sure he didn't die on the marge of Lake Labarge. That was Robert Service's idea.

William Samuel McGee was working in San Francisco when news of the Yukon gold rush hit the headlines. He was 30 years old, single, of no fixed address. Of course he went north but by the time he got there the gold was petering out, the good spots had been claimed. So he did what he'd been doing all along—worked on road and bridge building crews. On his days off, he built a log shack in Whitehorse and called it home.

Somewhere along the way, he decided he wouldn't be William anymore. William was too sissy for the north country where every second man seemed to be Big Bill or Fat Bob or Deadeye Don. So William became Sam and that's how Robert Service first met him—as Sam McGee. Service was a teller in a local bank. When Sam McGee came into the bank and signed his name at Service's cage, Service did a double take. **"I've**

been looking for the right name to rhyme with Tennessee," he said, or words to that effect. **"Mind if I use yours?"**

"Be my guest," McGee said, or words to that effect, and that's how come there is a real Sam McGee behind *The Cremation of Sam McGee*. That poem and its mate about the north, *The Shooting of Dan McGrew* are Service's most famous poems, much to his dismay because he wanted to be known as a more serious poet. Many of the poems he wrote after he left the north achieved critical success but none caught the fancy of the public and the spirit of the place like his Yukon pieces.

McGee shared his name with one other important person—18 year old Ruth Warnes whom he met in Ontario while visiting his family. They were married June 5, 1901, and went immediately to Sam's cabin in the north, where Ruth would have had a few months to get used to the north before the lights went out. There they stayed until Ruth had had enough of cold, and Sam had decided reluctantly to give up any notions of getting rich quick. He never gave up entirely, however. Years later when he was 70 years old, he flew into a remote area of the Yukon and prospected for a whole summer. Still no luck, but he always thought it was out there, just waiting for him to find it. Gold.

What he did find was a bag of his own ashes, or so the sign in the tourist place in Whitehorse said. Genuine Sam McGee ashes, from the barge on Lake Labarge presumably. He bought some. Two years later in 1942, he died at the home of his daughter in Beiseker, AB, and was buried in a nearby churchyard. Without the genuine Sam McGee ashes.

Robert Service should have sent flowers or condolences or something. Sam McGee's name had made him rich and famous, after all, but he was living in France by then. It's interesting that the names Robert Service and Sam McGee always fall off the lips together but there's never any mention of Service's real family. His folks homesteaded in the Mannville area east of Edmonton in 1905 and Robert visited occasionally. Once he organized a community dance but since he didn't know many people, he fell asleep on a pile of coats on the stage behind the orchestra. Maybe Mannville wasn't as exciting as the Yukon!

1901...So Much For Free Love...

As far as is known, there were no strange things done on Malcolm Island in BC in 1901, but there were plenty of rumors. After all, Matti Kurikka believed in free love and that sure hinted at something out of the ordinary.

Matti Kurikka was a good looking charismatic Finn who wrote and preached about a socialist Utopia where all people would be equal, where work and profit would be shared, where harmony and freedom would prevail. The vision went to the heart of the Finnish immigrants who were working in the mines on Vancouver Island where

Ruth and Sam McGee, 1901, Whitehorse, YT

anything but peace, freedom and equality prevailed. James Dunsmuir prevailed, that's who, and he treated his workers with a cold contempt. Finns had lived under autocracy when Russia ruled their land; they wanted no more of it. So they were easily persuaded by Kurikka's plans to buy an island and establish Sointula, a place of harmony.

Nobody had money, of course, but Kurikka made a deal with the BC government that they would do a certain amount of logging in return for ownership of the land. Sounded ideal. They moved lock, stock, kith and kin to the island and prepared to live happily ever after. Five days a week they worked; the sixth and seventh they saved for cultural activities—music, theatre, reading, education, contemplation. But along came winter, and culture was poor company in the freezing rain. They had to work six days and then seven to get shelter built for the 100 or so people who first moved to the island. Then the logging operation was poorly equipped and managed, they fell behind. In other words, whatever could go wrong did go wrong, and by 1904 Matti Kurikka had to admit defeat.

Actually, he never admitted defeat. He moved away from Sointula taking about half the population with him, especially the bachelors who still rather liked the sound of free love. But they could never find mates who bought the theory so eventually most of the bachelors married. So did Kurikka, for that matter, marriage #2 for him. Moved again, first back to Finland, then to the US where he worked a bit, wrote a bit, raised chickens. So much for free love.

To be fair, his free love message was not one of unbridled license. He thought that marriage was a form of slavery and enforced morality for women especially, that women should be able to bear children out of wedlock and have them raised by the community without any fuss being made. **"Let us aid woman into a position of unconditional freedom and responsibility. Let us build marriage on a foundation of ideal love…let us refuse to acknowledge a marriage in which the relationship is not centered on love, goodness and tenderness."**

By the same token, men should **"declare only the rights of love, not the chains of marriage,"** he wrote in his newspaper. He wasn't keen on organized religion either, all of which added up to more than society in the early 1900s could bear. If only he had lived in the 1960s—he would have been right at home!

1902…Clara Clare and Cataline…

It's 1902 in northern British Columbia. There's a great mix of people there and they're all on the move—looking for gold, looking for land, building roads on the edge of mountains, driving stagecoaches on those narrow precipitous roads, riding the rivers, building the railways. Hardly anybody has a permanent address…which is why there are so many unknowns about the bride and groom in this picture. They are Clara Dominic and William Frank Clare, married December 2, 1902, in Yale, BC.

It was always assumed that Frank Clare was from County Clare in Ireland, but he also talked of England as his homeland. How he got to Canada, nobody seems to know, except for references he made occasionally to **"jumping ship off an old tub from overseas."** A carpenter by trade, he worked for the CPR and the BC government, laying out survey lines and timber berths.

As for Clara, who became Clara Clare, she was a homegrown British Columbian, that much is known, but her precise parentage is uncertain. Her mother was Amelia Kowpelst, and it is thought, indeed it is hoped by some descendants, that her father was the famous Cataline, aka Jean Caux. **"Compare their foreheads, eyes, noses and chins,"** a great granddaughter says. **"Don't they look alike?"**

Cataline was the most famous packer in northern BC. His business was the equivalent of the trucking business nowadays. He'd load food, equipment and supplies onto his mules—anywhere from 16-48 per trip— and then he'd lead them through the mountain passes, forests and rivers to a destination further north—often Barkerville or Hazelton. There he'd unload, figure out who owed what—all in his head—and start all over again.

Thus, it was his ability to get the goods through, come hell or high water, that first established his reputation but it didn't hurt that he was also one of the most colorful characters around. For instance, he liked a shot of whiskey now and then but he never took it internally without also applying some to his hair, **"A little on the inaside, a little on the outaside. Bon, she maka da hair grow."** And she did apparently because Cataline had a fine head of hair all his life.

He was from the Spanish speaking area of France but by the time he got to BC, he was speaking—if at all—a mixture of French, Spanish, Mexican, Indian and English. Mostly, he preferred to stay silent. His mules seemed to understand him best.

While packing out of Yale, he hooked up with Amelia who was another pretty interesting character. Born on the Spuzzum Indian reserve, she was descended from Chief James Kowpelst, an important Indian leader in the Fraser valley area. Cataline and Amelia had at least two children—William and Rhoda, and maybe a third—Clara. And that's where this story started.

Because Clara went to the All Hallows School for Girls, an Anglican establishment in Yale, she learned how to be British in all things…including her wedding dress with its high neck, tucked and lacy bodice, a flared modest skirt belted around a tiny waist. The shoes and gloves are likely kid gloves. The veil is likely held by orange blossoms. And the entire ensemble is likely very different from anything Amelia or her maybe father Cataline ever knew! But then that's how the young Canada happened. Mix together origins, classes, styles and characters, bake and refrigerate by turns, throw lots of curves their way and pretty soon you have Frank and Clara who in turn have Catherine, Leonard, Sidney, Elizabeth May and Dorothy and that's just the beginning!

1902…Soft Summer Air in Winnipeg…

Ontario still tried to play by old rules, marrying one's sons and daughters to others of the same class, fraternizing and patronizing within the largely British community. Helen Gregory, for instance, was born to old money and old influence, such that Sir John A. Macdonald was an old friend who gladly wrote up a recommendation for her when she asked for it. That's all she had to do—ask for it. And with that and a few other big names under her belt, she headed out for western Canada and thence Japan to report on what she saw.

It's not as if she came to the job unprepared. She had already demonstrated her mettle and ability by becoming the first woman in Canada to get three degrees in music and arts from Trinity College at the University of Toronto. But scholarship was one thing; travelling by herself across two countries was quite another. Her parents, especially her old-fashioned father, thought she should stay home, attend teas and afternoon "at-homes" and marry suitably and soon.

Little did they know how soon she would marry! Maybe it was the wide open prairies that did it, maybe it was the soft summer air in Winnipeg, maybe it was just the old story—two young people who fall in love like lightning hits a tall tree. Helen and Lee Flesher were married within a week of meeting one another, but they decided to keep it their own delicious secret for awhile. And therein lay trouble, for Helen got pregnant, her folks heard about the pregnancy before they heard about the marriage. Her father, for one, could never be convinced that a proper wedding had taken place, so another was arranged in Helen's home town of Hamilton, ON. Mind you, it had to wait until Helen got back from her assignment in Japan by which time baby wasn't that far off. It was a very awkward situation for a very proper family.

From then on, Helen's life took all sorts of bends and twists. She and Lee with their two sons moved around the US until Lee died of a bacterial disease he had picked up in medical training. Helen kept on writing, ran several newspapers, looked after her family, did it all until in 1902 she married James MacGill, a classmate from Trinity days, now a lawyer in Vancouver. After their marriage in St. Paul, Minnesota, where she was given away by the president of the national Bank of Faribault—she still had those good connections—they returned to Vancouver. The local paper welcomed them back, describing Helen as **"a clever and well known literary woman."** Not bad press for a newcomer to the city!

The MacGill household grew by leaps and bounds, or so it must have seemed to James who was used to a quiet bachelor life. Suddenly, he had two stepsons, then two daughters of his own—Helen and Elsie, then a Chinese cook and various household help, then a suspicious number of meetings in his own front room. The energy that Helen had used in her first marriage to make a living was directed this time to various social causes and they required lots of meetings. The Canadian Women's Press Club, the University Women's Club, the National Council of Women, church groups, all ended up in Helen's living room or in her world generally, all espousing changes of one sort or another to make the world a better place for women and children. It was because of those meetings and the subsequent study that Helen made of BC law that she was appointed a judge of the juvenile court in 1917. The first woman judge in BC. She served as such for 23 years.

More and more did her daughters hear the dreaded tease: **"I should worry, I should fret, I should marry a suffragette."** In fact, they didn't have to worry about marrying a suffragette. They became one—at least Elsie did who years later served on the 1967 Royal Commission on the Status of Women. Elsie, in fact, has her own amazing story to tell. The first woman to earn a master's degree in aeronautical engineering at the University of Michigan, she headed up the design and production team that built Hawker Hurricane fighter planes in WW11. When asked how she could manage such an unwomanly task, she replied, **"I'm an engineer and I do what all engineers do, that's all."**

1903...Wedding Freeze Frame...

It's called Prairie Wedding, this picture from the Provincial Archives in Edmonton, AB, this picture with no names, no date. A picture that says so much in spite of the lack of information.

That it is a prairie wedding can't be contested. Look at the horizon, look at the expanse of sky—⅔ sky to ⅓ earth. Sometimes on the prairie, there's nothing but sky. The earth seems to drop off beneath your feet but for this day, for this wedding, there's just enough earth to stand on and be married.

That it is a wedding is also likely. The groom waits beside the altar, his hat off for this occasion, his white forehead attesting to the fact that he's a farmer. He hardly ever takes his hat off. This is a big occasion. The priest is there too with his Bible open and ready. He, like all the rest, is waiting for the bride to step into the picture.

Is she reluctant? Is she scared? Has she even spoken to the man who has taken off his hat for her? Is that why she hasn't stepped into the picture? Or is it the prairie that takes her breath away, keeps her hesitating at the altar? Has she come from a place that has trees perhaps, roads, houses, even a church? Would it be too much to ask for a church to be married in? Yes, in this case, it would. There's nothing here yet except hopes and dreams and fears, and maybe on the right side of the picture, a sod hut where there will be tea and cake following the ceremony. Maybe just tea.

There are neighbors, she can see that, and women who will help her, she hopes, to get along in this bowl of sky over a mere saucer of earth. But why are they not coming forward to greet her? Why does she have to come into this picture all by herself? Are they telling her that her first step into the frame freezes her there forever, like they are?

Maybe she's all dressed up. Maybe that's why the women stand back. They have no fine clothes anymore; they've been made into baby clothes or curtains or rags. Good clothes don't belong here on the cold dead prairie. What belongs on cold days like these are coats and sweaters and shawls and kerchiefs tied tightly to keep the wind out. The men put on their underwear today. She can't see that but they're not as bundled

as the women. That can only mean tough warm woolen underwear. Her man, the one clasping his hands up by the altar, he has his underwear on too and from now on, if she steps into the frame, it will be hers to wash and mend and sleep beside.

And why the chair? Only one? It looks so lonesome, so temporary. She's almost afraid to walk toward it for fear she'll cause noise as she walks across the dead grass. There isn't a sound; sound has left the world, sucked out by the sky. Not a bird even. All she can hear is silence. How do you hear silence? Couldn't there be a bit of music to soften this picture? Why is there no music? Maybe this is all a dream, a nightmare.

But no, she has said yes to this arrangement, or her father has said yes. She'll have to do it. She'll have to step through the looking glass.

1903...Mail Order Brides...

A man in the Kootenays sent $5 to a marriage agency in London, England, requesting a suitable wife. One of good English, Welsh or Scottish stock, one who could read, write and cook. That's all. Just come to Canada and read, write and cook, although the first two weren't nearly as important as the last one.

Three months later, he heard from the agency that a candidate was on her way. He could keep her for a month and if not satisfied, the agency would send him another and then another. Goods satisfactory or money refunded in full, they promised. Just the $5.00, mind you. The money he paid to bring his hoped-for bride to Canada was not refundable, but most men were satisfied with the very first woman that came their way. They didn't often send them back. It was supply and demand. The agency depended on that.

On a dare, a young British woman, third daughter of a gentleman farmer, signed up. She wanted adventure, wanted to be free of the social distinctions that British people lived by, and that she got. The rest was a bit of a surprise. After landing in Vancouver, she took the train to the Kootenays. The man in the seat next to her spent the night practicing his spitting technique. There was a spittoon but because he seemed rather new at the art, he didn't always hit the target. She had to stay awake to stay dry.

When she dared look out the window, she saw trees. Just trees. She had no idea there could be so many trees in this world. And then at Grand Forks, she saw her man. At least, he was the only man on the station platform wearing a suit. Obviously, he was dressing up for someone. For her, probably. So they had lunch together, got married that afternoon, and went to his cabin among the trees. She never did get to use the silver bell she had brought along to use to summon the maid, but she did use her linens and china. She was, as advertised, of good British stock who could read, write and cook.

1904...Complete With a Merry Widow Hat...

Martha Purdy surprised even herself when she got all dolled up for her second marriage. This is how she described the ensemble she wore August 1, 1904, in Dawson City, Yukon: **"My wedding dress made by Redfern, New York, was a very beautiful creation of pearl gray velvet, and I laugh to myself now as I recall it. The floor length skirt, lined with blush-pink silk, was gathered into a 16-inch yoke, with rows and rows of shirring, and fell in a short train. The high-necked bodice was fashioned with a lace yoke over blush-pink silk, the leg-o'-mutton sleeves being** trimmed with lace and pink silk piping, fastened tightly at the wrist. I carried a "granny muff" of flat pink roses, with long loops of pale pink ribbon reaching almost to the floor, while cozily nestled among the roses were three small birds, one white, one pink and one pale yellow. I wore a merry widow hat made entirely of pink roses, the brim raised at the left side and three little birds like those on the muff reposing under it. It all sounds too ridiculous now, but at the time the outfit was considered very swanky."

It does sound ridiculous but this is 1904, after all. Women's formal clothes were still more decoration than function, and women's bodies were still expected to conform to fashion rather than the other way around. At least, Martha wasn't about to climb the Chilkoot Pass in the dress described above. She had already done that six years earlier wearing an "outing costume" which consisted of a long skirt lined and interlined with silk and buckram, a sealskin jacket, a blouse with a high stiff collar, a well boned corset and brown silk bloomers that fastened below the knee. As she huffed and puffed her way up the steep rocky incline, she shed the jacket, cursed the bones on her corsets and wished heartily she could pitch the bloomers that had to be hitched after every step. No wonder she decided to stay in the north. She didn't have the right clothes to go out.

Mind you, there were other reasons for her apparently mad decision to go north and stay north. She wanted more out of life—adventure, money and challenge—and as it turned out, she wanted less of her husband, Will Purdy of Chicago. None of him actually. He had promised to go north with her but at the last minute chickened out at Seattle and went to Hawaii instead. The writing was on the wall. The only problem was the little surprise that Martha carried with her over the Chilkoot Pass and through her first winter in the north. Baby Lyman Purdy was born in Martha's cabin in Dawson in January, 1899. It could have been an awkward situation—a woman without a husband having a baby in the middle of winter in the middle of nowhere. But Martha recounts in her book, *My Ninety Years*, that the miners flocked to see the baby and help her however they could. Their own families were far away. They made Martha and Lyman their surrogates.

Except for a trip out the next summer to see her other two sons and her parents, Martha stayed in the north. Eventually, the three boys joined her and she made a good life for them with her investments and a sawmill that she owned and operated. Then along came George Black, a Dawson City lawyer. Within two weeks of their meeting, he proposed but for once, Martha reported, she let her head rule her heart. It was two years before the wedding happened—in her house, not the church—since she was this slightly stained thing now, a divorced woman. Didn't seem to hold the pair back at all. George became the Territorial Commissioner in 1912, then went overseas with the Yukon Infantry in 1916, came home and served four terms as MP for the Yukon. Martha followed in his wake, but managed to leave a hefty wake of her own. For instance,

George was ill in 1935 so she ran for election in his place, successfully as it happened, so she went into the record books as the second woman ever to serve in the House of Commons.

Life in the north left her with a low tolerance for insincerity. During a visit to England, the Bishop of England invited her to speak to other important clergymen about the missionaries of the Yukon, but he forgot to introduce her, then patronizingly called her a sourdough, at which point she observed that she now understood why many suffragettes in Britain carry axes. That got his attention. She then explained her rules for a happy marriage—harmony in religion, politics and country. **"And so, because I married an Anglican, I am one. But had I married a Fiji Islander, I would probably be eating missionary now instead of talking missionary."** That shut him right up.

1904...Measured By Cans...

Annie Siddall and Frederick Gaetz were married in Red Deer by the groom's father Rev. Leonard Gaetz in 1904. A nearby bachelor visited Annie one day and told her about another new bride in the neighborhood. "She's a terribly extravagant woman," he said.

"How do you know?" Annie asked him.

"I know by the pile of cans at her back door. You can always tell if a man has an extravagant woman by the size of the pile of cans at her back door."

This was before the days of regular garbage pickup, you understand. Annie took one look at the pile of cans outside her back door and began burying them from then on.

There's more than one way to measure a marriage.

1905...Floating To The Wedding...

In 1905, the federal government made honest women of Alberta and Saskatchewan. Made them provinces in their own right instead of mere pieces of the North West Territories. Good thing too because each of the new provinces was filling up with settlers, thanks to Clifford Sifton's determination to fill up the middle of Canada with immigrants from the US and Europe.

In Saskatchewan, e.g., nearly 28,000 homesteads were claimed between June 1905 and June 1906. If each of those claims represented a mother and father with three children—a modest estimate—then 140,000 people came to that one province in one year. It was an amazing process—to go from so few to so many. Brought all sorts of social problems, of course, but that came later. First came the homestead. Even that word is a western phenomenon. Scratch most westerners and there's a residual understanding of homestead. It's more than 160 acres. It's the whole, often awful process that went into maintaining that land, building the house, learning the language, surviving. There's pride in the word now but many times in the beginning there was sheer terror. Still, things were looking up by 1905. There were trains—more than one! There were elevators sitting alongside the train tracks. There were seed varieties that would grow in the shorter season of the northwest. The place was being tamed, sort of.

Out in the boonies, life went on. Charlie Johnson and Augusta Lindquist decided to marry but with no minister in their area, they had to go by horse and buggy to the nearest town, Wetaskiwin, AB. Part of the route involved crossing the Schwan slough, normally a fairly mucky low piece of water but on this day an unusually deep piece of mucky water. Nothing for it but to carry on, but in the middle of the slough, the wagon box suddenly floated right off the wagon base. Charlie had to leap out of the box in order to hang onto the horses which left Augusta sitting high and—one hopes—dry in the wagon box as it floated aimlessly around the slough. Charlie couldn't get to her but fortunately a neighbor with a canoe rowed out and rescued Augusta. The wagon box was rounded up once again, put back on its base, and the wedding party continued its way to the altar.

History does not record if Charlie had dry clothes to change into.

1905...Driving To The Wedding...

The first automobile wedding was also recorded in 1905, this one in Vancouver, BC. Just what made it the "first automobile wedding" is not clearly defined in the archival records. Maybe the groom, Herbert L. Sacret, had the first automobile in Vancouver? Could be, although there's no indication he had money or came from a monied family. He had charm, that much seems evident from the friendly grin on his face in the wedding picture. Maybe that was enough to bring out a friend in higher places with an automobile on the wedding day. And maybe that friend drove bride and groom back to their house at 2314 St. George St. in Vancouver after the wedding reception. See—there couldn't have been a lot of money since there's no mention of a honeymoon of any sort in the wedding write-up. So the automobile reference has to remain something of a mystery, especially since Henry Ford hadn't even invented his Tin Lizzie yet. The only cars putt-putting around in 1905 were open two seater affairs, hardly big enough to hold the bride and her beautiful dress. Maybe the groom ran alongside?

According to the newspaper account, the bride, Louise Allen was a well known young lady on the Hill. In modern terms, that description sounds a bit dubious but in the innocent days of 1905, it just meant she lived with her parents on the rise east of the city known as Mount Pleasant. The groom in turn was " a prominent member of

Louise and Herbert Sacret, 1905, Vancouver, BC

the Mount Pleasant lacrosse team." They received many "handsome" presents and then went home…in a car, presumably.

By 1938, Sacret was a Captain and secretary of the Canadian Merchant service Guild in Vancouver. There the trail goes cold.

1905…Crossing the Ocean To A Wedding…

Catherine couldn't have had a more mournful farewell when she left Scotland that June morning in 1905; her mother couldn't speak, she was so upset, so her brother decided to fill the silence with some mandolin music. The music he selected? Old Scottish hymns. Her heart cracked. How could she go?

But she had promised James Neil that she would come, so she climbed on the ship and came. So many new experiences for a young woman who'd never been far from home—on the ocean for what seemed like months, then on a train crossing a country that seemed like forever, then arriving in Medicine Hat for a joyous reunion with a man she hadn't seen for four years. Would she even know him? There was only one man at the station and she gave him a very hard look, but no, it wasn't James. Now what?

The strange man turned out to be the police chief who helped her find a room for the night, and more important, explained that James would be there in the morning. **"I was up and dressed by the time the clerk told me there was someone to see me. I went out of my room and there found Jim waiting for me. He was as brown as a berry with being so much outside, and the years had changed him quite a bit, but in manner, he was still the same as the man who had gone to Canada from Scotland four years before."**

The wedding was arranged simply; they got a license at the jewelry shop and found a minister up and about at the Anglican Church. **"By the time I got there, I found the minister's wife and a friend ready to stand as witnesses. I owe them quite a debt of gratitude for they had decked the altar with flowers to make me feel that somebody cared."**

But if Catherine thought a 17 day journey across unfamiliar worlds followed by a wedding in unfamiliar circumstances was enough stress for a lifetime, she was wrong. She had never been on a farm except as a city visitor. Imagine the adjustments she had to make once she got to the Neil sheep ranch on the wide open grasslands and coulees south of Medicine Hat. It was shearing season; the men were away all day long. Instead of "living happily ever after," as romances are said to do, she felt she was living "alone ever after." Then she had to figure out how to cook out of a camp wagon as they followed the herds from pasture to pasture through the remaining summer months. As she said in her memoirs, everything was a new experience. There was no orientation;

she just had to figure it out.

Had her mother been nearby, it wouldn't have been so hard, Catherine recorded in her memoirs. **"I was an only girl and had been raised by one of those reserved Scot's mothers who think it time enough for a girl to learn things about married life after they are married, always in the hope that she will be at hand to tell a young wife all she should know. Unfortunately for me, my mother was far away."**

So she soldiered on. Bread making was immediately her domain. She read the instructions on the yeast cake box, but the dough rose above the pans and ran all over the oven. She needed higher sides on the pans, she decided, so in went cardboard inserts. They burst into flame in the oven, and when she hastily pulled the pans out, the bread went flat. Her sourdough method turned out loaves that were so sour, she had to feed them to the dogs, and so on. If only she'd had a mother or a consumer hot line to help out now and then!

But that's the point of this book. Every generation has its challenges.

1906...Air Like Champagne...

In 1905 when Alberta and Saskatchewan were created out of whole cloth, the newly hatched town of Lloydminster was cut in two. One half was in Alberta; the other in Saskatchewan. But Lloydminster residents barely turned a hair. They had already survived the Barr-Lloyd split. A mere political decision to cut their town in half was nothing compared to what they'd already lived through.

Thus by the time Catherine Holtby and Frank Jones were married on Nov. 20, 1906, the immigrants known as the Barr colonists had begun to cope with their new lives in contrast to three years earlier when they first arrived and couldn't cope. Rev. Isaac Barr, who came up with the idea that British immigrants should settle together in a piece of northwest Canada, was a better talker than doer. He persuaded some 2000 people to follow his dream but he mismanaged the money they paid, misunderstood the reality that awaited the settlers, messed up arrangements right, left and center. It was left to another minister Rev. G.E. Lloyd to sort out the mess. Imagine it—2000 men, women and children arriving in the middle of nowhere, all wanting to know where their land was, how to get to it, where they were supposed to live in the meantime, and where their next meal was coming from. It was utter chaos, and speaking of coping, Barr couldn't. He left under a cloud of suspicion and anger. Lloyd took over, and that is why the town with a foot in both provinces is called Lloydminster.

The Holtby family barely survived the first winter. They built a shack with sod walls and a sod roof supported by wooden pillars. When the walls settled, the roof didn't. Winter walked right in under the roof. The oldest son Oliver went for help and nearly froze to death. Then he got scurvy. The doctor recommended lime juice which by then was so highly prized that it cost $5.00 a bottle. They had to move into Lloydminster to the already crowded Immigrant Hall, but come summer, they built a proper house, planted a garden, traded their horses for oxen. Began to get a handle on Canada.

Canada had begun to get a handle on them too. Oliver said Canada had **"air like champagne."** That was one of the reasons the Holtbys came—because Oliver needed better air. He had been an artist with the Coalport China works in England but couldn't continue because his lungs suffered in the poorly ventilated factory. So he knew air. When he said it was like champagne, it was like champagne.

The Jones family came out with the original Barr colonists as well. In fact, Nathaniel Jones was one of the 12 directors selected to help Rev. Lloyd make sense of the chaos, which left son Frank in charge of the homestead out near the Holtbys. It was a lonesome existence so he often visited his neighbors and that's how he and Catherine met.

Their story continues the theme of coping—how they went into dairy farming, how they joined the co-op movement as a means of improving the lot of farmers generally. Many years later, their son Harry mused on the lives of those original settlers. **"What has happened to them all?"** he asked in a letter to his aunt. **"What have they accomplished? We look around the few survivors of that hardy band. Was it worth the chance? Few became famous, even less made the fortune they were seeking."**

Never mind fame and fortune, he concluded. They succeeded and then some. **"Arriving with nothing in the middle of the parkland prairie, they cultivated mile upon mile of it. They built their own roads, they grew their own food. Their energy was their social security; their cunning their insurance."**

Beautiful words from a loving son who incidentally went on to become a politician—a Saskatchewan MP for seven years.

1906...Dear Sister, Please Come

Energy and cunning weren't always enough to make a successful transition to a new country, no matter how beautifully they were phrased. In the Provincial Archives of Alberta is a letter to break your heart. It's written by William Magee to his spinster sister Jennie, January 12, 1906.

"Dear Sister, You will be surprised to hear from me after so many years. Well, I have bad news for you. My Dear little wife is dead and I am the Lonelyest Man in all the world. She gave Birth to little daughter on the 27th of December. Three days after she went out of her mind and on the 7th of January she took Pneumonia and Died about half past three in the afternoon. We Buried her Tuesday afternoon in a little Cemetary on the Prairy about 5 miles from here. I am writing to you to see if you will come and keep house for me and raise my little Baby. I would not like to influence you in any way, as I am afraid you would be lonely when I have to go

from home as I will now and again. You are used to so much stir in the city. I have 400 acres of land and I have 9 or 10 cows and some hens. If you come you can make all you can out of the Butter and eggs and I might be able to pay you a small wage besides. Write and let me know as soon as possible what you think about the proposition."

Jennie likely came, although that's just a guess. Sisters were awfully good about helping their brothers, even if they had to milk the cows and feed the chickens in order to make any money. And what often happened was that Sister found a husband in the district and Brother remarried. Life had to go on.

1906...The Politician's Secret Wife...

Tell that to Marion Castellain who seemed to spend most of her life griping and grumbling even though she had one of the most powerful men in western Canada at her constant beck and call. She was young, lovely and lively when Frederick Haultain, the premier of the Northwest Territories first met her in Regina. She was 18, he was 36, he was hooked. But she danced out of his life and married Louis Castellain, a sometime merchant and soldier, who never lived up to her expectations. In fact, he misbehaved something awful if we are to believe this August 20, 1900, letter from Louis to Marion:

"Many thanks for your letter received last night. I cannot begin to tell you how sorry I am for causing you so much unhappiness, and on my knees I ask you to try and forgive me. I love you dearly and am always thinking of you. I can offer no excuses for my behavior but regret most sincerely that it happened. I came out here hoping to die as I was so ashamed of myself, but now I am anxious to live if only to see you for a short time and try to gain your forgiveness."

Apparently, he succeeded in that Marion agreed to go to live near his parents in England while he served with the Strathcona's Horse in the South African Boer War. And then there was a baby. Louis wrote on May 26, 1902:

"I just long to see you with your baby. As that can't be done at present you must write me long letters about the little Darling. I don't like Fidele for a name, too Frenchy altogether. If you don't want Hildegarde, how would you like Olive or Winnifred? They both mean 'Peace'."

On June 9, 1902, he wrote, "I hope you had a good time at the Coronation festivities and did not tire yourself. I suppose F.W.G. was delighted to see you again. Fondest love Darling and loads of kisses for Fiddle dee dee." (Baby must have been called Fidele after all, although she is always referred to as Mimi.) As for the F.W.G. reference, that was Canada's own Frederick William Gordon Haultain who just happened to be in London for the coronation of King Edward V11, and just happened to have a quick visit with Marion. He couldn't believe the state of her finances and mental health and from that time on sent money and encouragement.

By 1904, Louis was out of the picture, and Marion was in the US waiting for a divorce. There was a gentleman in the wings but apparently he wasn't gentleman enough to wait for Marion. Once again, she called on F.W.G. for help. Once again, he came across with more money and advice, but no matter how much was done for Marion, it was never enough. She always needed more money, more treatments, more nurses, more attention. It never stopped. So F.W.G. did the only thing left to him—he married her. That was in March of 1906 but he never told anyone. She never came to Regina to live with him; he never joined her in her various homes (and it must be admitted, in her various institutions) in England or Ontario. It remained one big fat juicy piece of news that somehow escaped public notice.

Her father knew, however, and wrote an accusatory letter to Haultain in 1910. Haultain, for once, lost his cool: **"…I do not like the way in which you have written and telegraphed to me. I have not been neglecting Marion at all but have been doing the very best I could under exceptionally difficult conditions….I will not take you over the history of the last eight or nine years at length but in receipt of your letter to me, I feel it my duty to remind you of a few facts…After she got her divorce, she was very ill and unhappy…She wanted to go back and live in England so I made arrangements for that and undertook to see that she would not want ordinary comfort so long as I was alive and well. I was, of course, very fond of her but didn't dream of her marrying me at that time and felt that I couldn't ask her to as long as she was dependent on me. She knew I would marry her at any time and finally made up her mind that she would not allow me to do anything more for her unless we were married. A bold statement of the conditions of that time will not explain how easy it was for me to agree. It was probably weak but you must make allowances for me. We got married then in March, 1906, on a few hours notice…and with the understanding that it was only to be a marriage in name until she had at least a year in England to settle down."**

Apparently, it remained a marriage in name only. Haultain did talk of bringing her west—once he was out of politics, once he had a house, once his practice was thriving, etc—but something always prevented it, usually Marion herself. So Haultain soldiered alone in the west and did very well for himself—became chief justice of SK, then chancellor of the University of SK, then Sir Frederick Haultain when he was knighted for his contributions to the public life of the west.

His final accomplishment was a real marriage. When Marion died in 1938, Haultain married Mrs. W.B. Gilmour and this time he told the world about it.

1907…Blood on the Hem…

On New Year's Day, 1907, Ruth Peacock put on her Paris designed wedding dress, put on her coat, boots, mitts and scarves and headed for Central Methodist Church in

Calgary, AB, to marry Norman Young.

Meanwhile, poor old Norman Young was in the basement of the church trying to get the blasted furnace going. It was 40°F below outside and about the same inside. If Norman and his crew didn't get the furnace going, then Rev. G. Kerby would have to conduct the fastest wedding ceremony on record. And Edith's wonderful wedding dress would remain under her coat, boots, mitts and scarves.

Fortunately, the furnace finally obeyed and began to warm the place up. But Norman had cut his hand in the heat of the battle and when he stood beside Edith at the altar, he inadvertently bled a few drops on the hem of Edith's wonderful dress. The stain never came out, and Edith always mourned the loss.

It was different from other dresses of the time in that it was designed and assembled by a Paris fashion house. The fabric, trimmings and pattern were all included in a kit and sent to faraway places—like Hamilton, ON, where Edith saw it and knew immediately that's what she wanted for her own wedding

dress. So even though she did the sewing herself, she could still say...From Paris.

It wasn't the first time Edith had shown a preference for something out of the ordinary. A few years earlier, she had talked her sister into going to England and the continent—without chaperones. It was unheard of, that two single women would travel alone but they did and had a fine time, by all accounts. Then she signed up for an Epworth League trip to western Canada which, if not as exotic as Paris, still had a cachet of its own. The Epworth league was a creation of the Methodist Church, and when the 25 young women from eastern Canada arrived in Calgary, the minister of the Methodist Church urged the young single men in his congregation to **"squire the young women around."** Norman did as he was told and on an outing to the Banff Cave and Basin met Edith.

Norman Young came west at the turn of the century and was a merchant in High River, 30 miles south of Calgary, when the town was incorporated in 1906. With a new town had to come a new town council. Norman Young was elected to that council, but it couldn't have been a lot of fun since newspaperman Bob Edwards kept taking potshots at them in his columns. They were **"amateurish, weak, ineffective and costly,"** he claimed. On top of that, they imposed a license fee of $200 on every saloon in town which really made Edwards mad since he was known to be a great friend of saloons. The saloons did more for the goodwill and growth of the town than the council ever did, Edwards preached.

And so on it went until Edwards moved his wit and barbs to Calgary. Norman Young, of course, stayed on the side of the angels since he was a good Methodist and good Methodists did not approve of liquor.

There were three Young daughters, all of whom admired the Paris wedding dress but none of whom could wear it at their own weddings. They were bigger than their mom, or they didn't have the same undergarments for control. Control was big in more ways than one in the good old days!

1907...Twin Shacks on the Line...

Control in the Peace River country was exercised by weather, distance, bush and inaccessibility but there weren't a lot of man-made rules. Maybe that's why Fletcher Bredin liked it. Want to build some trading posts in opposition to the Hudson's Bay Company (HBC)? Who's to say no except the HBC and they don't rule the world anymore. Want to move about the country, homesteading wherever you feel like it? Why not? What about a transportation company in partnership with Jim Cornwall, aka Peace River Jim? Sure, fine, if you think you can tame those northern rivers, go right ahead.

They had fun, those men who were first and foremost in the north. At least, it was fun for those who survived, and Fletcher Bredin survived. Thrived might be a better word.

On one of his rambles through the north, he met Anna Marsh who was working with her brother, Rev. Canon Marsh, at the Hay River Mission on Great Bear Lake, NWT. She too must have been infected by some kind of northern virus that makes its victims willing to put up with the most incredible circumstances. Anna was a nurse and teacher at the mission. On one occasion when her brother was absent for a long time (read—couldn't get back all winter long), Anna got so sick she feared she'd die. Knowing that natives were superstitious about building coffins before death had actually occurred—and she did want to be buried properly even if she was in god-forsaken country— she came up with a plan. She asked one of the natives at the mission to build her a window seat, about six feet long, three feet deep and wide. Just a box, she said, that I can sit on. And so it was done. She covered it with fabric, remarked casually here and there that it would make a good coffin, wouldn't it, and waited for death.

Death passed her by this time. Fletcher Bredin came instead. They were married in her hometown in Ontario in September 1907 and came back west in time for Fletcher to attend the first sitting of the new Alberta provincial legislature. He served two terms as the MLA for Athabasca, then had his final homesteading attack and settled on Bear Lake near Grande Prairie. Here, they built the famous Twin Shacks, two separate houses built very close to the line that divided Fletcher's quarter of land and Anna's adjoining one. Thus did they meet the regulations of the Land Act that said each landowner had to live on his or her land at least six months of every year. They just added one long verandah to link the two houses and presto, they met the letter of the law.

Another example of northern ingenuity. What do you bet there was a window seat somewhere in one of the houses as well…just in case!

1907…Bread and Roses…

Two other notes about love and marriage in 1907. Gordon McLaren married Mabel Hannah Phillips on Dec. 11, 1907, in Heward, SK. When he brought her home to his homestead shack, she looked up and saw there a loaf of bread nailed to the ceiling. It was a product of his batching days, flat and heavy, and its presence on the ceiling was meant as a lighthearted (but very sincere) welcome home gesture. Meanwhile, Frank Hubka from the Claresholm area of Alberta went to Texas and picked up the bride that he had met through the Lonesome Hearts Club, one of various matchmaking organizations that were advertised in farming magazines.

Never underestimate the power of a woman.

1908…The Rubber Boot Bride…

When in Rome, do as the Romans. When in Prince Rupert, BC, in 1908, put on your rubber boots. Even if it's your wedding day, put on your boots. You can't really see them in the wedding pictures taken that day. What you see is Marian Lengen-Burton in traditional wedding finery— white dress, long veil, cascading wedding bouquet— with Capt. Harold Roberson walking on a boardwalk some three feet above ground level. It was not put there especially for the wedding day, as nice a notion as that might be. It was put there to enable the citizens of this town-in-process to get around the mud and jagged tree stumps that covered the whole area.

Prince Rupert was just being unpacked, as it were, getting ready to be the new western terminal for something called the Grand Trunk Railway. Charles Hays of Montreal had had this bright idea—that Prince Rupert would be that much closer to the Orient. Therefore, ships from the east would come to his seaport first without even bothering to go down to Vancouver and Victoria. With his GTR, he'd leave the CPR and CNR languishing down in Vancouver and Victoria, eating his dust, although there was certainly no dust in Prince Rupert. It was forest, rain and mud.

The idea might have worked if Hays had not been on the Titanic that fateful night in April, 1912. The GTR didn't materialize but Prince Rupert did. Once the sun got at it and dried up some of the mud, it grew to be a good-sized and attractive town.

Harold Roberson came to Canada from England, got himself a job as captain of the CNR vessel "Prince Rupert," and then sent for his fiancée Marian. She came, loaded with all the trimmings for a traditional English wedding, and that's what they had June 1, 1908. They were the first couple married in the new Anglican Church. After a honeymoon on a friend's boat, The Constance, they came home to a tent like dwelling—wooden walls with a canvas roof. That's what a lot of places were like in the town then—half house, half tent, half hole in the ground. It didn't take long, however, for real houses to spring up and a real town to emerge from the mud.

Along came WW1. Harold Roberson joined up and served overseas, part of the time with the mystery "Q" boats, boats that looked like fishing trawlers but apparently had a more important task in mind than fishing. Marian returned to England and drove ambulance while she was there. Back home in Prince Rupert, he continued to captain coastal vessels while she gardened, started a Girl Guide organization in the area, raised two children and took on an orphan bear cub. That's what she seems to be most remembered for—her bear cub called Fuzzy that followed her tamely around town. Eventually, it was released into the bush but Prince Rupert folks still point to the sidewalk ring to which the bear was chained when he came downtown.

In the 1920's, the couple moved to Victoria, Harold to become an independent pilot for larger ships plying the BC coast, Marian to continue in church work and her beloved garden.

1908...Mrs. Pidcock and Another Mrs. Pidcock...

Another bride that balmy June 1 day in 1908 was Ella Marguerite "Dolly" Smith of Comox, BC, who married Herbert Heber Pidcock of Quadra Island, BC. No sign of rubber boots on that pair! There's a good looking house behind them in the wedding picture— a wide verandah, greenery twining around the corner posts, sun shining on a very proper wedding party. The bride is wearing a high necked white dress, her waist impossibly small, the veil over her bright red hair held in place by flowers. The bridesmaid is similarly tucked, flounced and draped in white but she has a marvelous

black hat that must have taken great balance to maintain. And the flower girls, well, they're just what flower girls should be, right down to the tippy flower baskets and the how-much-longer-can-this-last expressions.

The groom isn't nearly as grand, but then grooms never are. He's wearing a black suit with the requisite boutonniere and white gloves. Most of all, he looks young and therein, lies a story. It seems that Dolly and Herbert fell in love several years earlier but his mother would not hear of a wedding until the pair were of age. Even then, it seems she wasn't too keen. When the newly weds arrived back at the Pidcock establishment at Quathiaski Bay on Quadra Island after their honeymoon, someone on the wharf introduced them as Herbert and Mrs. Pidcock.

Herbert's mother corrected the introduction immediately. **"You mean Mrs. Herbert Pidcock,"** she said, **"I am Mrs. Pidcock."** Dolly, no slouch in the stubborn department herself, never quite forgave her mother-in-law for that comment and paid her back later by keeping the news of her pregnancy secret for many months. **"She was highly chagrined when she found out,"** Dolly remembered. That pregnancy resulted in their only son, Reginald.

The Pidcocks Sr. came to Vancouver Island from England in 1862, Mr. and Mrs. and five sons—George, Reginald Jr., Harry, William and Herbert. They began with the first logging and sawmill operation ever in the area around Courtenay, then moved the operation to Quadra Island. Pidcock Sr. also took on the job of Indian agent and had to deal with the fallout of the Potlach Law, a decision made by Ottawa to outlaw the gift giving and partying that comprised the Indian ceremony known as potlach. The natives both resented the law and often disobeyed it. In the meantime, son Herbert became a guide for hunters and fishermen, his customers including the likes of the King of Siam and the Governor General of the time, Lord Tweedsmuir. It was said of him that he knew every inch of the country, that he could find game or the famous Tyee salmon where no one else could.

Life would have been pretty good for Dolly and Herbert had not WW1 intervened. He joined up, of course, since BC and the Pidcocks were still very loyal to England. Dolly and baby Reg followed him to England—so many wives did that during the first world war. And when Herbert was confined to hospital suffering the after effects of nerve gas, she was right there. Unfortunately, the effects of the gas could not be overcome; he was weakened for the rest of his life. He died in 1938, aged 53.

Dolly lived to be 104 and for much of that time, she gardened. She became famous for her gardens, as a matter of fact, being one of the first to ever incorporate native plants into her outdoor arrangements. She also lived long enough to become as redoubtable as her mother-in-law. She was the Mrs. Pidcock.

1908...Good Catholics...

On June 1, 1908, on the other side of the country, Annie Ouelette and Albert Bureau were married. Annie was born in Madawaska, the French republic in New Brunswick; Albert in Lac Megantic in Quebec. Thus, they were French Canadian and Roman Catholic and those two facts made their lives very different from the Robersons and Pidcocks who were English and Anglican. Not that Anglicans didn't take their religion seriously, they did. Pidcock Sr. never left home without his prayer book, for instance, but there was an extra element of devotion and sacrifice that was demanded of Catholic adherents. Good Catholic adherents, at any rate. They could not take any measures to prevent conception. Therefore, they had large families.

After Annie and Albert Bureau had had five children, they met a Father Boucher who told them of new land opening up in the west, land where they could build from scratch the kind of church and community that they thought best for their family. Since the Bureaus were determined that their children would be religious, honest and hardworking, they decided to make the big move. The area they selected was near Bonnyville in northeastern AB. The year—1919.

Like pioneers all over the west, they had to work like crazy to make a living. Albert cleared and broke land, built a house and barn, worked in sawmills, blacksmithed, built roads. Annie served as postmaster for awhile, but eventually there were 12 children and that was enough work for anybody. They did not neglect their spiritual life, however. The first mass ever held in their area was held in their home, and as the children got to school age, some were sent off to a boarding school in Bonnyville run by the Sisters of Charity of Evron. Others went to local schools. All spoke French until they went to school.

It was with great pride that the Bureaus saw four of their daughters become nuns within the Sisters of Charity. It was also with great pride that they saw the remaining eight children marry and have a total of 67 children. It was the way that God intended Catholic families to live. It was not easy, however, and Catholic women had to rely heavily on their faith to get them though.

In 1939, for example, the Bureau's son Leon married Therese Labonte of Beaumont, AB. She was #17 in a family of 18. She knew all about large families and the expectations of the church but she had no idea how hard it would be. Their first baby died at birth; it was a breech delivery and the cord was around the neck. Four more followed in regular intervals, all healthy, but Therese herself was sick for a long time. During this time, she had a vision of her patron saint Therese who told her to be faithful to her marriage and welcome as many children as came. From then on, she did just that, with the assurance that the saints were with her, watching over her and the children. She often told her daughters later that a woman must offer her work as a sacrifice to God. God doesn't give us more than we can bear, she used to tell them.

Therese and Leon had 13 children in all. A son and a daughter are part of Carmelite orders; that much resembles earlier generations. The remaining members of the family are married with children of their own, but the count is way down. That's the difference.

Catholic women still won't talk about birth control. Most of them use it in one way or another but because the Vatican forbids it, they avoid the subject. Ninety years ago, at the time of the 1908 weddings, no women would talk about it except in whispered conversations and in doctor's offices. Pregnancy itself wasn't talked about. Women were expected to hide it from the world for as long as they could, and then go quietly to a "lying-in" where the baby would be delivered without fuss or bother or blood. Of course, it wasn't always so neat. Birth was a scary business; the mother could die, the baby could die. Women knew that but there wasn't much they could do about it except to pray. It wasn't just Catholic women who put their faith in God; that was about the only option most women had when it came time to have a baby. They could work to have hospitals and doctors available in larger communities to make birthing safer, but the prevention of conception was the impossible problem. Condoms had been invented but the average farmer in the middle of nowhere had little opportunity to get some. Various contraceptive jellies and devices were occasionally advertised in newspapers but they were a gamble that women generally lost. Abstinence was about the only reliable birth control method. Fatigue also helped. Work all day long and the only thing you want to do in bed is sleep.

The birth control pill was developed in the 1960's. It changed the world.

1909…No Excitement Please, We're Canadian…

In August of 1909, Alfred James Vale married Mary Etta Nash at the Hay River, NWT, Anglican mission and wrote about it as if it were just another task at the school, like cleaning the barn or something. Here is what he wrote in his diary two days before the event. **"Very much delayed in our haying this year on account of rain."**

On his wedding day, he wrote, **"Steamer McKenzie River returned from Smith in quite a strong wind bringing Archdeacon and Mrs. Lucas, also Miss Nash who comes as my fiancée. Miss Kelly whom we expected did not come. Our freight was all on board. Steamer arrived at 6 p.m. We had divine service at 7 p.m. and this was followed by the marriage ceremony, Miss Nash becoming my Bride. Everything went off very nicely indeed. All the steamer men attended. We were then obliged to attend to the mail bags and other small matters of business which kept me engaged the whole night."**

The next day he wrote, **"About 4:30 am. Capt. Mills called me to breakfast on the steamer and we began to unload our freight. Unloaded it and had it carried to our new Warehouse by evening. After prayers we invited the men in to taste our Wedding Cake."** He underlines and capitalizes wedding cake. That's the end of any discussion re wedding or the Mrs. for that matter, although there is a vague reference several years later in the diary about "regaining" her strength. It is thought there may have been a child who died at birth.

For the next 18 years, he continued as teacher, principal, minister, carpenter, cook, you-name-it for the residential school, and Mary Etta toiled right along with him.

1909…Much Excitement Thanks, We're Old Edmonton…

Status is often conferred by money, but in Edmonton, AB, it was also defined by who came first, who stuck it out, who could be called a pioneer.

Some explanation first. John A. McDougall came west in the 1870s and established himself as a free trader in competition with the Hudson's Bay Company. He was not connected to the Rev. John McDougall of the Methodist missionary McDougalls, although both John McDougalls were invited to all the right parties and saw one another regularly. In 1878, trader John returned to Ontario to marry Lovisa Jane Amey who prepared for her life in the isolated northwest by having all her teeth out. It seems a bit extreme but she had heard horror stories about the suffering brought on by bad teeth and no dentists, so she had a plate made and stopped fussing.

Anyway, trader John prospered, hooked up with Richard Secord and they prospered. By 1909 when the eldest McDougall daughter married, the sky was the limit. The wedding account in the Saturday News went on for pages and pages, but it began with a tribute to those who came first:

"The marriage of Miss Alice McDougall and Mr. W.C. Inglis took place with great beauty and eclat at the First Presbyterian Church, punctually at 11 o'clock on Wednesday morning, November the 24. In more senses than one, the occasion was a memorable one, almost an historical one, for it assembled together such a company of Old-Timers as has probably not foregathered in several decades. There were men and women present who were living in the west thirty years ago, and thirty years of life at such a flood embraces a century of existence under ordinary settled conditions...."

The Old-Timers would not have come out for a "mere" society function, the paper goes on to explain. **"But this wedding was to be different, it was to be a return to the hearty good fellowship of the spacious days so dear and green in memory, and knowing this, the splendid old sports of palmy trading post fame with their wives and sons and daughters donned their Sunday-go-to-meeting clothes, and braving a stormy day, turned out to such purpose as will make Alice McDougall's wedding a memorable one as long as any who were privileged to be present shall live."**

With the important stuff done-the real society of Edmonton defined, the writer goes on to explain the mere wedding details. **"The church as she entered was a perfect bower of beauty, the dais end being a solid bank of palms and ferns intermingled with great bunches of white carnations and magnificent 'mums. Trailing over the railings and suspended from invisible wires were long streamers of smilax caught with white 'mums while from the large electrolier under which the rope of the latter to ring them by, marriage bells, one large one of 'mums and fern and a smaller one of white roses and smilax, with a long green rope of the latter to swing them by."**

"Over the organist's mirror, a beautiful design in white carnations was carried out while the corners of this end of the church were banked in solid green. Bows of white satin ribbon caught with a knot of 'mums marked off the large space allotted for the seating of the invited guests, and about a quarter of an hour before the time set for the ceremony, Mr. Vernon Barford commenced playing in his own fine fashion some beautiful and appropriate numbers. The splendid new organ was a perfect instrument in his hands, and waiting the arrival of the bridal party those present enjoyed a rare and much appreciated treat."

There's a whole paragraph devoted to the bridesmaid, Annie McDougall, who looked "remarkably pretty," the reporter said, a comment that seems on the stingy side, but never mind, here comes the bride.

"The bride followed on the arm of her father who gave her away and murmurs

of admiration greeted her fair, youthful beauty and radiantly happy face, admirably set off by an exquisite gown of softest Duchess satin over which fell a magnificent lace over dress of darned silk dotted net, the pattern being a floral design of raised daisies and panels of basketwork. The gown was made semi-empire, the corsage being trimmed with rose-pointe lace, while silk ball fringe edged the loose bolero like effect, and satin bugles and frogs of narrow braid finished the yoke and sleeves. A tulle veil and crown of orange blossoms and white heather rested on her simply but admirably dressed dark hair, and she carried a beautiful shower bouquet of bride roses, fern and lily-of-the-valley, the long graceful strands being caught with tiny bows of baby ribbon, and the stems swathed in tulle and long satin streamers. The groom's gift, a pair of diamond earrings, were the only jewels worn."

And so they were married. Many more descriptions of the bride's mother's gowns, the wedding breakfast, the floral decorations in the hall, the toastmaster with the "merriest eye and the wittiest tongue," the speeches by one and all.

"But it all had to come to an end sometime, the train had to be caught and so the bride scurried off to don her travelling suit, a smart tailor-made of London Smoke broadcloth with silver and gold braiding of soutache, touches of velvet and pearl grey buttons, worn with a lace blouse of coin spot net. The smart little turban was of grey satin and squirrel with a knot of pink flowers and foliage at the side. As the day was so severe, in place of the suit coat, a stunning seal jacket, the gift of Mrs. McDougall, was worn. Tossing her bouquet to her girl friends and which, mark you, was caught by Miss Eleanor Taylor though Dr. McInnis did steal a sprig of it and cake walked down the aisle kissing it rapturously, at length they were off. Flowers and wreaths were tossed off the tables as they passed by the guests until they formed a path of flowers for the departing newly weds. An omen, let us hope, of their voyage through life, for the sun came out just in time to add his blessing, and surely happy is the bride whom the sun shines on."

Last but not least, the gifts are mentioned in the write up. Apparently, they were "legion," and included a piano from Alice's father, a cabinet of silver, a mahogany chime clock, an English silver tea service and lest we forget, a cheque **"from Mr. McDougall's long time friend and Partner, Mr. Secord, of such generous proportions that most young people would be happy to set up housekeeping on it."**

And so the prince and the princess rode into the sunset and lived happily ever after. Well, not quite. That's not how the real world works. Billy Inglis was killed in a drilling accident near Edmonton in 1932, only 23 years after the magic wedding. Alice lived into her 80's, died in 1962. Their only son became a cardiac surgeon in Montreal.

1909…Rhubarb to the Rescue…

When Walter Smart married Elizabeth Mathews in Regina in 1909, they got two wedding gifts from a neighbor—fresh meat and rhubarb roots. The meat would have lasted for mere days but that rhubarb root is probably still alive—behind an abandoned log house somewhere near Morse, SK.

Rhubarb was a faithful friend to homesteaders—seemingly indestructible, able to grow where it was planted. After a long cold winter, it obligingly produced pink tender stalks of fruit long before any other fresh produce was available. Never mind the first robin or the last drift of snow, spring was official when the rhubarb came up. And once it was turned into rhubarb sauce, rhubarb pie, rhubarb pudding and rhubarb jam, the pioneers knew they had lived through another winter. They had another chance. There should be monuments to that faithful plant.

When Walter Smart arrived in western Canada from Scotland, he had a brand new revolver with him. Didn't know the first thing about guns but hed read about the wild west. Guns were absolutely necessary as far as he could tell. Trouble was he didn't know how to shoot, so he walked out onto the prairie somewhere, set up two empty whiskey bottles and took aim. The first bottle exploded in a shower of glass, the second ditto, and for a few minutes Walter thought he was as smart as his name. However, he was never able to hit the side of a barn from then on and eventually traded the revolver for a pair of blankets.

He and Elizabeth were married in Regina on November 1, 1909. For awhile, it looked as if they'd spend their wedding night on a pool table in one of the city's hotels, the city was that full, but they did find a proper bed. And then they moved to their homestead shack where those blankets kept them warm until spring. Until the rhubarb came up again.

THE 1910s

**War brides and VC winners, from Eyebrow to Elbow,
a Paris original, and the Titanic honeymoon**

The Mock Wedding, 1918, Nelson, BC

1910...Deep South Moves Far North...

In 1910, the emigration of long, short, fat, thin, rich, poor, beggarman, thief continued into western Canada, and western Canada continued to open its arms to one and all...as long as they were white. Be just a little bit yellow and there were murmurings about heathen Orientals, and be just a little bit black and there were murmurings about Go Home.

The black settlers who came north to SK and AB in 1909-1911 thought they'd be welcomed. There had been newspaper articles and government pamphlets about the "open" west in Canada, about land for everyone, about freedom. It was hard to resist for the blacks of the southern US who still labored under terrible Jim Crow laws and discrimination of all kinds, so several groups from Kansas and Oklahoma headed north. Two things were immediately evident when they got here: the country was colder than anything they'd ever imagined, and the racial prejudice didn't stop at the border. It wasn't as bad but it was there.

Jefferson Davis Edwards decided to stay anyway and join other southern blacks in Amber Valley, a district east of Athabasca in Alberta. To his girl friend waiting in Oklahoma, he wrote that she'd have to come to him if she wanted to marry him. He wasn't going back. So Mattie Murphy got on the train and headed north. At the border, she was stopped. By law, she had to have $50 cash money as well as her ticket to Edmonton. No money, no travel, no marriage. So she wired Jefferson who got the money to her somehow, and they were married in Edmonton November 21, 1910.

Their house in Amber Valley that first winter was so ramshackle **"you could throw a cat through the cracks,"** Mattie wrote years later. And toilet facilities must have been the nearest snow bank because Mattie wrote, **"You had to go outside and you know, just newly married, a girl feels ashamed. You know how that is."** But like homesteaders all over the west, they got through that first awful winter, prepared better for the next one, and made it through many more years.

Amber Valley with its mostly black population was fairly isolated and didn't suffer the stings and arrows of public opinion as much as other black communities like Breton, Campsie, and Wildwood in AB, Maidstone and Wilkie in SK. In Edmonton, e.g., the immigration agent argued that there should be a law prohibiting black immigration, and this had nothing to do with discrimination. Oh, no, this had to do with the weather. The climate would prove too difficult for people whose native land is in tropical regions, he argued. Then the Edmonton Trades and Labour Council weighed in with concerns about blacks lowering the standard of living. Petitions were circulated, editorials ran in local newspapers, it was the US south all over again. The only saving grace in all of this was the fact that most of the new settlers were in such remote regions they didn't get papers, and they couldn't afford them anyway.

The weather was a surprise, it must be admitted. Gwen Hooks who lives in Leduc,

AB, remembers that her father arrived in Edmonton on Christmas Day 1911. He wore everything the stores in the American South had recommended for a cold climate but he still couldn't believe the cold. In fact, he looked down to see if he was actually wearing clothes.

Another Mattie—Mattie Hayes—settled in Maidstone, SK, in 1910, with her family. Born on a plantation in Georgia, the daughter of slaves, she spent her childhood serving in the Big House where she was in charge of shooing flies off food in the dining room. Maidstone, SK, wasn't always a picnic for the Hayes family, but when they shooed flies, they shooed their own flies. Makes all the difference.

1910...First to Eyebrow, then to Elbow...

William and Mable Bennetts were exactly the kind of emigrants Canadian officials wanted. They were of British stock, they were white, they spoke English. But they were no more prepared for Canada than the immigrants from the southern US. Married on March 30, 1910, in Cornwall, England, they sailed April 1 for their brave new world, first stop Eyebrow, SK. Truly.

They lived in Eyebrow for a few years, then William went looking for better land near Elbow, SK. Truly.

In the end, they settled at Glen Bain near Vanguard. There, they experienced the usual litany of farming, the good and bad years that follow inevitably upon the decision to take up the plow and walk! 1928 was a good year—great crop. For a moment, they thought they might get ahead. Then 1929 brought high winds, drought, grasshoppers, Russian thistle piled high along all the fencelines. An awful year, in other words, which led to a decade of awful years through the Great Depression. Nothing to do but hang on. They did.

In 1944, daughter Kate wore her mother's wedding dress for her own wedding, and in 1969, granddaughter Karen wore it again. A cream colored silk in a classic design, it survived, like the Bennetts did.

1910...Dreams and Wives Die Hard...

Ancel M. Bezanson went one step further. Besides being white, speaking English and determined to settle in the west, he decided to promote the west and fill it with people, especially the Peace River part of AB and BC. It seemed to him to have it all— good soil, wonderful rivers, a long enough growing season for the new strains of grain, space enough for towns and cities and most of all—railways. Once railways reached the Peace, it would be unbeatable, as far as Bezanson was concerned, and he laid out the plans for the town of Bezanson.

In February of 1908, he married Dorothy Robillard in Ottawa. Dorothy was lucky in that there was train service to Edmonton by then; otherwise Bezanson would probably have headed out across Canada with his team of horses and caboose. As it was, that's how they traveled from Edmonton to the Peace River country over some 400 miles of the dreaded Edson Trail. In the middle of winter. Welcome to the north!

Dorothy died in childbirth two days after Christmas that year. The baby survived but only because Dorothy's sister Lois had the guts to wrap herself and baby Frank in as many blankets and furs as possible, and drive horse and sleigh over 35 miles of frozen wilderness to the only neighbor who had cows.

In 1910, Bezanson married Lois and back she came with young Frank to the log house on the edge of Bezanson town. And there the dream died. The railway did not go through where Bezanson expected and wanted. His planned town was left high and dry off the main line. Most of the businesses moved to nearby Grande Prairie and Bezanson and Lois, with Frank and baby Jim, moved to Pouce Coupe and Vancouver. They left behind the shell of a town, the grave of Dorothy and the graves of their first born—twin girls. Dreams sometimes die hard.

1910...Marry Me Or Else...

George Henry Wheeler used a tried and true method of getting a wife, although he added some flourishes of his own. He seduced a young lady, all the while promising to marry her. That's the tried and true part. Then he seemed to forget his promise. That's also tried and true. But this particular young woman was not going to take this guff lying down, as it were. She took him to court for seduction under promises to marry.

On the day of the trial, the judge heard the case first thing in the morning and then put it over for decision that afternoon. George knew he'd met his match. He hustled around, got a ring, found a preacher, and married the girl in the parlor of the Commercial Hotel in Gravelbourg, SK. Case was dismissed.

1911...Lace on Father's Nightshirt...

Freeda Hume is the young girl beside the bride. She's 11 years old. This wedding is the most important thing that's ever happened to her and she's never going to forget it. And she never did. Years later, she wrote about it for a book called *Happiness is Remembering*, all about the history of Nelson, BC, and area.

The bride is her adopted sister, Eva McKay-Hume, who became part of the Hume family when she was orphaned at eight years of age. Older than the Hume children, she was almost a second mother to them, a very important part of their lives...which is why they almost turned inside out with excitement when preparations for her September, 1911, wedding to Leigh McBride began. This is how Freeda remembered those heady days.

"Mother made the wedding cake a couple of months before the date of the wedding and we all had a hand in its making...and I do mean all. Currants and raisins had to be carefully washed. You never would believe how dirty they used to be, especially the currants from which we picked bits of sticks and even tiny pebbles. Raisins had to be seeded. Oh, what a sticky job. Almonds had to be shelled, blanched in boiling water to remove the skins and shredded. Walnuts had to be cracked and "picked out." Huge chunks of lemon and citron had to be cut into fine pieces."

"Mother weighed sugar and flour on her scales and Jack and I made several trips to the cold storage house to fetch eggs...What a heavenly smell in the kitchen. When done, each cake was wrapped in cheesecloth that had been soaked in brandy, and put in a crock in the cold storage house "to ripen" with mother checking periodically to redampen the cloths."

"A few days before the wedding, the cakes were covered with a delightful paste made of ground almonds and powdered sugar (marzipan) and that in turn covered with a butter icing. Never anything so beautiful, we thought, when they were put together, topped with a beautiful pair of cooing doves and swathed around the base

with French tulle and wax orange blossoms matching the bride's veil and coronet."

"The cake wasn't the only pre-wedding preparation. Never had mother's sewing machine hummed so busily or for such long hours. Mrs. Duck, our favorite seamstress, came from town to help. Not only was there a trousseau for Eva but it seemed we all needed new things—lace trimmed panties, petticoats, corset covers. Dad said it wouldn't surprise him if he went to bed some night and found lace on his nightshirt! I had a beautiful dress of pink mull around the hem of which mother embroidered white daisies with yellow centers. I carried similar daisies in my role as maid of honor. Maid of honor—not flowergirl!"

"For the day of the wedding, dad made arches across the wide cement steps leading from the boat dock to the house. (Note—the Humes lived at the north end of Kootenay Lake.) **Alf Jeffs** was also responsible for three wire frames in the shape of wedding bells that were covered with white flowers for the ceremony on our wide verandah. Early on the morning of the big day, sister Dawn, brother Jack and I rowed down to Hoover's Point for armsful of Golden Glow to be added to the greenery with which dad had entwined the arches. It was a busy day for the two boat businesses responsible for ferrying the guests back and forth across the lake in their launches. The guests were attired in the height of fashion: men in striped trousers and frock coats, women in silk and satin, white kid gloves, gorgeous hats and feather boas."

"Oh, it was a beautiful wedding…and a beautiful day. Hardly a ripple disturbed the serenity of the lake."

"And such refreshments! Chicken salad (dad had been fattening hens for weeks), homemade bread, cherry olives made from our own Queen Anne cherries, mouth watering mocha balls, huge bowls of punch kept cold with ice cut from the lake and, best of all, ice cream brought in special containers from the creamery in town."

That's the end of Freeda's memories of that day except to say that she and brother Jack got into the leftover ice cream the next day and had to be put to bed with blankets and hot water bottles.

As for Eva and Leigh, their story together came to a crashing end when Eva died in childbirth in December, 1912, along with a premature baby girl. Leigh later married a friend of Eva's, Winnifred Foote. Freeda explained in her memoirs that they loved her too.

1912…Divorce Just Wasn't Done…

Fraser Biscoe wanted to be a drummer boy in the Boer War, but the man sitting next to him on the train advised him to stick to his studies instead. The man sitting next to him was Winston Churchill, a friend of the family.

That was the social circle that Fraser Biscoe came from—a father with an important government position in India, a grandfather who was a justice of the Indian high court, and an ancestor even further back who helped Capt. Vancouver explore the coasts of BC and gave his name to Burrard Inlet. No wonder Biscoe thought nothing of coming to a new country to "learn farming." That's what the brochure offered—an opportunity for young men to gain the skills they needed to be successful farmers in Canada, the land of milk and honey. Too good to be true, of course. The school was simply a scam to get cheap labor, but Biscoe liked Vancouver Island and decided to stay for awhile.

He liked it so much that he married into one of Vancouver Island's pioneer families—the Carwithen family who were among the very first white settlers into the Comox Valley. He and Margaret Bluhm Carwithen were married Jan. 21, 1912 in what the local paper described as a "pretty" wedding. With all the adjectives that newspapers had in those days to cover weddings, "pretty" seems pretty tame, but indeed it looks like a pretty wedding. A picture shows the wedding party on the front porch of the Carwithen house, the bride in the requisite white dress with a veil held in place by orange blossoms, the bridesmaids with big picture hats, the best men and ushers lolling on the railing of the verandah, looking as if they haven't a care in the world. Maybe they haven't, because the mother of the bride near the front door looks as if she'll break into an apron any moment and bring on the food. Only the bridegroom looks a little glum. A portent perhaps?

After a sumptuous repast, the newspaper account tells us, the newly weds left by

automobile for a honeymoon to Victoria and parts of California. An automobile yet. Henry Ford didn't invent the Model T until 1908, so to have a car in the Comox Valley of Vancouver Island in 1912 was an accomplishment indeed. Not that it meant Biscoe had come into money apparently, for when he got back from the honeymoon, he scrambled from venture to venture—a farm and logging operation on Kye Bay, a theatre, a general store, delivery services.

Then he met Annie Ellen Andrew, 20 years his junior, and was smitten. That's how his second family—a son and two daughters—describes it. His first family—a son and daughter—may describe it differently, but Biscoe fell like a ton of bricks. He divorced Margaret and married Annie, not in a church, of course, because divorced people were not allowed church marriages. There was considerable stigma attached to divorce in those days.

With a new wife and no money, Biscoe went into real estate and oyster farming. In case you think oyster farming is like grain farming, it is. You put oyster eggs on a beach and wait for them to hatch. Then you harvest them. That worked nicely until a pulp mill moved in nearby and stank the oysters out, that or poisoned them with toxins from the pulp process. Biscoe was never sure what happened to his oysters and he fought till the day he died for compensation. Never got it.

Margaret, wife #1, never re-married. Described as a gentle soul, she stayed until her death in the Comox Valley.

1912...A Residential School Wedding...

The Sarcee Indian Reserve in Alberta beheld a wedding of social note in 1912. Winnie Crowchild married Alec Bull and in their wedding picture, they're with a group in front of the reserve's day school. Winnie is wearing a long white wedding dress with a picture hat that would have been right at home at any stylish wedding. Her sister Lucy as bridesmaid—likewise. The groom is wearing a black suit, the Rev. J.R. Timms is wearing his collar and his wife is properly enclosed in European clothes. Only Winnie's mother and father give away the fact that this is happening to a native family. Her mother's outfit includes a headscarf and blanket; her father has braids under his heavy hat.

It's a picture of culture clash, of transition, of old ways meeting new ways. Lots of wedding pictures are like that frankly—the young people up front in the latest fashion with the old folks in the background wearing their babushkas or felt boots or traditional shawls. But this one has the Christian minister in the picture as well, and that adds a whole other element to this story. Christian churches and government agencies set up residential and day schools on Indian reserves to teach the Indian children how to read and write English, to preach the Christian gospel to those who were considered "heathens" and to change the native children into nice little British/Canadians.

Didn't work very well. The methods were far too draconian, especially in the residential schools where children were taken from their families and forced to speak English, to abide by institutional rules, to give up their culture, in other words. Some of the teachers/preachers were cruel and those who meant well and behaved well got lumped into the same barrel as the bad ones, and so on. Churches and governments are apologizing and repenting all over the place now, but it's not that simple. How do you make amends for the mistakes of other people?

1912...So Much History in One Place...

There are a couple of boys in the Nanton/Cameron wedding picture who are rapidlylosing interest. Paul and Augustus Nanton are the page boys in the front row, getting more and more restless in their white satin suits "of the Louis Quinze" period. No matter that their half sister, Mary Georgina Nanton, is marrying Douglas Lorn Cameron and it's the biggest deal Winnipeg has seen for years, they'd still like to get the itchy outfits off. Paul's feet are hot besides. It's September 6, 1912, and one of the hottest days of the year.

Absolutely every element of a society, expensive, no-holds-barred wedding is present in this wedding—the clothes, the gifts, the decorations, the food, and most of all the guest list. The groom's father is the Lieutenant Governor of Manitoba, Sir Douglas Cameron. He brings all the big government names. The bride's father is Augustus Nanton. He brings to the occasion old and rich Winnipeg. The bride's grandfather is William Hespeler. He brings Manitoba history to the table. It's a feast in so many ways.

The bride herself represents an awful piece of the history of the west. Her father, Augustus Nanton (the man behind the two little flower girls in the front row) married her mother Georgina Hope Hespeler in 1886. A year later, Georgina died after giving birth to a baby girl, the cause of death quite surely childbed fever brought on by a careless doctor who hadn't washed his hands and equipment between deliveries. Three other new mothers died at the same time, all patients of the same doctor.

That baby girl, Mary Georgina, lived with grandparents in Ontario until her father married again, this time to Ethel Clark by whom he had four more children. They are in the picture—the two reluctant train bearers in their satin suits and the two bridesmaids left of Mary on the top step, Constance and Marguerite Nanton.

It's hard to see much of the wedding dress in the picture, covered as it is by the enormous bouquet of lilies-of-the-valley and silver tissue streamers. However, the train is there, silver embroidered chiffon bordered with seed pearls and silver tissue roses and knots. **Altogether exquisite**, according to the Winnipeg Saturday Post.

The five bridesmaids all wear the fashion of the day—the mob caps of chiffon ruffled with lace and banded with blue satin. They are, besides the bride's half sisters, Phyllis

Rose, Marian Meredith and Marjorie Coombs. The best man is George Culver.

Now, for the history lesson. Sir Douglas Cameron, named Lieutenant Governor of Manitoba in 1911, made a fortune in lumber and milling. He's on the far left of picture. His wife, the groom's mother, has the biggest hat in the picture. She's in the second row, third from left.

The Hon. William Hespeler is also in the left-hand group. He's the one whose face you can barely see. He came west as a government immigration agent and was responsible for the settling of Mennonite immigrants in Manitoba. Later, he was elected to the Manitoba legislature where he served as Speaker for four terms.

On the right hand side of the picture is A.M. Nanton, father of the bride, who came to Winnipeg in 1883 as an up and coming banker who soon became an up and coming entrepreneur with fingers in many financial pies across western Canada. The town of Nanton in AB is named for him. Behind him and to the right of his shoulder is his wife Ethel who discovered to her horror just before the wedding that she and another guest had exactly the same dress, one bought in England and one

bought at the French Room at Eaton's in Winnipeg. Ethel got another one. Her mother is the older lady seated in the chair. It is said that she thought she looked like Queen Victoria so always arranged to be photographed in profile, holding flowers. Ethel's

brother is the distinguished looking gent on far right holding his shiny top hat.

As for the bride and groom who could almost get lost in all the notables around them, Douglas worked for his father in the Rat Portage Lumber Co., and then went overseas with the 27th Battalion. Mary made her way to England as well and stayed with Nanton relatives until the end of the war. Their only daughter Elspeth was born there.

1912...Women and Children First...

In the fall of 1911, Albert and Vera Dick of Calgary left on an extended honeymoon to Europe and the Middle East, the culmination of which was to be their trip home on the amazing new ship that **"even God himself couldn't sink."** Everyone knows the end of that story by now—the Titanic hit an iceberg and sank April 14, 1912 with a loss of 1500 men, women and children.

The Dicks survived, both of them, and therein lay the problem. The gallant order of the day was **"Women and children first."** Men weren't supposed to survive. No matter how much Albert Dick protested that the officer in charge had assured him there were plenty of boats, that he was welcome to get on one with his wife, he was never quite accepted in society again. The local paper ran a headline that said, **"No Charge of Selfishness Against Dick."**

There may not have been a formal charge but Albert and Vera were quietly shunned. They had wealth and a beautiful home, but they had very few friends. Albert had broken the code of a gentleman while returning from his honeymoon overseas.

1913...Picture Bride and Groom...

Tsuki Hironaka is the very picture of a very proper bride—modest ensemble of white blouse and dark skirt, a straw hat with flowers on the brim, black leather shoes with bows on top and a parasol. Most of all, a parasol. Maybe if she opened that parasol, it would hint at Japan. Give us a clue that Tsuki just arrived in Vancouver from Japan the day before. She doesn't know English, she doesn't know Canada and most of all, she doesn't know Yoishi, her groom. But her back is straight and her head high. She will do her duty as an obedient Japanese woman.

Yoishi Hironaka is equally determined to honor the arrangement that his family has made for him. He stands tall in his black three-piece suit, his shoes shined and his hair combed just so. His hat will likely mess up that hair as soon as he puts it on but for now, he and his new wife are frozen in their wedding picture. Considering that pictures brought these two together, it is fitting somehow that their story be continued in pictures.

Tsuki and Yoishi are "picture" bride and groom. That means that Yoishi sent his picture to his family in Japan and said, Can you find me a suitable wife? I am established in Canada now and can support a wife. His family then approached Tsuki's family and showed them the picture. Might they allow their daughter to marry the Hironaka son way over in Canada? They might. So a picture of Tsuki was sent to Yoishi. He had final

Yoishi (Harry) and Tsuki Hironaka, 1913, Vancouver, BC

right of refusal but why would he? Tsuki was a lovely young woman. The deal was made. They were married by proxy in Japan June 13, 1912, and Tsuki moved immediately to the home of her mother-in-law and father-in-law. That's where she stayed for a year, doing as she was told in the household of her husband's parents.

Not until the following year did Tsuki finally get to meet her husband. She had to wait until he sent enough money to pay her passage. She arrived April 9, 1913. The following day they were married again in the Canadian way, with a civil service.

As for her thoroughly modern Canadian clothes, they might have been bought in Japan because a lot of Japanese women were coming to Canada at that time as "picture" brides. They knew what Canadian women were wearing and could buy it in local stores. Or Tsuki could have started her life off in a Canadian way in a Canadian institution by heading down to the Eaton's store in Vancouver and buying herself an outfit.

They took the train back to Lethbridge, AB, where Tsuki (soon renamed Harry by his employers) worked in a restaurant. From there, they moved to Raymond and established their own restaurant, the Sugar City Café. That's how Tsuki learned English— by asking locals if they wanted ice cream on their raisin pie. The restaurant led to a garden to supply the café with fresh vegetables and that led to a small farm and that led to a bigger farm. The restaurant lost out—the Hironaka family became big farmers. There were eleven children; two died in infancy, one died in the flu epidemic of 1918.

Life was relatively good for the Hironaka family and other Japanese-Canadian families in southern Alberta until December 7, 1941 when Japan bombed Pearl Harbour. Suddenly, they were objects of resentment and suspicion, even though they assured their neighbors and the government of their loyalty to Canada, even though their kids spoke English and many of them were already fighting for Canada. There was such fear and paranoia in the country that the government passed a law ordering every man, woman and child of Japanese ancestry to be moved at least 100 miles from the west coast of BC. It was a mass evacuation in the course of which many of the Japanese lost their homes, boats, livelihood, and pride. At least those established in southern Alberta didn't lose their homes and livelihood but they had to struggle to keep their pride. It was an awful time. Some 2,250 evacuees eventually ended up in southern Alberta. The Japanese Society and the Buddhist Church did what they could but many of the evacuees were not prepared for the colder climate, for different kinds of work, for the betrayal that they felt. Why would they be?

Florence was one of the younger Hironaka kids and remembers now that 1941 changed everything for them. The discrimination that had been more or less overcome through the years immediately reared its ugly head again. Store clerks got snippy and wouldn't wait on her. Her brother wanted to join other Japanese Canadians in the army but received a letter that made no sense. All they could conclude was that "his" kind were no longer being accepted. Her dad sold Victory Bonds and helped the evacuees as much as he could, but there were those who resented the fact that he hadn't lost everything. He was still solvent and successful.

When Harry came to Canada in 1907, his homeland expected him to come back. He was only supposed to stay away until he could **"Return home rich and successful and in glory."** That was a Japanese saying. He did return to Japan once. Tsuki went several more times, but their family and life was in Canada. They were Canadians by then.

1913...The Sauer-Pickle Wedding...

George Murray and Margaret Lally, married in Vancouver in 1913, had a wedding much like their lives—unpredictable, disorganized, all over the map, but interesting, always interesting. For one thing, Margaret was a sassy American of Irish descent who barely stopped talking long enough to say I do. For another, George practically had to hog tie Margaret to get her to the church. She kind of liked the guy but wasn't sure a Catholic and a Presbyterian would ever manage to get along. Besides, she hadn't had as much adventure as she had planned upon coming to Canada. She hadn't been to Calgary yet, hadn't seen a real cowboy, but George said he couldn't get along without her. The newspaper couldn't get along without her. They needed her. No woman can resist the "I need you" argument so they tied the knot and George never had a peaceful moment again. Mind you, he didn't seem to mind.

They ran a newspaper in Lillooet and then Fort St. John, BC. George was supposed to be the writer, the sober first thought, but readers just loved it when Margaret threw in the silly second thought. She couldn't spell, her grammar was atrocious but she could make people laugh. She'd be sued out of sight nowadays but she got away with murder. When a Miss Sauer married a Mr. Pickle, for example, she couldn't resist running a headline about the Sauer-Pickle wedding.

In the north, she and George went to different churches on Sunday morning, and one year, to the intense embarrassment of the family, Margaret ran as a Social Credit candidate in a provincial election against her husband who was running in the same election in the same riding as a Liberal candidate. She was incorrigible. People loved it. Neither won. George did become the MP for Cariboo eventually but even when he was in Ottawa he had to watch his back in case his wife said something so outrageous he'd hear about it in the Commons.

Once when they were delegates to an international convention of Chambers of Commerce being held in Virginia, USA, one of the chairmen called upon her to say a few words, seeing as how she came from so far away. Never one to refuse a microphone, she carried on about the Peace River country and how everything is bigger there. In the course of her pitch, the top button popped off her dress and hit a nearby water pitcher. Everyone got to see a bit more of Margaret's 44" bust. **"It's just like I told you,"** she said. **"Everything is bigger where I come from."**

George, the ever diplomatic and courteous George, responded to his wife's performance thus: **"President Roosevelt is said to have included in his nightly prayers this one: 'Please God, Make Eleanor more tired tomorrow.' But like Eleanor, my wonderful wife is never more tired tomorrow. If anything, she is more enthusiastic, fresher for the task, and more dedicated than ever as the days go by."**

Now, there's a gentleman.

George and Margaret had a daughter and son who have carried on the writing traditions of their parents without the extremes. George died in a car accident in 1961, Margaret who by this time was known far and wide simply as "Ma" Murray died years later.

1913...Remove That Mob Cap...

It's right out of an old movie—beautiful young woman sprains her ankle on a mountain climbing expedition. Thoughtful young man shows concern, helps her down. Maybe sees her ankle in the process—not an easy thing for young men to do in those days, especially young men in the ministry. And so Rev. Arthur Sovereign of Vancouver meets Ellen Fearnaught Ellison of Vernon and the violins in the background go crazy.

Arthur is a young cleric, educated in Toronto and Oxford, England. Ellen is a young scholar also, educated at Havergal in Toronto and McGill in Montreal. Her father is the well known Price Ellison, MLA for the Okanagan for 20 years, minister of finance and agriculture among his portfolios.

They were married on an absolutely gorgeous Okanagan day, June 12, 1913. Everything was in bloom, the lawn and gardens in front of the Ellison house outdid themselves as background for the wedding breakfast, the entire wedding party looked like an advertisement out of a New York magazine...except for Ellen whose mob cap drooped and almost covered her face. Why didn't someone tell me, she moaned years later when looking at the wedding pictures. Mob caps were the latest thing in bridal headpieces in those days, sort of a dust cap made of lace and sheer fabric. Here's how the Vernon News described the wedding outfit: **"The bride wore a model gown of ivory charmeuse satin, draped with crepe ninon and Brussels lace, embroidered with pearl and iridescent motifs. The full court train of satin lined with chiffon fell from the shoulder and was finished with a large bow and sprays of orange blossom. She wore an elegant veil of Brussels lace, arranged under a mob cap and falling to the end of the train."**

In other words, she was lovely. If only people could have seen her face!

Arthur was quite lovely himself. In the wedding pictures, he's shown wearing his clerical collar, a black morning coat, shoes so shined that Ellen might have rearranged her mob cap had she taken a peek, a black silk top hat and gray gloves. The very model

of a modern major general, which is about what he was, except that he worked within the Anglican Church, first in Vancouver for years, then in Dawson City for one year, and finally in Peace River. By then he was Bishop of Athabasca, an area that, some say, covered one-sixth of the total area of Canada. It was huge at any rate, and Sovereign had to somehow travel that endless north country, bringing church services and personnel into areas that had no roads, no church buildings, no money. Good thing he was tough, organized and devoted. Good thing that Ellen's bridesmaids showered her with silver paper horseshoes when she left on their honeymoon. She needed luck among all the other qualities she needed in her career as wife to minister and bishop.

1914...A Garden Wedding...

They're in the potato patch, the bride and groom and all, and that's exactly where they should be. After all, the potatoes will see them through the next winter, the potatoes and carrots and the other garden produce that we can't see in the picture. Life was pretty basic for farmers in southern SK in 1914. Best not to forget the garden.

The house behind the potatoes belongs to the bride's mom and dad. It doesn't look very big but remember, this is southern SK. There aren't a lot of trees on the prairie so you don't go building a mansion when there are fields to be plowed and potatoes to be planted. In fact, the lumber for this house had to be hauled by oxen from Gull Lake, some 50 miles distant. It's a wonder houses got built at all until the railway came in 1913.

The bride is Marie Arcand, the first ever teacher in the Dollard area. She was a great catch; schoolteachers always were in the early days when single women were few and far between. Besides, schoolteachers made honest-to-goodness money before they married which accounts for the fact that Marie and Delphis have a bedroom suite and a sewing machine back in their own house, waiting for them.

Her dress is white silk and lace, her headpiece a simple white band. However, her daughter Georgette remembers a large white picture hat swathed in tulle that used to reside in her mother's steamer trunk. That was the wedding hat, she's sure of it. Maybe Marie removed the hat for the ceremony, for the pictures, for the potatoes?

The groom is Delphis Gregoire, born in Quebec. His ancestors came to Quebec as early as 1653 which makes him a mere pup in this pioneering business! However, he and his family were pioneers in the Dollard area, south of Shaunavon, SK. That's where Delphis settled after he came west with a harvesting excursion. Now, a harvesting excursion was about as far from seminary school as it could be, but Delphis had had enough of priestly training. He wanted adventure, challenge, hard work, and a trainful of men heading west for jobs in the harvest looked to supply all of the above. It did, but what a switch from ecclesiastical studies.

Father Kugener married Marie and Delphis July 21, 1914, at the Catholic Church near Dollard. The service was in French, the guests were neighbors with French names like Sicotte, Coderre, Villeneuve, Roy, Dufresne, Audette, Maurice, Buoffard, Pattyne and Lambert. In other words, not all French Canadians live in Quebec. The prairies had numerous communities like Dollard.

A month after the wedding, England declared war on Germany and WW1 was underway. Canada was part of the British Empire. We were also at war, but farmers didn't have to go. They were essential to the war effort in that they produced beef and grain and potatoes, so Delphis stayed where he was. Conscription was still voluntary and the government of the day, trying to appease French Canadians who did not feel all that much loyalty to England, promised that it would remain that way. They changed their mind later but that's another story. The war ended in 1918.

In 1919, Marie and Delphis had their own private awful war. Not war exactly, but certainly tragedy. There were four children by this time—a new baby just days old, a toddler and two little boys who one day found some matches and tobacco in the barn. The hired man slept there; they were just kids snooping where they shouldn't. The babysitter thought they were with their father, Delphis thought they were with her, so even when they first noticed fire in the barn, they didn't look for the little boys. It was only when the barn burned to the ground that they found the two little bodies. It was too awful to stay near that patch of scorched earth; they moved to another farm site.

There were more babies and more farms, sometimes even more money except in 1924 when the crops were hailed out. No crop insurance in those days. When you lost your crop, you lost your living and had to make do. Every householder knew those dreaded words, **"We'll have to make do."** That year, Marie's brother came up with a unique solution to the fact that Santa Claus would not be paying a visit. He went out back of the woodshed and fired two shots from the shotgun. Then he came back in and told the kids that Santa had committed suicide and wouldn't be able to leave anything under the tree. A solution that was original if not exactly comforting.

The Gregoire farm survived it all and is still in the family. There were eight children eventually counting the two little boys who perished in the fire.

1914...The Trapper Takes A Wife...

Louis Houle made up a much happier story about Christmas for his kids. He was a trapper in northern Alberta, often away for three or four months at a time, but when he came home, he'd have—with any luck—lots of furs to sell. One year, he came back just before Christmas and took his furs to the trading post in Peace River. There, he made his deals, exchanging the furs for groceries, gifts, candy and cash money. It must have been a good catch because his sleigh was loaded with stuff when he got home. Just like Santa. But before unloading it, he went into the house and told the kids he'd seen Santa Claus and his reindeer. Listen, he said, you'll be able to hear Santa and his sleigh bells.

And they did, or at least that's the way his daughter Bertha Houle Clark remembers it. Santa was there; she could hear him and see the gifts! The power of suggestion.

In 1913, Louis Houle was in great demand. He played the meanest violin in the north and everyone wanted him to play at the dances in their homes or communities. One evening in Athabasca, he saw Emilie St. Arnault and said, **"There's the girl I'm going to marry."** Meanwhile, Emilie knew nothing of this declaration. Young women weren't allowed to look at young men. The only time she saw Louis was in church and the extent of their conversation was **"Hello."**

On January 9, 1914, he came again to Athabasca, this time as part of his freighting job. He went immediately to Emilie's grandmother and asked for Emilie's hand in marriage. She was 17. Her grandmother decided he'd be a good husband and accepted his offer. Then she informed Emilie of the plan. Emile wrote years later in a local history book, **"I never really knew him because in those days we were raised differently. We were told who to marry."**

Four days later on January 13, 1914, they were married in the Roman Catholic Church in Athabasca, and the day after that they left with a load of freight for Grouard, even further north. Fifty sleighs in all and on top of one of them was Emilie covered with a feather robe. That was her honeymoon which considering that some brides went directly to cooking for threshers or milking the cows, Emilie at least had ten days on top of a sleigh, doing nothing but enjoying the scenery. Louis made a flying leap to give her a kiss one day and missed her, ending up in a snowbank along the way. The other freighters loved that.

Louis wasn't the only strange man at her wedding. Her two younger brothers were there, Miles and Robert. She hadn't seen them since they'd been taken to the Catholic residential school in Grouard four years earlier. Obviously, this was not a 9-5, five days a week school. It was a permanent residence where children lived until they were old enough to go out on their own.

The first two Houle children, Josephine and Flavien, also went to mission school, the one near Peace River town called St. Augustine. However, community schools soon opened up near their homesteads and the kids went to them. There were 14 children in all, all but two delivered at home with the help of local midwives or Louis, if there was no one else nearby. All were healthy. All, incidentally, had to work in the garden once they were big enough to distinguish a pigweed from a petunia. The older kids had three rows of potatoes about forty feet long plus one row each of carrots, turnips and peas to look after all summer long, and their dad made sure they did it. No whining allowed.

When Josephine, the oldest of the Houle children, herself got married, her father told her, **"Now, you're going to make your bed. You lie in it and don't come home to us with your troubles."**

As with the garden, so with marriage. No whining allowed.

1915...Will This War Never End?

Phoebe Sanders and Archer Toole were married in Calgary, AB, far from the guns of war, but their wedding date, the honeymoon-that-never-was, even their first three years of married life, all were controlled by the war. WW1. The War to End All Wars, as it was known. The War That Went On and On, as Phoebe knew it.

Phoebe should have known something about war. Her father, Col. Gilbert Sanders, C.M.G., D.S.O., joined the NWMP during the Riel Rebellion and continued to serve with them in northern Alberta until 1908. When he retired to Calgary, he couldn't quite leave police work so became a city magistrate.

By contrast, Archer Toole was not from a military family, but was one of 13 children in the Toole family of southern Ireland. If a storm hadn't bankrupted his civil engineering dad's plans for a land redevelopment scheme, he'd be there still, albeit by now buried in the local graveyard. But finances got tight for papa Toole, so much so that he sent his oldest son William off to try the colonies. Canada, in other words. That was 1894. William cottoned onto Canada right away and ended up as a partner with one George Peet in a real estate and insurance company in Calgary. Younger brothers Archer, Ned and Jack eventually joined him in the city.

Archer hadn't been in Canada long before there was talk of war, so he signed up for officer's training. On January 2, 1915, his fiancée Phoebe wrote in her diary:

"Archer was sworn in today and has a commission in the 50th Battalion (3rd contingent.) I never dreamt that he would be taken on account of his poor eyesight. I am very sad at the thought of it and my only hope is that the war will be over before the 3rd contingent goes."

No such luck. Archer and Phoebe tried to fit a wedding into his training schedule, but it was difficult. On April 30, 1915, Phoebe wrote:

"Was at a bridge party at Edith Lilley's when Archer phoned in the middle of it to say that he and three other lieutenants, one captain and 250 men had been chosen

to go to England at once to reinforce the Princess Patricias. My heart was in my mouth and when I had finished playing bridge, I came home. I couldn't wait for tea and I felt so badly and I met Archer just coming to our house. He doesn't know when they are to go but I am feeling so sad and can do nothing but weep. After all the Canadian casualties the other day, so many we knew, and to think Archer will be there soon is too awful. I am very very sad."

Finally, the date was set for May 29, 1915, but even that got adjusted by the military. This is what Phoebe wrote on May 26:

"Our Wedding Day. Mother, Con (her sister), Marjorie Lumbe and self were downtown all morning getting my suit to be married in and hat, etc. and only arrived home at 2 in the afternoon to find Archer and Jack in from the camp. Archer got word to say he was leaving in the morning and wanted to get married this afternoon. My suit couldn't be altered in time, nothing could be got, so Con went down and brought me a new pair of shoes and Marjorie Lumbe gave me a lovely set of dainty combinations, all lace and ribbons, out of her own trousseau, and this morning I had got a silk vest and stockings and the sewing girls had finished a delf blue skirt which matched my silk jersey. So wore that and a dainty muslin blouse and my delf blue silk jersey and my panama with the satin colored ribbon round—and a big sprig of white roses and ferns. Con wore her salmon pink jersey and cap and roses and my darling mother her old grey silk dress and roses and my dad a tweed suit and white rose. Archer wore his uniform. Dad gave me away and Jack and Con were best man and bridesmaid. Jack was also in uniform. Only the relations knew of my wedding and were present—Barney and Alice Toole, King and Ella Graburn, Chris, Bill and Arthur Graburn, Percy and Jane Heliwell, Eileen and Edith Thompson, Cassie Toole and Mr. and Mrs. Lumbe came also and afterwards we had champagne and cake (my wedding cake was still in the oven) and I forgot to say we were married at 6 o'clock this Wednesday evening and after our health had been drunk and various photos taken Archer and I went down to the Palliser and had dinner and then took room 432 and stayed there until 11:15 when the motor came for us. Poor old Archer had to go back to the Sarcee camp. They couldn't give him leave as they didn't know at what moment they would have to pull out so it was very sad. He took me home and gave me $30.00. My first money. It is 1:30 now of my wedding day and I am just writing this before I pop into bed all alone. I wish my darling Archer was here."**

Her sentences ran on, her emotions ran away, but it was her wedding day, after all, and she was all alone. Three days later, there was better news:

"Archer got the weekend off so we took a room and bath at the Palliser Hotel, the first time I have slept with my darling Husband."

Archer left to go to England on June 9, 1915. Two months later, Phoebe got a cable from him saying simply, "Come." More rushed arrangements had to be made and it was all very exciting except for the news that the ship she was to take from New York to London had been torpedoed by a German submarine. She and two friends, Gwen Bacioi and Cassie Toole, boarded the SS New York instead.

"I would have given anything to have been able to dash off the boat and go home. I was so homesick and wept bitter tears. It is a terrible thing to leave a dear home….All Saturday and Sunday, we were in the war zone so the life boats were lowered even with the deck and all dead lights closed and all the watertight doors in the boat closed…The American flag was painted on either side of the boat and well illuminated and the flag flying at the back of the boat had search lights on it so the Germans couldn't mistake us. We carried our flashers in our pockets while we were in the war zone. The meals, etc. etc. were dreadful but I should say nothing as I am very thankful she landed us safely."

Archer was there to meet her and helped her find lodging in London. He couldn't stay with her, however, since the soldiers had to stay in camp. Thus, she experienced this alone:

"**Zeppelin raid 2 miles from here at 9:30 in the evening. I nearly died of fright, 15 soldiers killed in the guard tent. We could hear the beastly zips overhead as plain as day. It was too awful. The explosions were dreadful.**" (Zeppelins were cigar shaped, hydrogen filled airships that were used by Germany in WW1 to drop bombs over Britain.)

The diary entries got shorter, sadder and less frequent. Archer spent time in the trenches in France as a musketry officer which pretty well put him in the thick of things. Phoebe could only wait and hope for the best. On Sept. 16, 1916, she recorded, "**Ernest (Pinkham) and Ned (Toole) were killed instantly within a few yards of each other by machine gun fire at Courcellette, France. Too sad for words.**"

The war dragged on. Archer got good promotions all along, and Phoebe filled her days with occasional work at hospitals and war related offices but mostly she visited relatives in Ireland and England, and waited for Archer. On September 9, 1918, she wrote four words only, "**Dear old Jack killed.**" Jack was Archer's brother, the second of his brothers to be killed in action. Archer was promoted to Captain and got the Military Cross. "**Best news I have heard for many months,**" Phoebe wrote.

Then came Nov. 11, 1918: "**Peace declared. Too wonderful for words. Was shopping in Knightsbridge with mother and Con when the sirens went off giving the signal, and London then went mad. We tried to get to Buckingham Palace but the crowds became so great we got as far as Trafalgar Square and stood on Nelson's Monument up by the lions and watched the seething crowds go mad with joy. Wish Archer were here.**"

What a memory—to have been in London on Armistice Day and to have seen it all from Nelson's Monument. The only thing better would have been no war at all.

They were back in Calgary Jan. 13, 1919. Phoebe worried that Archer would find civilian life pretty dull but he went into the family real estate and insurance business and that was exciting enough for him. She had one son, William, and that was exciting enough for her. Son William had sons and so the family firm is still in the family.

1916...Time Out From Trouble...

What a mixed up year 1916 was. Overseas, the horrors of war got worse when Germany introduced mustard gas as a new weapon. Thousands of Canadian men were killed or permanently injured by it.

Back in Canada, the war of words about female suffrage was finally settled somewhat when the four western provinces passed legislation allowing women the right to vote in provincial elections. Nellie McClung, the commander of this particular battle, thought maybe women would use their new toy to vote against war and liquor. She was half right—liquor got the boot for a few years during prohibition but war remained a part of our thinking.

Chinese, Japanese or East Indians did not get the vote, however. Nor did Canadian Indians. They were still living on reserves, their children in residential schools, day schools, industrial schools or no schools at all.

It's an Indian industrial school that provides the setting for the 1916 wedding. The industrial school just north of Red Deer, AB, was intended as a place where native children could learn practical arts—how to farm and garden, cook and sew. Sounds good in theory but this school seemed to have more trouble than theory—not enough students, unhappy students, government cutbacks, smallpox and other deadly diseases, arson, looting and to top it all off a matron that disappeared one day and created a mystery that has never been solved. If ever a place was under an unlucky star, this was it. By 1916, it was on its last legs but that didn't stop romance. Of course not. Gertrude Hornby and Claude Bills, both staff members, were married at the school March 10 at 8 o'clock in the morning. This is how the Red Deer Advocate described it:

"The ceremony was performed by Rev. Principal Woodsworth in the presence of the staff and pupils of the school, taking place in the schoolroom which had been beautifully decorated for the occasion by Mr. Dodson and his wife with the assistance of some of the boys. Immediately after the ceremony, the bridal pair received congratulations in the staff reception room while the children were at breakfast and enjoying also a treat of oranges and peanuts provided by the bridegroom. Then followed the wedding breakfast proper in the staff dining room to which all the grown-ups were invited. The room presented a very festive appearance. The color scheme here was white and gold. A fifty pound three story cake—made and decorated by the bride who is an artist in this line—graced the center of the table and, as a finish to a sumptuous meal, was cut by the bride, assisted by her maid, and each of the family of staff and children received a generous slice. Then came the toasts, the speeches a pleasant mingling of grave and gay and showing the high esteem in which the happy couple are held. Mr. and Mrs. Bills left amid showers of rice and good wishes for a honeymoon trip to Calgary and Lethbridge, after which they will resume their duties at the school."

As you can see, a fair amount of editorial comment was allowed in wedding write-ups in 1916. There was more editorial comment a week later when the editor of the same paper said this about women getting the right to vote: **"I am not one of those who think that the millenium will come now that women have votes but I believe no state can flourish unless its legislation and administration is based on justice, not on privilege."**

Amen. (That's more editorial comment.)

1917...The VC Winner and His Bride...

When Gertrude's father realized the young man in the pub was a Victoria Cross winner, he invited him home to tea right there and then. VC winners were almost as important as royalty; everyone admired them, feted them. So Chipman Kerr from Spirit River, AB, had dinner with the Brigdor family of London, England and there met Gertrude. On November 7, 1917, they were married.

Chip looks mighty pleased with himself in the wedding picture, and Gertrude does too although we can't see much of her under her fashionable hat, behind her fashionable furs. Does she know what awaits her back in Spirit River? Does she know about the homestead shack on 160 acres of bush and muskeg, far from stores or trains or fashionable anything? Does she know that her new husband took no persuading at all to enlist the minute he heard England—and by extension—Canada was at war with Germany? In fact, he could hardly wait to be gone, taking time only to pack a few things and write a note for the front door that said, **"War is hell but what is homesteading?"**

Does she know all that? Not likely. Perhaps he was trying to tell her the night before their wedding when he responded to a toast to them with this comparison: **"As near as I can figure out, marriage is like war—the first seven years will be the worst."** Not the most encouraging news for a woman who's about to be married the next morning, but never mind. Gertrude also had the right stuff.

Another joke was made that night about a plot by Canada to rob England of her marriageable women. General Sir Sam Hughes responded to that assertion by saying, **"I have never been afraid to trust the Canadian soldier to shoot, fight and conduct himself as a gentleman, and I have no hesitation whatever in trusting him, without any aid of any society, to pick himself a good wife in England or elsewhere."** So there.

Fighting for one's country was a family tradition, according to Chip's mother who wrote him soon after he'd enlisted and she listed off all the ancestors who had preceded him into battle. There was the great grandfather who fought in the Revolutionary War in the US, on the British side, of course. He had to move to Canada, of course, since the Americans didn't approve of British sympathizers. Then there were the great uncles who fought in the War of 1812. Your own father fought in the Nova Scotia Militia, she added, and you have a brother and 14 cousins in khaki at this very minute.

Chip's brother Roland died in his khaki. Chip, on the other hand, got lucky. Somehow, in the heat of battle between enemy trenches and Allied trenches in France, he single-handedly confused and overwhelmed German soldiers on their side of the line so that he and his fellow soldiers were able to take 62 prisoner and capture 250 yards of trench.

That's how WW1 was measured—in feet and yards of trench taken, trenches being

Chip and Gertrude Kerr, 1917, London., England

143

exactly what they sound like—long ditches dug into the earth where soldiers could be protected somewhat from direct enemy fire. Eventually though, the men had to leave the safety of one trench and get to another through mud, gunfire, bombs and gas. It was awful, all of it. Some men were lucky, some weren't. Chip admitted as much when he said later about his actions, **"Just an ounce of opportunity and a ton of good luck."**

After the war, the conquering hero and his bride went back to the little gray shack near Spirit River and lived there like every other homesteader except for brief bursts of glory, like the time the Prince of Wales asked him to dinner at the palace in 1929, and ditto in 1956.

It doesn't seem fair that the men and women who fought in WW1 should be the ones whose sons and daughters have to fight in WW11, but that's what happened with the Kerr sons, four of them. All wanted to go fight the Hun. One was too young. So was another but he lied about his age and was overseas by the time he was 17. One died in a training accident in Yarmouth, NS. **"That's the only time I saw dad cry,"** his daughter Shirley remembered. But Chip himself couldn't stay out of it. He lied about his age too. He was 53 but somehow talked himself into the RCAF where he served on Sea Island, BC, as a military policeman and sergeant of the guard.

The old soldier finally died in 1963.

He would have loved the Port Moody Legion ceremonies on November 11, 1997. A granddaughter laid the wreath that cold morning at the base of the cenotaph beside the Chip Kerr branch of the Canadian Legion. There were more Kerrs there as well, a whole table full in the hall enjoying the traditional Remembrance Day fare—beer, pickles, cheese and crackers. And when the Simon Fraser pipe band filled the hall— and some of the outdoors—with *Amazing Grace*, there wasn't a dry eye in the place. People were doing what old soldiers would have them do—remember.

1917...A Paris Original in Hamiota...

Elizabeth Gutteridge meant to wear a good blue suit for her wedding. That's what she told her brother when she wrote to him in France to tell him that she and Norman had decided to go ahead and get married. Her fiancé wasn't going overseas after all. There was no reason to wait.

Yes, there was, her brother wrote back. Just wait long enough for me to get you a dress from France. Send me your measurements. So she did. John, an officer with the RAF, took them to the nuns at the convent where he was recuperating from wounds received during the fighting. The nuns set to work with needle and thread and a few weeks later, a parcel arrived in Hamiota, MB.

And that's how Elizabeth Gutteridge wore a handmade designer dress instead of her good blue suit when she and Norman Jordan were married December 12, 1917. It was made of a soft blue crepe de chine, full sleeves gathered to a tight wrist band, full

Norman and Elizabeth Jordan, 1917, Hamiota, MB

skirt with a belt the like of which no one had ever seen in Hamiota. A wide cummerbund almost with sculpted pink and blue fabric flowers across the front. Years later, her daughter Norma Jordan remembered that her mother loved that dress and wore it "for good" for many years.

The wedding picture was taken the next spring in Brandon. That often happened with weddings in years past; the picture was taken months, sometimes years after the wedding, depending on when money and a photographer were available.

For the first ten years of their married life, the Jordans continued to live in Hamiota. Norman was a carpenter and got work where he could. Elizabeth was, like most women of that time, a full-time homemaker, a faithful church worker, a sometime campaigner on behalf of women's rights (Nellie McClung was one of her heroes) and in time, a mother. Norma was born in 1921, and her younger brother in 1925.

He lived for seven weeks only. Norma can still remember how hard her mother tried to make her baby well, but he had a kidney infection and it could not be denied. Now, it would take a routine application of antibiotics but not then. The little white casket sat in front of the living room window, and it was open for the funeral service. Norma can remember it all—her father took her on his knee and broke the news to her, her mother just went silent. There were no more children.

A few years later, the family moved to Saskatoon where there seemed to be more jobs available for carpenters. Elizabeth died in 1962, Norman in 1978. Norma never married. There was someone once, she admits, but he went to the Second World War and never came back. There's an eerie echo there. Just as Chip Kerr's sons had to go to WWII, so did the Jordan's daughter remain single because of WW11. War has so many ripples.

1918....Mock Weddings For Fun and Profit...

No wonder the Tom Thumb wedding packed the house in Nelson, BC, on April 30, 1918. No wonder it had to be repeated by popular demand two weeks later. Who could resist such cute kids? Who could resist a wedding, for that matter? Put the two together and you've got a sure fire hit.

To be fair, the kids didn't just stand around looking adorable. They had lines to learn and choreography to remember. The bride, Miss Wilson, and the groom, Gerald Stibbs, had to learn their vows, for instance, and the minister David Proudfoot had to know where to stand and when to ask for the ring. Mother of the bride, Jean Lambert, had to be escorted to her seat by one of the ushers, and Vera Whalley had to learn to play the Wedding March on the organ. The Tom Thumb wedding, in other words, had all the elements of a regular wedding except it was little kids playing all the parts. Performance art is what it was, although the moms who made all the costumes and spent hours in rehearsal told everybody it was just this year's way to make some

money for the church. Instead of a rummage sale, we'll have a Tom Thumb wedding and charge everybody who wants to see it, they must have said. And then when it was such a success, they did it all over again with proceeds going to the Red Cross.

The Nelson Daily News said the whole affair came off in **"a magnificent manner."** Indeed, the editorial writer added, the local ministers and justices of the peace could take a few pointers from the little people.

Other communities certainly took pointers. There was a regular spate of Tom Thumb weddings in various BC communities in the late 1910s and into the 1920s. That they seemed to lose favor after 1929 is likely related to hard times, not enough money for satin waistcoats and fancy white dresses. Too bad. They were lovely.

Mock weddings using adult players were also great sport, but these were used for fun and frolic rather than profit. Generally, some good-natured guy with a heavy beard and likewise belly was talked into donning women's clothes with an old curtain for a veil perhaps and rhubarb leaves for a bridal bouquet. The possibilities were endless, but rubber boots were generally featured in some way. The groom was inevitably little and henpecked, the bridesmaid was inevitably in curlers, and so on. In the Nampa, AB, local history book is the account of one mock wedding where the mock minister read the vows from an old Eaton's catalogue. This is before television, remember. People made their own fun.

1918...A Manitoba Mennonite Wedding...

There was no nonsense at the wedding of Henry Friesen and Anna Penner, July 21, 1918. Not that it was a cheerless affair, it wasn't that. It's just that Mennonites take their religion seriously. That's why they came to Canada in the first place. They wanted a place where they could practice their religion in peace, where they could build communities based on brotherly love, adult baptism and non-violence.

It was that non-violence business that caused problems in their native Russia. One government would say...OK, be pacifist. The next government would retract that promise and say...No you'll have to fight like everybody else. And so on. Eventually, to be truly Mennonite, they had to move, many to South America, some to North America—especially Manitoba.

Henry Friesen was born in 1889 in Niverville, just south of Winnipeg. His father was a farmer, he became a farmer. That's what Mennonites did—they farmed, although it must be admitted that only one of Henry's three sons became a farmer. Daughter Anna married a farmer, does that count? Anyway, it's a sign that Mennonites had to change right along with other Canadians. The one thing that didn't change, however, was their opposition to compulsory military service.

Pacifism was not the most popular point of view in 1918 but because conscription was not compulsory in WWI, Mennonite men did not have to go through the process of finding alternative ways of serving. As conscientious objectors, that's what they had to do in WWII. It wasn't always easy being a Mennonite.

But it was, that summer day in July when Henry and Anna were married. Anna wore an ankle length dress of royal blue, Henry his best dark suit. Most of the other women that morning wore white blouses and dark skirts, most of the other men wore their best dark suits. They were at church, after all. The wedding would happen after the regular church service was finished. First things first.

A wedding dinner was served at the home of the bride's parents, Mr. and Mrs. Erdman Penner. Everyone came; there was no need for invitations. Everyone knew what would be served—borscht, cold meat, buns, plume mousse. Everyone enjoyed the break and wished the young couple well.

Henry and Anna picked up her wedding dowry—a good milking cow with calf— and moved in with his mother and younger brother. There they had two sons, then moved to another house and had another son and daughter. And then Anna had the dubious distinction of being the first patient in the tuberculosis sanitarium in St. Boniface. It didn't help. She died of the disease, aged 31. Nowadays tuberculosis can be prevented by vaccination and treated with drugs but in 1918, it was a killer.

Various family members helped out with the kids, and many years later Henry remarried.

1919...Wedding Within A Riot...

Frances Forrester and William Sharman were married in Winnipeg on Bloody Saturday, June 21, 1919, although by six o'clock that evening, the downtown streets had been cleared of most strikers and the bodies of dead and wounded had been taken away. Not the most propitious day for a wedding, certainly, but what could they do? The church was booked, the preacher waiting.

So, the bride wore a gown of white satin, the bridesmaid a gown of pink taffeta, and while the register was being signed, the soloist sang, *All Joy Be Thine*.

Outside on the streets and in the north end where many of the disenchanted workers lived, there was no joy. The General Strike called six weeks earlier was over with no clear winners. The 30,000 workers who wanted higher wages, better hours and the right to collective bargaining were no closer to their goals, or so it seemed that awful night. By the same token, the government and civic leaders who had refused to consider the demands of the workers looked coldhearted and inept, especially after they fired the city police force and replaced them with 2,000 "Specials" with vague instructions to keep the peace. Give a man a gun or a club and how does he keep the peace?

On that bloody Saturday, while Bill and Frances were trying to have a nice peaceful wedding, the pent up frustration of the strikers erupted in a downtown mass demonstration of pushing, shouting and vandalism. The Mayor came out on the steps of City Hall and read the Riot Act, which was about as effective as spitting in the wind. Finally, the "Specials" lined up against the strikers in the street and like Cossacks of old proceeded to push the strikers back. That was just too much. Was this Canada, the land of freedom and opportunity that attracted so many of the immigrant workers, or was this their worst memory of the old country?

The strikers pushed back, and inevitably someone—one of the police forces—fired into the crowd. One man was killed and others were wounded. Shock and disbelief stunned both sides, and many left the scene but there were still knots of angry people left on Main Street. When Frances and Bill left the reception at her parents' home to go to the CPR station, they had to have police escort to the train station. It was the longest day of the year in more ways than one.

J.S. Woodsworth emerged as the good guy of the strike. Always a spokesman for the underprivileged, he took the socialist cause into Parliament when he became an MP and eventually the founder of the CCF party, the Co-operative Commonwealth Federation, which in turn became the ND Party. Other leaders of the strike were elected to the provincial government and represented the working man and woman at that level. It was through these legislators that the words "**old age pension**" and "**unemployment insurance**" came into the lexicon of politics.

So in the long run, Bloody Saturday made a huge difference to all Canadians.

As for the Sharmans, they had a seesaw life. It was not Bill's idea that he should be a doctor. That was the cherished dream of his mother, the cherished dream of many mothers, for that matter, and even though Bill spent most of his life in the medical field, he told his son once that he would have liked to be a commercial artist. As for Frances, she would have liked to be a concert singer. Her vocal coach cried when she heard that Frances was going to get married because, of course, marriage meant the end of any professional career for a woman. There were two daughters, one son. Both daughters had careers. The world changed after that generation.

THE 1920s

Old Country weddings made new, new fangled airplane weddings, the Rabbi's daughter and History's son

The Church/Ion wedding, 1927, Medicine Hat, AB

1920...Ring Around the Cow Pie...

1920 is the year of the Florences—Florence Elliott who married Jack Tooley, Florence MacKenzie who married Charles Henderson and Florence Hawker who married George Askin.

The Tooleys were the first couple to tie the knot that year—January 7, 1920, in Blackfalds, AB. They must have depended on that old cliché—their love to keep them warm—because their house that first winter was so drafty, they could see daylight through the cracks. Anything freezable inside the house froze—the slop pail, the water pail, the chamber pot. Since chamber pots have already been explained and water pails are pretty well self-explanatory, here's a word about slop pails. They were a crude necessity; every new bride in charge of a household had to establish one somewhere in the vicinity of the kitchen. Into the bucket designated as slop pail went the slops— the potato peelings, the dirty dishwater, sour milk, rotten apples, etc. In other words, the stuff that would go into a garburetor or garbage pail nowadays. Once the slop pail was full, it was either flung into nearby bush or fed to the pigs. Emptying the slop pail became one of the tasks that the children in the family fought over. Whose turn it was, and who did it last time, and so on.

Here's another detail about housekeeping in the early days that isn't often shown on nostalgia TV. Florence was expected to look after killing, plucking and cleaning the chickens for household use. She saw what had to be done but just couldn't bring herself to do it—to catch a poor innocent chicken, lay its neck upon a wooden chopping block and then chop off its head with an axe. Finally faced with yet another meal of eggs, she decided she'd have to manage this task. Every other farm woman could do it. So could she. So she caught a chicken, spoke to it gently, **"Come on ducky, put your head down there,"** and was poised with the axe when the chicken winked at her. That was more than she could take. It was eggs again for a few more meals. Eventually, she got the knack but it was never her favorite household task.

Maybe it was during one of the chicken episodes but somewhere along the line, she lost her wedding ring. Had no idea where it went. Much later, it turned up in a cow pie on a nearby farm. Don't ask how it got there, and don't ask how they found it.

Jack Tooley had some learning to do when he first came to Canada too. He was an orphan, 14 years old, being sent from England to Canada to live with relatives, so what did he know? He arrived wearing short pants and a pistol on the belt that held up his short pants. At least the pistol would have discouraged jokes about the short pants. When WWI was declared, he joined up right away, and that's when he met Florence in England. When WWII was declared, he lined up again and went overseas, this time as a tradesman. Three of their five children also served in that war.

Florence stayed home with the remaining children and the chickens.

1920...First Airplane Elopement...

The next Florence wedding in 1920 was that of Florence MacKenzie and Charles Henderson who were married on June 16 in Dodsland, SK. It was a record setting event for two reasons: it was the first airplane elopement on the prairies and it was brought off right under the noses of a town full of people.

The people of Dodsland suspected a wedding was in the offing and they had elaborate plans for all the pranks they would play on Charlie and Florence. Especially Charlie. Charlie had played enough tricks on other people that they were determined he would not escape his turn. Neighbors were assigned to watch the Henderson house for signs of unusual behavior, ditto for his newspaper office. The rice, the cans, the noise makers, the nuisance makers, all were in readiness.

But they were having too much fun at the first annual Dodsland sports day to notice that Charles and Florence had slipped into the newspaper office. There, they had the fastest wedding on record. The editor whistled the Wedding March for them as they galloped into place, the minister barely had his Bible open before they both said I do, and off they went in a cloud of dust toward a field outside of town. That's when the townspeople got suspicious and began the chase in their own cars.

At the field, Lieutenant H.S. McClelland had his Curtiss Jenny biplane warmed up and ready to go. He'd been there earlier in the day to give a barnstorming demonstration as part of the sports day events but now he was waiting to whisk the newly weds off into the wild blue yonder. They barely made it. Charles almost threw Florence into the forward cockpit, he climbed in, they were off. Those left on earth could only shake their fists and vow revenge. **"To say the event created a sensation would be putting it mildly,"** the newspaper reported next week. It also reported, incidentally, that a subscription had been taken of the Dodsland community to buy the newly weds a gift. The total collected was $141.75, most of which went to buy a 96 piece dinner set, the request of Mrs. Henderson.

Charles Henderson came from Nebraska to SK originally as a representative of a land development company but he soon branched out into the newspaper business, his own farm and by 1940 into politics when he became Liberal MP for Kindersley. Not surprisingly, he made his maiden speech in the House of Commons about fair play for farmers. Florence came with her family from Ontario and trained as a teacher. One of her first teaching jobs was in Dodsland, and the rest is blue sky.

There were two sons, two daughters. Charles died in 1957, Florence in 1987.

1920...Three Centuries for Florence...

There'll be no talk of dying for the third Florence in this trilogy of weddings. Florence Hawker was born in 1899 and intends to live into the 2000s so that she can say she lived through three centuries. At last count, she was 99 and holding, living on her own in Arcola, SK. She had to give up driving at age 98 but she continued to be useful—her words—by making afghans.

There's a hint of that determination in the wedding picture of Florence and George Askin, married November 3, 1920. Florence is standing beside a seated George, her hands on her hips as if to say, OK George, let's get this show on the road. She says that wasn't the case, that the photographer suggested the pose, but it does look pretty natural nevertheless.

As for the wedding day, she remembers it was cold and windy with sand and grit blowing through the dry grass and along the dirt road to the farm. George couldn't put his stiff collar on before he came into the house; it would have gotten dirty. She wore a white silk dress that her mother had made, and as soon as she got back from their honeymoon trip, she cut the thing off and turned it into a dress for good. Wore it out, she said proudly on the phone. Couldn't waste in those days.

Did they have a reception? Well, sort of. A turkey dinner in her mom's kitchen. Then they took the train at Kisbey, thus foiling the pranksters who awaited them at the Arcola train station and went to Weyburn to visit relatives. Then back home to George's farm to get the show on the road.

By 1927, they thought they were far enough ahead to buy a car so got a Chevrolet Landau sedan for $1,099 cash. That was nice, but when the Dirty Thirties came along, it went into the shed, and the old horse and buggy came back into use. With little or no

George and Florence Askin, 1920, Arcola, SK

money on a farm, you could get hay for the horse but no gas for the car. And so they bumped along through life, Florence always ready to tell their six children that hard work is the answer. Never mind the question.

They were together for 62 years.

1921...Unto the Hills Around...

You can rest assured that Jasper is as beautiful as it can be on this 15th day of June, 1921. For one thing, there won't be any laundry flapping on the clotheslines around town, no long underwear or ladies' unmentionables hanging around for everyone to see. Park Superintendent S. Maynard Rogers has decreed that washing shall be

done on Mondays only and that by Tuesday there shall be no stray socks or stubborn overalls left outside to distract the eye from the town's natural beauty.

Since most housewives obeyed the old adage—wash on Mondays, iron on Tuesday, mend on Wednesday, etc.—the rule was seldom broken but one has to wonder about the baby's diapers by Friday! But that's another story for another day. For today, Beatrice Rogers and Alvin Mills are being married in beautiful Jasper, on a Wednesday, a day that the sun shines on everything but laundry.

Beatrice was the adopted daughter of Lt. Col. S. Maynard Rogers, the first superintendent of Jasper Park, and his wife. She came to them when she was eight years old after her own mother, Mrs. Rogers' sister, had died. The groom was Alvin Mills, most often referred to as Millsey. He came to Jasper in 1919 after he returned from service overseas with the Seaforth Highlanders.

The wedding was about as grand as it could be, considering that nothing could ever outdo the grandeur of the setting. That was always Maynard Rogers' first concern— that human habitation should always come second to the setting or should at least fit into the setting. That's why he had famed architect Alexander Calderon design a park administration building and residence that would look rustic yet substantial, one that would use local materials as much as possible—logs, stones, rocks. It's still there, doing yeoman duty in Jasper as the park Information Center.

But when Beatrice and Millsey were married, it was "The Boulders," and it was where Mrs. Rogers hosted an "At Home" just prior to the wedding. This is how the newspaper described it.

"Mrs. Rogers received her guests in the large lounge room with its massive artistic boulder fireplace, one of the sights of Jasper. She was assisted by Miss Beatrice Rogers who was wearing a lovely frock of shot blue and pink silk faille. The skirt being cut in petals, while the simple straight bodice in jumper effect with no defined waist line was caught to the left hip with a cluster of silver roses. With this she wore dainty silver slippers and stockings of silver hue."

"Tea was served in the bright dining room and was poured by Mrs. Fleming while Mrs. W.S. Jeffrey presided over the coffee urn. Mrs. Jackman and Mrs. Fred Brewster assisted while little Phyllis Fleming in a dainty white net frock, girdled with pink, acted as doorkeeper and sweetly admitted the guests."

"During the afternoon, Mr. J.B. Suape, who is the possessor of a delightful baritone voice sang *Thora* and being heartily encored responded with *Tommy Lad* and *Mother O' Mine* (words by Kipling). Miss Rogers sang charmingly *Alice Blue Gown*, an appropriate song, and Mrs. A. Dayton contributed *A Little Grey Home in the West*, and *One Fleeting Hour*."

The newspaper also indicated that no invitations were being issued to the wedding since everyone in town was welcome to attend both the ceremony at St. Mary's Church and the reception to be held, where else, at The Boulders.

Thus, it's at The Boulders where the wedding party had their pictures taken, Beatrice and Alvin Mills are in front, flower girls Phyllis Flemming and Dorothy Fulton on either side, and Mr. and Mrs. Rogers barely visible on the steps behind. The boulders are visible, however. Col. Rogers would be pleased.

Jasper Park was first set aside as a Reserve in 1907. Only the most independent and most intrepid lived there or traveled through but by 1911 when the Grand Trunk Railway made an appearance, it began to attract some permanent residents and many more non-permanent. Tourists, in other words. Not that Rogers was going to allow any nonsense. In 1915, somebody brought in a motorcycle. Rogers had it shipped right out again. Imagine bringing a noisy smelly machine into this peaceful mountain sanctuary. Mind you, it wasn't many more years before cars started shattering the peace of the place and Rogers had to accept that change. In fact, during the depression of the 1930s, the government established work camps in the mountains. The unemployed men who were sent there were put to work building roads. First, the road to Edmonton was made somewhat passable and then a road linking Jasper and Banff was opened. The place was under siege and has been ever since. Col. Rogers would not be pleased.

Beatrice and Millsey moved to Vancouver during the depression years and lived the rest of their lives there. They had two sons, Allan and Robert.

1922...A Marriage Made in History...

Juliette Lagimodiere and Arthur Goulet represent so much Canadian history, it's a wonder they can shoulder the load. In truth, they're textbooks, they're Canadian heritage moments, they're symbols of the way we were. They're also newly weds.

Juliette's story goes back to Jean Baptiste Lagimodiere, a French Canadian adventurer, and Marie Anne Gaboury, his wife, who became the first non native woman to travel west beyond the Red River area. Into the west, she took their first baby, Reine, and had another one enroute. Why that experience has not been made into a movie is hard to understand. Picture this—a pregnant Marie Anne riding across the prairie, baby Reine in a bag at her side. Suddenly, her horse spots a herd of buffalo and runs headlong into their midst. There's no stopping the horse; it's trained to chase buffalo. All Marie

Anne can do is hold onto the reins and the baby and hope that someone comes to her rescue before she and Reine are thrown beneath the thundering hooves of thousands of buffalo. Thankfully, Jean Baptiste sees her plight and rides through the stampeding buffalo to bring her horse to a stop.

A few hours later, baby #2 is born, and his mother gave him a name that would forever evoke his birthplace. She called him La Prairie. A few years later, a baby girl was born while camping near an evergreen forest. Marie Anne named her Cypres. And even later when the family was settled permanently in the Red River area, she gave birth to another girl, this one without any reference to her birthplace, but Julie's name was destined to go down in history too.

Meanwhile, Arthur has an even longer lineage in Canada. One of his ancestors came over with the expeditions of Champlain in the early 1600s and saw what he liked in New France. So he brought the wife and family and settled on land near the present cathedral in Quebec City. Thus, he got the title of "first farmer" in settled Canada. Others of Arthur's connections came with the explorer La Verendrye in the 1700s and also settled in Quebec. Some eventually wandered west; it was an occupational hazard in the 1800s, this wandering west, and some settled in the Red River area. Add to that mix a Hudson's Bay Company factor called Severeight who came from Scotland to work in the west, and you have a family that's been in Canada a long time. Which sets the scene for the wedding on November 15, 1922, of Juliette, the great great granddaughter of Marie Anne and Jean Baptiste, and Arthur, the who-can-count-anymore descendant of some of the very first visitors to Canada.

They look remarkably calm in their wedding picture, as if the load of their shared significant history was for the moment forgotten, which it probably was. They were married in the Catholic church in Lorette, a French Canadian community just south of Winnipeg. Juliette wore a jersey blouse, which she had embroidered and beaded herself, along with her good dark skirt. Arthur wore his good dark suit. As soon as the wedding picture was taken, they had a wedding supper with Juliette's folks and then went home to their own place. Nothing fancy. Arthur was a labourer.

They had eight children. One died in infancy, one was adopted, and one became an unofficial historian for the family. It is she, Agnes Goulet, who sorts out the family connections. Her mother Juliette was descended from William Lagimodiere who was the son of Elzear Lagimodiere who was the son of Jean Baptiste Lagimodiere (more commonly known as La Prairie) who was the baby born to Marie Anne and Jean Baptiste that wild night on the prairies. The night that should be immortalized in movies!

However, there is one part of the family story has made it into movies and then some. Marie Anne and Jean Baptiste's youngest daughter was Julie. She married a Mr. Riel and they had a son named Louis. And it is Louis Riel about whom books, plays and songs are written. It is Louis Riel who gets the statues and the titles. History does that, picks one name and loads all the past on it. But the Lagimodiere/Goulet names get a mention here and there as well. There's a major thoroughfare, Lagimodiere Boulevard, in Winnipeg, a Lagimodiere School in Lorette, a Goulet Street in St. Boniface, and a Goulet chapter of Knights of Columbus.

1922...Blindsided By Love...

When Harry Taylor brought his new bride to the farming district of McCord in SK, one of the neighbors remarked, **"My God, Harry, you must have got on the blind side of that gal."**

In other words, she was about the prettiest thing to set foot in McCord and how did a poor farmer like Harry bring it off? How did he get her to leave a nice job in New

York—a paying job, mind you—to come to a log shack on the Canadian prairies?

It was love, by all accounts. Pure and simple.

Harry met Maude MacNish when she was a student nurse in Brockville, ON. They corresponded during the time he was overseas in WW1 but there was no understanding as such. Just a friendship, or so she thought, but once Harry was back from Europe, he went to work. Found out she was nursing in a New York hospital, found out she was engaged to another guy. Nothing ventured, nothing gained, he figured, so he went to New York, wooed and won her away. They were married March 7, 1922.

She wore a cream colored satin dress in a shade that was called "Pussy willow." The pearls were a gift from, who else, Harry. As for other gifts, Maude asked her family to give her money so that she could ship her furniture from New York to her new home, to her little gray house in the west. She and Harry traveled on the same train as the furniture and whenever the train stopped for any length of time, they made excuses to go back to the freight cars to make sure everything was OK. In reality, they wanted some time alone.

It was that love bug again.

Apparently, the furniture fit into the house or the house fit into the furniture, whichever, and they settled down to be a proper old married pair. It was hard at first—fun kept breaking out. Harry liked to tease Maude. Whenever she settled into the outdoor biffy for a good read, for instance, he'd throw rocks in the general vicinity of body parts. Or he'd threaten to set the little house on fire. She'd react by chasing him around the garden path, and so on. They were young, they enjoyed one another.

But life has a way of interfering with fun. It was winter, it was wash day. Maude was holding their second child, Bettie, sitting in front of the stove as she waited for snow to melt in tubs on the woodstove. One of the tubs was already boiling when Harry came in with another tub full of snow. As he moved the tubs around, he accidentally knocked the hot one off the stove. As it fell, the boiling water dumped all over Maude's lower body. All she had time to do was throw Bettie over her shoulder onto the chesterfield behind her. Bettie still has a patch of rougher skin on the back of one of her hands but Maude was burned very badly. She spent months in the hospital, so long that the baby she was expecting at the time of the accident was born there. That was George. She came home shortly after his birth, and she coped from then on with stiff knees and scarred legs. It was a terrible accident.

The oldest child, Margaret Alice, stayed with Harry while Maude recuperated but Bettie was cared for by her Aunt Emma in Herbert, SK, for the next 2-3 years. In fact, the whole family moved to Herbert when Harry finally admitted he wasn't much of a farmer. He got a job in town, but never made much money, especially during the late 1930s when the west was gripped by worldwide depression. Thus, when war was declared in 1939, he lied about his age and joined up again. Lots of men did that—lied about their age. Made themselves younger than they really were so they could get a steady job and pay cheque. Harry worked with the service police in Canada.

On the back of the wedding picture that daughter Bettie Hall has in her home in Herbert are Maude's words to Harry, **"To the dearest boy in the world."** A love story to the bitter end.

1922...If He's Dancing, It Must be Serious...

Saidye Rosner always said it was her new brown wool cape trimmed with red fox that caught the eye of Sam Bronfman one cold day in Winnipeg. Whether it was that or something else—her energy, vitality or that elusive thing called love at first sight, it quickly took hold and Sam watched for the chance to meet her. One day he saw her in the front row of the women's section during synagogue. During a break in the service, he suggested a walk. That was the beginning of what they called their "Holy Courtship."

Sam followed that up with an invitation to a B'nai B'rith dance. She knew something serious was in the air because he didn't really like dancing. If he was asking her to a dance, then she'd better pay attention. She did, and a month later on Valentine's Day, 1922, they got engaged. A day later, two dozen American Beauty roses arrived at the Rosner residence, blooms so lovely that Saidye's mother couldn't stand to throw them out once they lost their freshness. Instead, she made rose petal jam of them.

Sam Bronfman wasn't yet the Seagram's baron but he was on his way, which meant he traveled most of the time. Thus, the courtship continued by letter, lovely old-fashioned lovey dovey letters. **"I could cry because there are no flying machines to be had, even for a few hugs and kisses, the kind we love so well,"** he wrote from Calgary. Saidye responded, **"Your thoughts are so noble darling. And all I can say on my own is that I love you and your sweet and noble thoughts more than I ever knew or dreamed was possibly within me."**

After the wedding announcement appeared in the paper, Sam wrote, **"One month. Then and forever we are one."**

They married June 20, 1922, at the Shaarey Tzedek in Winnipeg. Saidye wore a wonderful dress, according to the Manitoba Free Press; her sister as matron of honor wore a remarkable hat trimmed with ostrich plumes; her younger sisters wore mauve, and Sam wore a morning suit with a top hat. There were many more adjectives and much more detailed description, but one detail was missed. The bride did not wear the gift of the groom as was common in the 1920s—a necklace or earrings or some such bauble. No, Sam presented Saidye with a new Studebaker coupe. Try wearing that around your neck.

It was a long way from Wapella, SK, where Sam's folks homesteaded in 1899, but it proved that indeed Canada was the land of opportunity.

There were four children, Charles, Edgar, Mindel and Phyllis.

1924...Double Wedding, Double Trouble...

Someone once told Shirley Smith that double weddings were unlucky. She pooh-poohed the superstition at the time, but when she looks back on the fate of the two couples in this picture, she wonders.

Shirley is the daughter of Daniel Thomas and Elsie Mohr, the couple on the right of the picture. The other couple is Frank Mohr and Ruth Thomas. In other words, brother and sister married brother and sister. The date—November 19, 1924.

Why a double wedding? Simply—money. It cost a lot even then to bring off a big wedding reception, so two weddings for the price of one reception was good value

Frank and Ruth Mohr, Daniel and Elsie Thomas, 1924, Josephburg, AB

indeed. Besides, the families lived and worked so close together in the Josephburg area near Edmonton, AB., it seemed natural to share a wedding day as well. And if you're going to share, you might as well match. Elsie and Ruth obviously bought the same dress and headpiece—likely from Eaton's catalogue. And Daniel and Frank seem to have bought the same suit and shoes, but then men's suits in the 1920s looked alike anyway—dark, three button, worn only for good.

It was the first double wedding ceremony in the community, so it was a good party at the Philip Mohr home. But once the party was over, both couples went to their respective homes and settled down to farm. Thanks to the wisdom of their fathers who emigrated from Germany and did not settle until they found the right place, they had good land. It was their luck that turned bad.

Six months after the wedding, Daniel Thomas was sawing wood with a tractor-powered saw. Somehow, the saw blade broke loose from the shaft, swung out of control and cut Daniel's leg off just above the ankle. He said later that it was a good thing he had his legs apart at the time or both would have been cut off. Now comes a saga of health care that's hard to believe in the face of modern systems for such emergencies.

A neighbor had a phone. One of the wood sawing crew ran there, the neighbor phoned the doctor in Fort Saskatchewan, some six miles away. The doctor came part way by car but the roads got too muddy for him to go further. A horse and buggy had to be found to take him the rest of the way. Once at the Thomas farm, he stabilized Daniel as much as possible, loaded him back into the horse drawn buggy and took him to town. There, they waited for an ambulance to come out from Edmonton, but it wasn't until 4 p.m. that afternoon, some seven hours after the accident, that Daniel was finally delivered to the hospital.

He didn't even have the comfort of unconsciousness because he remembered the whole awful trip and he remembered, even worse, the doctor at the hospital asking for the saw. His leg was amputated just below the knee and somehow he recovered. But that was just the beginning of this saga. Then he had to find himself a prosthesis, although they weren't called anything that polite in 1925. They were called 'peg legs' and they weren't easily available. Daniel finally found an ad for one in a farm newspaper. Wrote away to Winnipeg, wired it on with copper wire, and managed. That was the first of many. All cost a lot and all of it came out of his own pocket. Give thanks for modern health care.

Meanwhile, Ruth and Frank toiled away at their own farm. A son, Earl, was born and then in 1932 a daughter, Violet. Whether childbirth so weakened Ruth that she couldn't mount a resistance, or whether the pneumonia was that strong, nobody knows, but Ruth died two months after the birth of Violet. Antibiotics would have helped but they hadn't been discovered yet. So the other half of the double came to the rescue. Elsie and Daniel moved in with Frank to help out. Four years later, Frank remarried, so they went home again.

Life was kinder after that. The farms flourished. Antibiotics became available after 1945, health care became—by stages—a government service, roads and cars moved people much more quickly. Everything moved faster and further; it was hard to keep up sometimes. In fact, grandpa Thomas wouldn't believe that men had landed on the moon. He watched it on TV but wasn't convinced. It was an elaborate sham, a send-up, he said. There couldn't be that much change in one lifetime.

1924...Famous Bush Pilot Crashes...

Space ships blasting to the moon, Grandpa Thomas couldn't believe, but airplanes would have been commonplace to him by the 1920s. He was in Wop May territory, after all.

Wop May became an Alberta and Canadian legend in WWI when he accounted for the death of the famous Baron of Richtofen, the Red Baron. May didn't shoot him down; that accomplishment belonged to squadron leader Roy Brown who saw Richtofen closing in for the kill above May's plane. Just in time, Brown fired from above, sent the Red Baron spiraling to earth, and made Wop May a hero. That's right; somehow Wop May became a bigger hero for almost getting killed than Roy Brown did for actually killing the dreaded enemy air ace. Go figure.

Back in Edmonton after the war, he kept up his airborne heroics. At first, he used airplanes to entertain—barnstorming at local fairs and exhibitions—but it wasn't long before he got serious with the possibilities of air flight. For one thing, he and another pilot, Vic Horner, flew in an open cockpit plane in the darkest and coldest part of winter to Fort Vermilion in northern Alberta to deliver diphtheria antitoxin. Had they not flown it in, it would have taken weeks to get there. Many would have died. On another occasion, he and his plane joined the search for the Mad Trapper in the Arctic, the first time a plane had been used in a manhunt. In between the feats of derring-do, he established the role of bush pilots in opening the west.

Naturally, when such a public figure got married, the papers went all out. **"Wop Crashes,"** one paper announced in big headlines. Another said, **"Warrior of Many Battles Bows to Cupid's Dictates."** There was even a poem that went on and on about the "reckless lad" who knew how to "squirt the lead." This is how it ended:

> **But now he's crashed—no whizzing shell**
> **Has brought him down or cramped his style**
> **His epitaph will read: "He fell**
> **Before a charming woman's smile."**
> **And yet us single chaps won't sigh**
> **Because he's left our ranks that way**
> **We're all too glad to cheer and cry**
> **"Good luck to Wop and Mrs. May."**

On November 24, 1924, Wop married Violet Bode, a young British born woman who was way more keen on horses than airplanes. They were earth and sky, but then earth and sky have been getting along forever.

1924...Before the Beans

Bow Island, AB, has a bean as tall as a house on the outskirts of town now. A sign announces proudly that **"Bow Island is the Bean Capital of the West."** All around the town are prosperous looking farms, big houses, machines that are way bigger than the bean, but when Ralph Schlachter arrived with his folks in 1909, **"there wasn't a neighbor in sight,"** he wrote later. **"Just a lot of tall prairie grass."** And no beans either.

They came in two CPR box cars. One held a wagon and farm machinery; the other held mama, papa, four kids, five horses, nine cows, and one dog. Luckily, the trip from Regina to Bow Island was short. The next part of the trip was longer. All the stuff had to be unloaded from the boxcars, reassembled, rounded up and organized in order to get on the road for home. Except there was no road and no one knew where home was. They had the legal description of the land but it was still a job to find the surveyor's stakes, especially since they also had to find a way across the wide open prairie. It was like landing on the moon in many ways. Uncharted, unknown.

That they managed, that they built themselves a cave-like structure in a hillside to live in for the first while, that they built more buildings and plowed the land, that they succeeded, is a story told again and again in the west. It almost gets boring except that it was an incredible achievement over and over again.

The oldest Schlachter son, Ralph, established his own farm nearby and on November 11, 1924, he married Katie Shatz in Sacred Heart Church. See—they had even built a church.

The Shatz story was much like the Schlachter's, except they had three boxcars full of stuff instead of two, one for machinery, one for cows and one for eight prize horses. The family got to ride in the passenger coaches but George stayed in the boxcars with his animals. Someone had to feed and water them. He might still have been in North Dakota had it not been for a Canadian agent who came around singing the praises of free Canadian land. It was hard to resist free land, a new start. So they up and moved north, built up another good farm. In 1914, when WWI started, the eight prize horses were sold to the government to be sent overseas. One matched pair went for $1,000. It was about then that he bought his first Model T Ford for about $500. Shows you what was important in 1914.

Ralph Schlachter and Katie Shatz met at a country-dance or at church. Those were the two possible venues for courting. Mind you, Ralph improved his chances by obtaining a good matched team of high-spirited horses and a handsome buggy, the better to impress his girl friend and her father. The better, also, to cover the 15 miles between the two homes. Once they decided to marry and got permission from the folks, the date was set for November 11. There were two reasons for picking that day: it was a holiday so people who worked in town could come and it was the day that the parish priest would be available.

Katie's mother made her dress of white satin, pearl beads and lace. The headpiece, veil, shoes and flowers were all purchased in Medicine Hat. There were no formal invitations; everyone was invited to both the wedding and the three-day reception at the Shatz home. Not that everyone stayed for every minute of the three-day party—neighbors came and went throughout the celebration—but it was such a welcome diversion from work and worry that most stayed as long as they could. Besides, the food was great— chicken soup, roast chicken with dressing, fruit pies, and traditional kuchen. Everything was homemade, even the chokecherry wine.

But once the party was over, it was over. Time to get real. So they did, built up a good farm within eight miles of both sets of parents, had three children, managed through good times and bad, and celebrated 69 years of marriage.

1925...Wooed on the Princess Patricia...

If ever you're tempted to think Canadians all came out of the same box, read on. The four weddings of 1925 are about as different as they can be: a maritime wedding, an Icelandic wedding, a Jewish wedding and a double wedding that included a future prime minister of Canada, but he didn't know it at the time. Neither did she. Had she known, she might have said, **"I don't."**

The four weddings are an indication of the prosperity that Canada was experiencing in the mid 1920s. Everything is relative, mind you. Many of the very recent immigrants on the prairies were struggling like crazy, but the more established population on either end of western Canada was getting ahead. There were jobs, houses, streets, churches, big weddings.

The first wedding that year was the maritime one when Amy Kenilworth Gilchrist married Alexander Stuart Moffat on January 3, 1925, in Nanaimo, BC. Both came from seafaring folk—Alex's father served 32 years in the BC Coastal Service, Amy's dad 20 years. Alex added to the record with 38 years of service on ships, and his and Amy's four sons all took their turns, albeit shorter ones, with the coastal service. No wonder they never used the generic word "ship" in that family. They spoke instead of "The Princess Patricia" or "The Kathleen" as if they were part of the family.

Alex knew he was going to work on boats. He just didn't know how soon. After completing an apprenticeship in steam turbines with Todd's shipyards in Tacoma, Washington, he came home to Victoria to have a well-earned rest, or so he thought. But his dad had other ideas. He had him signed up as 13th Engineer on "The Empress of Russia" by week's end. Two years and several ships later, he was 3rd Engineer of "The Princess Patricia" with the BC Coastal Service. That's when Amy met him and his Patricia. They met on the ship, they got engaged on the ship, they left for their honeymoon on it.

And just in case you don't think our language and our sensitivities have changed in the last 75 years, here's how Amy's going away dress was described in the newspaper: **"The bride traveled in a smart coat of silk velour with a bleached beaver collar and a chic brown hat. Her dress was of nigger brown canton, trimmed with large moire blocks of the same hue."**

In 1941, the British Admiralty came calling in BC looking for ships, any ships that might be able to help the war effort. "The Kathleen" and "The Marguerite" got the nod. So did Alex Moffat. He left with Kathleen in November 1941 bound for the Middle East by way of the southern Pacific, an expedition made much more dangerous when the US declared war on Japan following Pearl Harbor in December 1941. The Kathleen survived; her sister ship The Marguerite did not.

Alex and The Kathleen returned in 1944 and both went back into domestic service, Alex as the ship's Chief Engineer. **"All went well,"** Amy wrote in her memoirs, **"until September, 1952. I went down to the CPR station to see a friend off to Vancouver. One of the officers of the ship in at the time came to me and told me he heard on the radio that The Kathleen had gone ashore at Juneau in Alaska."**

Sure enough, Alex's ship had gone down. Crew and passengers were OK, but The Kathleen was lost. It was like losing a family member. Alex grieved her mightily. Oh, he worked on other ships after that—a total of 21 in his lifetime—but he never forgot his Kathleen. Neither did Amy. She has pages of words and pictures in her scrapbook about The Kathleen's sinking, and never once does she murmur resentment about the attention paid to her rival. Naval wives must learn to share their husbands that way.

Alexander and Amy Moffat, 1925, Nanaimo, BC

1925...The Rabbi's Daughter and the Rabbi...

The Kahanovitch wedding in 1925 was the biggest event the Jewish community in Winnipeg had ever experienced. This is the wedding announcement, translated from the Israelite Press, June 19, 1925.

"A wedding ceremony of unusual interest will take place on Tuesday next, June 23 at 5 pm, when Miss Kahanovitch, daughter of our popular Chief Rabbi, I.L. Kahanovitch, will be united in marriage to the young Rabbi Wohlgelernter of Toronto. It is quite a unique event in Canada at any rate that a Rabbi's daughter should marry a Rabbi and given the esteem and great popularity that Rabbi Kahanovitch enjoys, not only in Winnipeg but throughout the west, as well as the fact that Rabbi Wohlgelernter himself has in the short time that he has been in Winnipeg, gained many admirers, it is expected that the wedding which will take place at the residence of Rabbi Kahanovitch, Flora Avenue, will be attended by the largest number of people ever present on such an occasion."

And so it was. In the post wedding write-up, it was estimated that 4,000 people filled the yard and street around the Rabbi's house during the ceremony, some 400 of whom sat down to dinner at the Talmud Torah Hall while another 600 attended later in the evening. (There were 19,000 Jews in Manitoba in the 1931 census, so an attendance figure of some 4,000 in 1925 probably means about ⅕ of all Jews in the province were present in one way or another for this important wedding.)

The ceremony itself would have followed traditional Jewish custom, with the bride and groom saying their vows beneath a canopy upon which is customarily written the words from the book of Jeremiah, **"The voice of mirth and the voice of joy, the voice of the bridegroom and the voice of the bride."** Under the canopy, the bride stands at the groom's right.

The service proceeds with blessings and readings, then the bride and bridegroom drink wine from the same glass, and the groom places a plain gold band on the first finger of the bride's right hand. **"Behold, thou art consecrated unto me with this ring, according to the law of Moses and Israel,"** he says at that point. The ring must be plain, not adorned with diamonds and other jewels because marriage is not about riches. There is no difference between rich and poor in the sacred ceremony of marriage. Then follows the reading of the ketubah, the marriage contract. In days gone by, the ketubah was an elaborately decorated document that laid out the rights and privileges of the bride. Nowadays, there's legislation covering most of the financial details formerly in the ketubah, but it remains in modified form a part of the Jewish wedding ceremony.

Finally comes the fun part—the breaking of the glass by the groom. Maybe in 1925 in the Rabbi's house, the young newly wed Rabbi was able to stomp on a glass and let the chips fall where they may. In modern times, the glass is generally placed in a bag

to prevent the scattering of fragments. There are several explanations for the glass breaking ceremony. Some say it has to do with the fragility of human marriages, a demonstration of how easily they can be broken. Others say it is done to remind Jewish people of the destruction of the Jewish temple in Jerusalem and the importance of the homeland.

One other custom that was observed in the Kahanovitch wedding is evident in the wedding picture. The bride, Shayna Faigeh, her mother (on the right) and mother-in-law (left) have all covered their natural hair with a wig. This was a Jewish custom right from Biblical times. At first, women wore a kerchief or shawl over their hair but by the end of the 1700s, many had begun to use wigs. Generally speaking, women no longer observe the wig tradition in Conservative or Reform synagogues—they may use small doily-like covers in synagogue—but there are Orthodox congregations whose women continue to wear wigs as a sign of obedience, chastity and modesty.

It was the assassination of Czar Nicholas in Russia in 1881 that prompted Jewish immigration to Canada. Because the Russian government believed that Jews were behind the assassination, they began a series of pogroms—organized massacres and looting of Jewish property. They'd just ride into a village, shoot, pillage and burn with impunity. So the Jews had to leave, which is why some 400 arrived in Winnipeg in the summer of 1882 without much more than the clothes on their back. Summer wasn't too bad but winter was terrible—starvation, disease, cold, poverty, all the awful things that go along with homeless people of no means. Many died, but somehow things got better the next year and eventually the Jewish community in Winnipeg became one of the largest in any Canadian city.

Rabbi Israel Kahanovitch was born in Poland but came to the USA in 1905, then to Winnipeg in 1906. In just a few years, he had organized a Hebrew School, the United Charity, a Jewish orphanage and Old Folks Home. His son-in-law, the groom Rabbi Wohlgelernter, served the faith in Seattle, Washington. During WWII, he traveled through Europe rescuing children whose parents had been killed in the war. He and Shayna, known as Fanny, had two sons and a daughter.

1925...How To Live and Die in Canada...

It has to be admitted that immigration to Canada sometimes seemed like a formula for death. Take the Icelandic people who left their homes in 1875 and 1876 to come to Canada. They had little choice in the matter—Iceland's volcanoes had once again covered land and lakes with volcanic ash. No way could they farm or fish, so it was Canada or nothing. Sometimes, it was Canada and nothing.

They got to their destination on Lake Winnipeg just as winter started. No houses, no crops or gardens, not enough clothing. Many died of scurvy, exposure and starvation. The next winter, smallpox swept the struggling settlement, further decimating the population. That some survived to set up the Republic of New Iceland is amazing. That they even wanted to stay in Canada is just as amazing, but where could they go? What could they do?

They coped, that's what, and finally figured out how to farm, fish, lumber and live. Gimli became the center of Icelandic settlement, the name meaning Paradise in Icelandic. There must have been times they were tempted to change the name. Eventually, other towns grew up in the area—Riverton, Arborg and Hecla Island, and eventually they became part of Manitoba, no longer an independent Republic. That helped; there was provincial money available now and then to provide roads and schools and health care. Life got better.

Helgi Sigurgeirsson and Emma Jonsson missed all those awful beginnings. They were 2nd and 3rd generation Canadians who were married August 29, 1925, in Winnipeg. Life had improved so much for their generation that one of their wedding gifts was an electric toaster, not that they had electricity at Hecla Island but it was a nice thought, they agreed.

Emma's wedding dress was the white dress she had worn for high school graduation. She just added a veil and flowers for the wedding, and then took them off again and wore the dress "for good" for many more years.

Helgi was a lumberman and then a commercial fisherman with a small fleet of

boats. When the fish stopped biting and the markets dried up, Helgi retired and in time, so did Hecla Island. Kids had to go away to get work, the school closed down. Only a few buildings were left and a lot of scenery, so the government stepped in and made it a park. Hecla Island Park, 18-hole golf course, a hotel, all the scenery you could want. It was the best thing that could have happened, according to Binnie Sigurgeirsson, one of Emma and Helgi's five children. He goes there every chance he gets—to help with maintenance and to tell tourists what happened there so many years ago.

That was just Hecla Island, however. Other towns with Icelandic beginnings figured out how to support its people. After all, it wasn't the first time that Icelanders had to adjust.

1925...The Two Sisters—Intrepid and Formidable...

They shared a double wedding in Winnipeg on August 22, 1925, but from that moment on, the sisters moved in very different circles. Grace Moody, the bride on the left of the picture, married Norman Young; Maryon Moody, the bride on the right, married Lester Bowles Pearson.

"Charming indeed were these two maidens in their bridal array, both so individual and yet differing so widely in the type of raiment," the Manitoba Free Press explained in the wedding write up. Just how the two wedding raiments differed is hard to tell from the picture, but the wedding bouquets are different, that much is evident. Miss Grace carried a **"large bouquet of lily of the valley with showers of bloom falling to her feet,"** while Miss Maryon's bouquet was **"Colonial in design and composed of sweetheart rosebuds centred with forget-me-nots and lily of the valley and collared with lace."**

In fact, everyone in the wedding party looks pretty swell in their best bib and tucker. Left to right, they are: Gordon Young, Norman Young, Grace Moody, Catherine Evans, Herbert Moody, Lester Pearson, Maryon Moody, Marion Hilliard, Richard Bonnycastle and George Binns. Two of the ushers are missing from the picture; they stopped off for a beer before the reception, knowing that the good Methodist Moodys would not be serving alcohol at their house.

Grace and Maryon didn't beg to be married together. That was Mrs. Moody's decision. Grace was the oldest. She would be married first and if Maryon couldn't wait, then she'd have to go along with a double wedding. Take it or leave it. Maryon was tempted to leave it, to elope or something a bit more dramatic, but her steady young professor fiancé said No, we'll wait. Thus, the double wedding.

While waiting, the sisters embroidered various parts of their trousseau, underpants and vests. That's what proper young women did in 1924 while preparing for a wedding—they embroidered, they attended and gave parties, they studied household arts, they waited. It's no wonder that Maryon who was not known for her patience used to sneak out with her brother for an occasional smoke, drink and lively game of cards.

The long awaited wedding came off beautifully by all accounts, followed by the reception and the brides appearing in their going away outfits. Grace was in a patterned crepe with **"a close fitting hat of plum velvet with pressed pattern of leafage in autumn tints of green and brown adorning the crown."** Maryon's ensemble was a long coat that showed a border of baby leopard skin worn over a dress of Riviern bengaline. Her hat was of **"Austrian velours in a deeper shade of penny brown, its only adornment being a side cluster of dyed quills with touches of gold and blue."**

The only thing not described with many adjectives is the embroidered underwear. And so the married lives of the two Moody sisters began. Grace and Norman

honeymooned in England and then went to the African Gold Coast, now known as Ghana, where Norman taught at the university. Then back to Winnipeg where both established and taught at Ravenscourt School.

WWII changed everything. Much to the dismay of many—especially his mother—40-year-old Norman Young joined the Queen's Own Cameron Highlanders. Maybe it was the fiery sermon that Charles Gordon (aka Ralph Connor, the author) gave at church one morning, all about God and country, or maybe it was simply the sentiment of the time, that all good men must fight for King and country, but Norman felt he had to go. And was killed for his trouble at Dieppe in August, 1942.

It was then that Grace had to show her stuff, and she did. Her daughter Sheila described her as "intrepid," because she figured out how to support the family of four as censor for the Manitoba film board. And when she was done that, she worked for and supported the worldwide movement known as MRA, Moral Re-Armament.

In the meantime, Lester Pearson climbed rapidly through the ranks of the civil service in Ottawa, and that was just fine with Maryon. She enjoyed the social life, organized the two Pearson children, enjoyed the attention that came with the Nobel Peace Prize that her husband won in 1957. But getting into elected politics was quite another kettle of fish. She wasn't comfortable with crowds or the baloney that goes along with campaigning. And when Lester Pearson became Prime Minister of Canada in 1963, she made the much-quoted statement, **"Behind every successful man there stands a surprised woman."**

While Grace was described as intrepid, Maryon was known as formidable. She didn't do speeches, didn't conduct tours of the Prime Minister's residence, never sucked up to the media. It just wasn't her thing and she wasn't about to change. Thus, she left politics up to her husband and he left the social life up to her. It must have suited them both, for when Pearson died in 1972, she paid him a high compliment, **"He was one of the most entertaining men I have ever known."**

1926....Three Day Wedding Parties...

Ukrainian settlers knew how to throw a wedding party. Even if money was scarce to non-existent, even if the weather did its worst, even if stores and churches were miles away, they still managed the best parties in town, especially the three day kind.

The bride might have been the only one who didn't look forward to the wedding party, because brides got to do some pretty embarrassing things throughout the two or three day event. It was easy enough to submit to the teasing and the threat of kidnapping, but it was not so easy to be led off to a special bridal chamber where she and her new husband were expected to consummate the marriage. Not only that but they were expected to prove the bride's virginity by later displaying her nightie suitably marked with blood.

Michael Ewanchuk, a Ukrainian scholar and writer from Winnipeg, tells the story of the clever pair who had a dead sparrow hidden in their chamber so that they could use its blood, if all else failed. He admits the story is probably apocryphal because he's heard it often, but it too is part of the legend of Ukrainian weddings. Talk of "deflowering," the rather crude expression for the loss of virginity, was part and parcel of the traditions of many European weddings, he explained. In the days when Scottish and English lords ruled over their own fiefdoms, for example, they would sometimes claim the right to be the first to lie with a virgin on her wedding day.

That kind of cruelty is gone but the teasing, crude jokes and innuendoes still exist on the fringes of most weddings.

Not every Ukrainian wedding included the bridal chamber chapter, of course. In fact, they varied a lot depending on the area of Russia, Austria or the Ukraine that the folks came from. Generally, however, there was lots of singing. It was almost operatic in that there were set pieces for the women to sing during preparations for the wedding, during the wedding itself and later at the receptions. That's receptions, plural. If the parents of the bride and groom lived close together, the reception would move from house to house, the better to eat, sing, drink and dance some more. Everyone who had an instrument would bring it to the party—a fiddle, cymbala, horn or accordion.

And a good time would be had by all, except maybe the embarrassed bride.

1926...A Picture Worth 1000 Words...

Henry Husak was born in the Ukraine but came to Canada as a child. Mary Malofie was born in Canada. As first and second generation Canadians, they would not have observed all of the old country traditions in their wedding, but they weren't so removed from traditional ways that they weren't going to have a good party. To that end, the fiddler is shown, his bow ready, in one of the wedding pictures.

It's 1926. You can see in the picture of the wedding party that Henry's mom and dad have made a good start in this new country. There's a frame house in the background, two storeys high and big enough to hold most of the wedding party. The groom Henry Husak and his brother Bill both have a new suit for the occasion. Little brothers Michael and Steve have new breeches and sweaters. Henry's dad wears a substantial fur cap. Only his mom in her old country cap and apron hangs onto old ways.

As for the bride's family, they must be managing as well. Mary is wearing a white dress, likely an Eaton's catalogue purchase that required cash money. The vines on the front of her dress are an Eastern European tradition and wouldn't have cost much, but her headpiece would have. Her mother, fourth from the left in the picture, is bundled warmly in a store bought sweater and hat; her sons around her wear store bought suits. That was the way to judge whether families were moving up the social scale or not—whether their clothes were store bought or not.

That they are store bought means that the gamble the Husak and Malofie families took in leaving the Ukraine is beginning to pay off. They have land, a home, some money; their children have a future.

All except Nick Malofie. He died in 1918 because soldiers returning from WWI brought along a terrible disease called the Spanish influenza. The flu. It mowed down whole families, and in the Malofie family, it was Nick.

All except Dan Malofie who went to fight for his country in WWII and was shot down over Holland. He's in the picture—the smiling boy second from left.

For their part, the bride and groom, Henry and Mary Husak, farmed in the Fisher Branch area of Manitoba for 47 years. There they brought up four children: Olga, Eugenia, Edward and Marilyn, all of whom are doing fine. Just as Henry and Mary expected them to go to school and do well, come chores or high water, so did they expect them to make something of their lives. The worst was over, after all.

Ukrainian immigration began because two Ukrainian men, Ivan Pylypiw and Wasyl Eleniak, came to Canada in 1891 to check out the rumor that there was good land here for the taking. That an ordinary man could get 160 acres for $10 and a dream. It seemed too good to be true but the two men assured their countrymen it was so. Go, they said. So Ukrainians began to trickle into Manitoba, then flood into Manitoba, then spill over into Saskatchewan and Alberta. Between 1891 and 1914, some 170,000 immigrants of

Ukrainian origin came to Canada, mostly from the Galicia and Bukovina districts. When WWI came along, Ukrainians were declared enemy aliens even though some 10,000 of their men enlisted in the Canadian armed forces. Didn't make sense but then war is a senseless thing sometimes. Naturally, immigration ceased until the war ended, but as soon as the laws were changed, immigration from Eastern Europe picked up again. By 1981, there were half a million Canadian citizens of Ukrainian origin in Canada.

1926...Even the Wedding Had To Be Co-op...

Maybe it was the stubborn oxen. Maybe it was their fault, but one day as he was trying to keep them together to pull the breaking plow through the prairie grasses, it occurred to Lewis Lloyd that cooperation was the answer. Not just for plowing but for the whole wide world. Why couldn't people co-operate to provide health care and education and a decent living for all? Why couldn't governments set up tax systems to even things out a bit between the haves and have-nots? Why shouldn't farmers, for example, get together to sell their product instead of each man working for himself? Made sense to him, and cooperation was his passion from then on.

Even his wedding turned into a co-operative affair. When he and Ruth Graham arrived at the preacher's house in Medicine Hat, AB, they found another couple there before them. The other couple needed two witnesses, Lewie and Ruth needed witnesses. They co-operated and stood up for one another. That was March 9, 1926.

When they got back home to Webb, SK, the community rallied around—gave them a wedding supper and dance, even a purse of money. Lewie wrote later, **"The result was that we were better off financially after the wedding dance than we were before."** He didn't make the point that it was a classic case of co-operation, but he could have.

From then on, it was one scramble after another for Lewie and Ruth to stay solvent on their farm. Crops weren't bad in 1927 and 1928. Lewie supplemented farm earnings by working with his brothers on a custom threshing outfit. That is, they went from farm to farm with a threshing machine and sold their services to farmers who didn't own a machine. But by 1929, the prices for grain were so low that it made no sense to bother threshing it. Lewie sold a crop of fall rye for 10 cents a bushel. It cost 12 cents a bushel to thresh, let alone buy seed. It was a losing proposition and the beginning of the awful 1930s for farmers in Saskatchewan. Drought and depression.

By 1933, nearly everyone in the area was on government relief. Lewie wrote, **"Can you imagine the Municipality so hard up that at times they did not have enough in the treasury to pay for a casket when some of our people died? It was so hot and dry. The sun came up like a ball of fire and went down like a ball of fire. The wind blew hot as if it came from a furnace. The soil drifted, covering up roads, fences and trees we had planted. Very few were able to pay doctor bills. Many, because of their pride, wouldn't even go to see a doctor because they owed bills for many years. Some were never paid."**

Lewie's brother Woodrow was a teacher at this time. He was supposed to get $500 a year, but didn't get his final cheque until many years later when, as it happened, he was Minister of Education in the Saskatchewan government. Eventually, he became premier of SK. His family teased him about the fact he was born in a two room shack on his parent's farm, a shack that later became a chicken coop. So, like Abraham Lincoln, Woodrow Lloyd was born in humble circumstances—a chicken coop.

During the worst of times, many SK settlers left for what they hoped would be greener pastures—the Peace River country of Alberta or BC. But Lewie concentrated instead on political action. He was present in Regina in 1933 for the first annual meeting of the Co-operative Commonwealth Federation, the CCF in other words, the forerunner of today's NDP. The goals of this new endeavor included the nationalization of key industries; the establishment of universal pensions, health and welfare insurance; children's allowances; unemployment insurance; all those things that Lewie had thought about as he steered the oxen over the prairies. He was delighted, and from then on he was a man possessed with his philosophy.

He traveled, talked, argued, organized, broke his toe, wrote letters—all in the socialist cause. It wasn't an easy sell in spite of the hard times. There were still people who asked why should they pay for other people's problems, but the idea gradually took hold. SK was the leader in social legislation, and Lewie was definitely a factor in that.

Even his choice of recreation reflected co-operative principles. He liked baseball; he and his eight brothers occasionally formed a team and played neighboring towns. He liked it, he said, because **"in baseball, everybody has a chance regardless of size."**

Eventually, he and Ruth left the farm and moved to Antelope where Lewie became manager of the local co-op and Ruth ran a restaurant. In 1963, after serving on the board of just about every co-operative venture in the province, Lewie was elected president of the Federated Co-operatives, the biggest co-op movement in the west.

Ruth was the quiet one of the pair, the one that looked after the three kids and kept things going at home. Lewie recognized that in this dedication to his book called *Memories of a Co-operative Statesman*.

"I dedicate this story to my wife, Ruth. Why? Because all my life I have been a high strung, restless, sort of a go-like-h— individual, never contented, always wanting to get on with the job of reorganizing the world so that every person born into it would have the right to earn an honest living provided they were sound of mind and body and able to work. Naturally, any person living with such an individual as I am had to go through some trying times. As I look back now, I appreciate what my wife had to put up with."

1926...The Horse, Then the Wife...

Joe Bellamy joined the Royal North West Mounted Police in 1919 and was told then that he could not marry—should he be so inclined—until he had 11 years of service under his belt. No problem, he said, but after he got his tonsils out and spilled his innermost feelings to a young nurse at his bedside, it became a problem. He and Marjory got officially engaged on Oct. 5, 1922, but had to look forward to waiting until 1930 to get married.

Fortunately, Joe performed his police duties so well that the powers-that-be in the RNWMP agreed to a special consideration that would allow him to marry with only seven years of service to his credit. So they were married on October 5, 1926, exactly four years after their engagement.

Once settled into her new home at the detachment in Hodgson, MB, Marjory quickly learned what it meant to be a part of a police family. **"One of the first things I was to learn about living with a Mounted Policeman was that, in the necessary order of things, a wife ranked somewhere below the horses."**

She was not putting herself down. She just knew that her husband's work and safety depended on horses, and she'd better pay attention to the stable routine. She did.

1926...Let the Play Begin...

Romanian weddings have so much significance and tradition attached to them that it's no wonder they are big beautiful affairs. They, more than most weddings, are theatre. There are two main characters but many supporting roles, there are songs that must be sung and dances that must be danced, there are stage directions, there are monologues and dialogues, and there are chickens.

Take the wedding of Annie Tarcea and Pahnait Ciuca (later known as Pete Ciuca.) They were married in Regina at St. George Romanian Greek Orthodox Church August 22, 1926. The two main characters are the bride and groom in the center of the picture. They are supported by 12 bridesmaids, all in white; four flower girls, all in pink; two ring bearers in white frilled shirts and buttoned on velvet pants—they must still get teased about those pants—and the four vatajale. They are the four extra men in the picture, one of whom is holding up the wine flask. It was the vatajale who invited the guests to the wedding so they are important and must be in the picture.

There is also a cast of hundreds off stage—the families, the priest, the whole tight knit Romanian community and last but not least the florists who supplied the flowers, all of them in shades of pink. See—even the flowers had to meet the script, had to add to the stage setting.

Annie and Pete both came to Regina from Romania with their folks. Annie's family tried Argentina first but it was too hot, too poor, so they joined the growing Romanian community around Regina instead. The wedding picture contains names from those very first families: Cuica, Zora, Capraru,Dumas, Sandu, Lupustean, Cissmus, Soporlo, Corkish, Bancescu,McRadu, Postelnicu, Tater, Orbean, Magda, and Tarcea.

Not all the elements of a Romanian wedding were incorporated into every wedding but likely Annie paused as she left her parents' home so that they could hold the round loaf of braided bread known as Kolachi over her head and say the traditional blessings. During the ceremony, the minister likely joined their hands with a special piece of cloth or lace, then placed a crown on each , all the while explaining the significance of each action. When they drank from the common cup containing both water and wine, they were told to expect both good and bad in the future, and when they walked around the altar three times, they were told that this was the beginning of their married life together.

And so the wedding likely progressed through more or less of the traditional steps, but the drama wasn't over once the wedding was over. There was still so much to come at the reception—singing and dancing and lots of nonsense rituals like the Dance of the Chickens. This is a task performed by two or three women who try to sell gaily decorated cooked chickens to the best man and matron of honour. If the saleswomen do their job well and sell the chickens for a good price, then the gifts to come from other family memebrs must be equally valuable. And so on through so many acts of the wedding drama that the party had to extend to two or three days sometimes.

Annie and Pete continued to live within the Romanian community in Regina. Pete established himself in dry cleaning businesses, Annie looked after home and the two children, Eleanore and Eugene. The warning of the wine and water came true when Peter died in 1950, only 49 years old. Annie eventually married again, lived for awhile in the US but when her second husband died returned to Regina and her Romanian roots there.

1927...Tiptoe Through The Wedding...

When Eliza was 14, a Scottish trapper came to call on her folks. Nothing unusual about that—lots of people came to call on her folks. They lived in the North, northern people welcomed company and never worried about an extra plate for meals or an extra body overnight. It happened so often that Eliza barely remembered the guy. But he remembered her and three years later, he came back and asked to marry her. He didn't ask her, mind you. He asked her dad, and her dad said OK.

Eliza accepted the arrangement, because that's the way it was in her culture. Fathers and prospective husbands made the deals—the girls went along with it. Love had nothing to do with it. Marriage was the way a girl started her own life and family. So be it.

She didn't even know that he was 33 when they married, some 16 years older than she was. Even if she'd had the nerve to ask him his age, she wouldn't have had the language. She knew a little English from the Eaton's catalogue, but not enough to ask such a personal question. She just knew this was her life and she'd better make the best of it. Which she did, incidentally. Eliza may have seemed powerless in the choice of a husband but she proved a powerhouse later on.

Eliza's people would be classified as Metis, the mixed blood people who got to

show the explorers where to go but never got their name on the discoveries. For instance, one of Eliza's forefathers was Joseph Cardinal, a North West Company voyageur who was with Alexander Mackenzie in 1789 when he followed a major northern river to the Arctic. That major river became the Mackenzie but it could just as easily have been called the Cardinal since it was he who knew the lay of the land. Not that any of that mattered to Eliza's folks, Felix and Mary Lapoudre (Powder), in the early 1900s in northern Alberta. They were too busy moving around in search of good hunting, trapping or jobs. Ten children were born to them, Eliza, born in 1910, was #4. She was born at home with the help of a grandmother but #8 child, Jack, arrived while the family was on a scow in the middle of the Athabasca River enroute to Fort McMurray for the summer. The expedition was halted for three days to give the new mother some time to recuperate, but once the three days were up, so was Mary.

Alex Stratton, on the other hand, was a newcomer to Canada. He arrived from Scotland in 1914 at the age of 17. For the next 13 years, he worked at farms, did construction work, and eventually found his way to the north. Even in Scotland, he'd had a notion he'd like to live an outdoor life, be a trapper maybe. And so he learned the trade and learned the country at the same time. He even discovered a waterfall that nobody else had named and gave it his own—the Stratton Falls on the Abitua River in northern Saskatchewan.

After awhile, he'd had enough of his lonesome travelling however. That's when he met Eliza and married her three years later. July 5, 1927.

Eliza had a white wedding dress. Her mother made it from material that they bought from the local store in Fort Chipewyan. The store didn't have anything that resembled a veil, however, so her mother bought mosquito netting and trimmed it round with narrow lace. Luckily, Colin Fraser's granddaughter had just been married a few days earlier and was happy to lend her waxed paper orange blossom headpiece for the bride and boutonierres for the men. Everything fell into place wonderfully except for the shoes. There wasn't time to order white shoes from the Eaton's catalogue so Eliza decided to paint an old pair of runners white for the occasion. For the pictures, Eliza tried to stand on tiptoes so the old runners would look like high heels but it didn't work too well. In fact, they were soon abandoned entirely when the dance started because they stuck to the floor, as runners have a habit of doing!

Not many attended the church service since it was held in the rectory of the Catholic Church. It couldn't be in the church proper because Alex was not a Catholic and even in the far north in 1927, that mattered. Everyone, however, came to the reception at the Fraser house. There were no invitations. People just knew and kept coming until the food literally ran out, which was taken as a signal for the dance to start. It was a good party, they still say.

The newly weds got exactly three gifts. Eliza could remember that so clearly because it was only the white people of the community who gave them gifts. The Cree and Metis believed it was an insult to give gifts because it implied the family was needy. It was never done.

And once the dance was over? That's easy. Eliza, now Mrs. Alex Stratton, packed up her few possessions, and followed her husband, first to Uranium City for the remainder of the summer and then to the bush for the winter trapping season.

Eliza and Alex moved from trapline to summer job and back again until Mary was born in 1932. Then they bought land in the Plamondon area near Lac La Biche and stayed put, raising a family of six girls and two boys. Alex took up mink and fox farming and did fine at it, but even if you can take a trapper out of the bush you can't take the bush out of a trapper. In this case, it was dogs. Alex always had to have his dogs around and eventually the kids went to school via dogsled.

Eliza in the meantime practiced all the arts necessary to keep a large and busy household on track. She sewed for the whole gang, cooked for their gang and more, learned to read and write as her children progressed through school, did every kind of handiwork, insisted on cleanliness and Godliness. She was a marvel, her kids say. Alex was right to wait the three years. He died in 1972, Eliza died in 1998.

1927...Married In White

Dorothy Ion was so keen on horses that she talked her husband-to-be, G.W. (Bill) Church, into an outdoor wedding—on horseback. Never mind that the date set was November 12, 1927, when the weather around Medicine Hat, AB, can be most anything—warm, cold, wet, dry, windy, white. Pick white. There was a huge snowstorm that day. Dorothy's father wrote in his diary: **"Dorothy was married today...on horseback near Medicine Hat in a blinding snow storm. 12 noon started to snow and blow from the east...10 pm, still snowing. 10 pm, wife and Willie came home from Medicine Hat. They were both at the wedding. They had a hard time getting through the snow as it is getting very deep."**

Never mind, Rev. Morrow got there, the bride and groom wore their best cowboy hats, and the horses stood up for them. Several months later, the picture of the five of them in the slanting snow was featured in a London, England, newspaper with the following cutline: **"A movie-like wedding group in the cattle lands of the west. Mr. G.W. Church of the 9 Bar Ranch and Miss Dorothy Ion of the southeastern Range were married in a snowstorm and are here seen riding over the prairie to their honeymoon."**

Sounds terribly romantic, but the truth was not so rosy. Bill was a ranch manager and horse trader who worked where his fancy took him. Dorothy would have liked to be a ranch hand; she had worked with horses on her dad's farm all her life. In fact, she and her brother made extra money for the family by breaking untamed horses for halter, bridle and harness. But a congenital heart problem slowed her down some, and then slowed her down completely. She died three years, almost to the day, after her wedding day. Rev. Morrow officiated at that service too.

The baby, six month old Patricia, was taken to Ontario to be raised by her father's sister. She didn't meet her Ion relatives until she was 19 when Grandma Ion asked to see her. Once in the west, she discovered that she too liked what she saw. No horses for her, however, even though she married a farmer. Her daughter is the horsewoman in the family now, and it gives Pat some connection to the mother she never knew.

Rev. Morrow deserves a word or two here. A Presbyterian and United Church minister in Medicine Hat for years, he was immensely popular. Liked to roll up his sleeves and help with harvest when needed, or push a car out of the mud, or marry a crazy couple in the middle of a snowstorm.

1927...The Trouble With Life...

The Anderson story has some of the same elements as the Church story, fortunately and unfortunately. Merle Anderson liked horses, raised them, trained them for chuckwagon races and won the big prize at the Calgary Stampede Chuckwagon races in 1958 with them. His wife Nellie wasn't that keen on horses but she was game to be part of that life. The trouble was she didn't have much life.

Nellie Mayes and Merle Anderson were married January 27, 1927, in Calgary. Eighteen year old Nellie never looked better. Her dress was an off white with an inset of beige lace on the side. Her hair was curled in the flapper style of the day, a look that she accomplished on her normally straight hair by heating the tongs of a curling iron in a lamp chimney, then rolling her hair over and over again until it was one curly bob. Merle at age 39 was pretty well established on a farm in the Carbon, AB, area and after the wedding they went home to the farm.

Nine months later, Vivian was born and several years later Lloyd was born. Nellie had pleurisy by then, or so the doctors thought, but it didn't get better. Finally, it was

diagnosed as tuberculosis, and Nellie had to go to the sanitarium in Calgary. Two years later, she died, 10 years almost to the day after her wedding day.

Vivian was nine. She knew they were taken to something called a funeral, but she still expected her mother to come home. There was no such thing as therapy for motherless children in those days. **"You just figured out how to get along,"** she said. It helped that her mother's sister lived with them from then on.

In the midst of the confusion and despair of Nellie's illness, in rode a Yodelling Fool, otherwise known as Wilf Carter. (His full name was Wilfred Laurier Carter; his Nova Scotia mother so admired the former prime minister of Canada that she named her son for him.) Wilf was nobody at the time, just a travelling cowboy looking for work like hundreds of other young men in the west. The only thing he could do really well was yodel and sing cowboy songs, but there wasn't much call for that for those talents at first. He had to ride and muck out barns and work in a café for awhile until he put together enough money to buy a ranch in the Carbon area in 1937. Then, wouldn't you know it, he got his big chance in the US as "Montana Slim" and never looked back.

That's not quite true. He did look back and returned to the Carbon area as often as he could, and in 1984, he came back as the Grand Marshall of the Calgary Stampede. For a cowboy or cowboy singer, there is no greater honor. Merle missed the stampede that year; he died in April, aged 96.

1927...The Marriage Commissioner's Mother...

Lillian Saltman decided she'd seen enough of Winnipeg. Time to see some faraway places like Japan, perhaps, so she headed west. First stop—Vancouver. Last stop—Vancouver. She met Ben Shapiro there, you see, and they were married August 14, 1927. She wore the latest flapper fashion—a long waisted white dress with V-shaped petals all over the short skirt. He wore a dark conservative suit that didn't quite hide his huge hands. Ben Shapiro, it was said up and down the west coast, had the strongest grip going.

Perhaps he needed it. Born in Russia and brought up in the US, he tried a number of jobs—most of them physical—until he bought an old car for junk one day and fixed it up. That led him into the automotive parts business and eventually into the manufacture of batteries. By that time, he lived in Vancouver.

Lillian knew something about business as well, having been the credit manager for a national food organization in Winnipeg. But once married, she put all that experience and energy into community organizations and became, as her daughter explains it, **"an amazing Jewish leader."** She chaired every level of Hadassah right up to council level, she worked to establish children's camps, the Jewish Family Welfare Bureau and the Jewish Home for the Aged. When WWII came along with the unbelievable news about Jewish death camps, she and many others raised money to bring orphaned Jewish children to Canada.

She was one busy lady, but never too busy to sing *O Canada* at official functions. She was the unofficial anthem singer, and she did it with great pride.

There were three children, one of whom—Nomi Whalen of Calgary—is a marriage commissioner. She estimates that she's conducted some 6,000 weddings—in airplanes, on mountain tops, beside babbling brooks. What a wonderful coincidence for a book on weddings.

1928...Toil and A Peaceful Life

There's an old adage that says, **"First comes love, then comes marriage."** Not so for a Doukhobor wedding. God comes first, Doukhobor beliefs come first, the community comes first, the parents come first, duty comes first. Love is a long way down the line unless you are talking about the love of God. Then there is passion in the Doukhobor soul. Then there is so much fire in the belly that sometimes the Doukhobors have to take off their clothes to make it plain.

That smart-aleck remark would not amuse Mike and Doris Verigin in Cowley, AB. It's Mike's parents who are in the picture, Mike and Annie Verigin. They were hardworking devoted members of their church and local communities. They never once broke a law or took off their clothes, yet that's what a lot of Canadians remember about the Doukhobors—that some of them, a dissident group known as the Sons of Freedom, took off their clothes to protest a BC law concerning the education of their children. TV and newspapers had a heyday with so many bare naked people; skin wasn't as common in the 1950s as it became in later years...which is why that's all a lot of us remember about Doukhobors. But there's so much more.

The Doukhobors came to Canada from Russia in 1898/99 in search of a country where they could live communally, where they could practice their pacifist beliefs and worship in their own way. Canada said OK to all those conditions in the beginning and the Doukhobors built a thriving settlement in Saskatchewan under the leadership of Peter the Lordly Verigin. There they lived their motto of Toil and a Peaceful Life.

Then the rules changed. Frank Oliver, the MP from Edmonton, decided the Doukhobors ought at least to swear allegiance to the King before they got title to their lands. How could they do that? God is their King. No way could they fudge that. So they up and moved to the Kootenay region of BC. Along the way, some 300 Doukhobors settled in the Crowsnest Pass around Cowley in order to be a halfway point for the move. The grandfather of the present Mike Verigin was one of the ones assigned to that duty, and that's where the wedding took place.

Courtship was an almost invisible process in the Doukhobor community. Young men and women were expected to marry—bachelors and old maids were very unusual—but there was no hand-holding, no dating, no overt displays of interest. Sometimes the young people expressed a preference and the parents took that into consideration. Sometimes they did not. When the arrangement was agreed upon, the young couple asked the blessing and consent of their parents, a ceremony that was as important as the actual wedding.

Annie and her female relatives made the wedding costume, the most important part of which was the shawl. It was often embroidered or painted, and always the fringe was hand knotted in a certain design. In the early part of the century, the skirt would have been hand woven of linen with a cotton and horsehair lining to emphasize the fullness of the hips. Big hips signaled strength and healthy babies.

On the wedding day, March 1, 1928, in Lundbrek, AB, Annie and Mike stood before the community of Doukhobors and made their vows to God and the congregation. There was no minister as such. There was singing and prayer, then the couple bowed to both sets of family and to one another as an indication of humility, respect and love. And that was pretty well it except for a special meal shared with the whole community. Then it was off to the part of the communal house that had been prepared for the newly weds and back to work the next day. Weddings were not a huge deal. They were part of God's plan.

Mike and Annie lived communally with their people in southern Alberta until 1939 when the rules changed again. This time, the government said all Doukhobors had to buy their own land individually; no more of this shared ownership business. So Mike and Annie bought their land alongside the Oldman River and continued to farm. Their six children learned Russian first, English later.

Mike the third bought his father's land eventually and owned it individually. What could he do? Those were the rules after all. Then along came the AB government in the 1980s and expropriated his land in order to build the Oldman Dam. What could he do? Those were the rules, after all. So he's become the historian of the community, telling and retelling the story of the Doukhobors who came to a land that promised them freedom to live as they believed, and then changed the rules time and time again.

1928…Water, Water Everywhere…

It was the best of times in 1928 when Emma McCoskrie and Fred Wastell were married. There was a new house waiting for them at Alert Bay, BC, a good job, family and friends who lived the good life too. What could go wrong?

It was the worst of times a year later when the stock market crashed, the good job evaporated, the family money dried up and the Great Depression descended upon Canada. That's what could go wrong.

Who knew? Fred's father was a British gentleman who managed a box factory at Alert Bay. There was enough money for a big house, tennis courts, a Chinese cook, a yacht, picnics and even a Chevrolet that Fred brought home from university. There were no real roads on the north coast of Vancouver Island but he tootled around the mill yard and out toward the Indian cemetery now and then. That's the only place where he and Emma could be alone occasionally. Emma was a nurse at the local hospital. Her background wasn't quite as privileged as Fred's but she was learning to enjoy the good things of life. It seemed, in those balmy days at the end of the 1920s, that nothing could go wrong. Investments kept growing, money flowed, parties happened.

They were married in Victoria, Emma in a white silk crepe de chine dress designed by a French dressmaker, mid calf length, straight from the shoulders, very flapper in feeling. For their honeymoon in California, she had other dresses especially designed for her trousseau including the one she's wearing in the picture. It's a jade green to match the jade necklace she's wearing. The necklace was a gift of the Chinese men who worked at the box factory. Even they had some money.

191

After October, 1929, all that changed. The box factory closed, Fred and his father lost their jobs, so did the Chinese men. Everyone had to scramble to make a living so Fred decided to go further down the coast to some waterfront land that his father owned at Telegraph Cove. There was a small rundown sawmill there, an old house, a lot of bush. No roads but they were on the water. What more did they need to establish a sawmill besides bush and water? Emma might have mentioned a few things like plumbing and electricity, a telephone maybe, but it was 1929. You did what you had to do.

It was water, water everywhere in the business that slowly developed—out in the boat to get the logs, to bring them back to the mill, to deliver the lumber, to get groceries, doctors, mail, workers. There was no way to travel overland; the growth was just too heavy. The two girls, Pat and Beatrice, never learned to ride a bike—no paths—but they sure learned to navigate a boat, to hook a log, to row a skiff. At first, their mother insisted that they wear life jackets while in the boats. She made child sized ones from some old adult ones around. One day Beatrice protested she could swim well enough now, surely she didn't have to wear the bulky jacket anymore. Her mother agreed, Beatrice pitched it off the side of the boat, and it promptly sank. Such are the experiences of those who **"grow up wet."**

That's an expression used by Pat Wastell Norris, who now writes about growing up wet. It's like prairie kids who grow up dirty. Wet or dirty, can't be helped. It's the place that makes the difference, and for the Wastells life on the water was the best place.

1929...On the Ground and In the Air...

Saskatchewan holds the record for two airplane weddings. First there was the Dodsland couple who married on the ground, then drove madly to a waiting airplane that whisked them up and away from any possible post-wedding nonsense. The first elopement by airplane. (See the 1920 chapter.) Then there was the Regina couple who reversed the order—they were married in a plane, then came back down to earth and drove to their honeymoon. The first wedding ceremony on a plane in flight.

It makes you wonder. Were Saskatchewan folk a more daring lot than other Canadians, or were they simply trying to see where the prairies ended? Without mountains, where else could they get a birds eye view? Where else could they feel equal to their great lone land? Or were the reasons for the interest in airplanes just that—an interest? Nothing too deep at all?

That's the conclusion of Margaret Nicks Frejd, the bridesmaid at the James-Robinson wedding. The groom was crazy about airplanes, she says. He had had some flying lessons and like the rest of the world was transfixed by the idea of flight. Therefore, why not combine one peak experience with another— a wedding and a flight over the city of Regina?

Thus did Howard Layton Robinson exchange wedding vows with Muriel Stuart

The first wedding performed in an airplain in Canada. Regina May 23 1929

James at 7:35 of the evening of May 23, 1929. The minister was Rev. J.D. Wilkie, the bridesmaid was the bride's cousin Margaret, the best man was the pilot Jack Wight, and the chapel was a Stinson Detroiter that had arrived from the Detroit factory the day before. The minister and the bridesmaid had never been in a plane before; the plane had never been a wedding chapel before. All elements of the wedding performed beautifully.

The bride and the bridesmaid, mindful of the setting, chose to wear leather coats over afternoon dresses. The bride's was a gun metal gray **"opening over a light tan ensemble suit with hat to match,"** the bridesmaid's a brown leather coat over **"a flat crepe dress in bonny blue tone and harmonizing hat."**

The ceremony must have been a short one since it started when the plane was over the Parliament buildings and concluded over the RCMP barracks. Just enough time for **"I do,"** and **"I do too"** and then a flying lesson, or as the newspaper account explained, **"Jack Wight explained the art of flying to the members of the party, and turns were executed for the edification of the wedding party."**

In Moose Jaw a year later, Mr. and Mrs. Robinson celebrated their first wedding anniversary with a short flight on a single engine Fokker monoplane then used in the prairie air mail service. It was to be an annual event from then on, but the Robinsons had no family so there's no one left to tell their tale. Muriel died in Victoria; Howard remarried and died in Nelson, BC.

After 19 years of flying over Saskatchewan, the prairie ended for the Stinson Detroiter in 1948 when it crashed at Conquest.

1929...Until The Lights Went Out...

Michael Luchkovich was on top of the world in 1929. The spats he's wearing in the wedding picture tell everything. If a man of humble birth could wear spats and know he looked good in them, know he deserved the respect they implied, then life was indeed sweet. Add a beautiful bride and who could ask for anything more?

Most of his pleasure derived from the fact he was the first MP of Ukrainian origin in Canada, elected in 1926 from the federal riding of Vegreville, AB. That was heady stuff. He ran under the banner of the United Farmers of Alberta, but it didn't really matter what party Michael Luchkovich represented. He could speak Ukrainian, he could understand Ukrainian problems, he was their man. Period. The fact that he could also speak English without an accent didn't hurt either. Anglo Saxons could hold their noses and vote for a Ukrainian as long as he spoke perfect English. They could even say things like that out loud; there was such prejudice and snobbery toward Ukrainians in those days...which makes Luchkovich's accomplishment all the more amazing.

Then there was his speech in May of 1929, in response to a letter that George Exton Lloyd, Anglican Bishop of Saskatchewan, issued to his churches in which he referred to the Ukrainians as **"dirty, ignorant, garlic-smelling unpreferred continentals who are flooding into the country."** Luchkovich stood up in Parliament that May day and spoke for several hours, without notes, without prompting, and blew holes in Lloyd's arguments. Also got in a few shots of his own. **"The central Europeans are neither dirty, ignorant nor unpreferred, and as for being garlic smelling, I consider such a weakness a thousand times better than filling one's mind with the hideous and discriminatory epithets....which appeal to the mentality of, and could be uttered only, by a moron."** Ouch.

He was suddenly the darling of both the media and other parliamentarians. **" How long did it take you to prepare that speech?"** one of his colleagues asked. **"My whole life was a preparation for that speech,"** he answered. No wonder he was very pleased with himself when he got back to Alberta that fall, and no wonder he decided that he and Sophie Nikiforuk shouldn't wait any longer to be married. Let's do it before the next Parliamentary session, he urged her. Come back to Ottawa with me.

So that's what happened. Sophie resigned her teaching job in the Vegreville area and went home to Edmonton. There her mother and aunts hustled up a wedding, and there it happened on January 25, 1929.

It was an evening wedding in the Greek Orthodox Church in Edmonton. Sophie's dress was trimmed with 12 inches of silk lace on the bottom, her headpiece was fashioned of seed pearls and flowers. Her cousin Phyllis and sister Olga were bridesmaids, their hats the very latest cloche style. Her little brother Allen wore his sailor suit and a pained expression, the flower girls had baskets overflowing with flowers. Everyone had flowers. It was a grand occasion—a beautiful young woman and the first MP of Ukrainian extraction. We can't forget that. It meant everything.

From then until 1935, life continued to shine for Michael and Sophie. She loved living in Ottawa; it didn't intimidate her at all. In fact, she remembered years later that she literally ran into Prime Minister R.B. Bennett one day. "I'm sorry," she said. "Don't worry," he said, "I enjoyed it." In 1931, Michael was crowned with more glory—he represented Canada at an international congress in Bucharest, Rumania. He loved it.

His motto was often quoted, **"I am first of all a citizen of Canada and to her I owe my absolute loyalty."**

But the lights went out in 1935 when William Aberhart's new party, the Social Credit party, swept the province, even swept some of the federal seats, Luchkovich's among them. He was devastated. He had put all his energy and talent into being a full time politician. He knew nothing else and wanted nothing else.

Back in Edmonton, they eventually bought and lived in a small confectionery store in the east end, but Luchkovich had never intended to live back of the store. Sophie became the mainstay of her family. Michael did some work with the Ukrainian community, he translated some books from Ukrainian to English, but he never got over the defeat. It would probably be diagnosed as clinical depression nowadays but then there was no counseling, no help. He kind of faded out of sight. It was a sad ending for such a bright beginning.

Being the lone representative (at that time) of the Ukrainian people would have been a heavy load. His daughter Carol tells about a certain MP who always greeted her father in the House of Commons with, **"Hello, Lucky Bitch."** A mean spirited play of words on his name. Her father finally responded with, **"Hello, you son-of-a-bitch."**

The Michael Luchkovich Scholarship for Career Development, one of a number of scholarships supported by the Alberta government, was announced in 1980. The family members—sons Myron, Dennis and daughter Carol— were not notified because no one knew the family existed.

1929...Home On The Range...

Ann Clifford has two pieces of advice for brides: Don't give everything away before you're married. After all, if the socks are already darned, why get married? And secondly, don't take your relatives along on the honeymoon.

That's what she and Raymond Clifford did, took six extra people with them for their two-day honeymoon in Banff. The relatives had never been to Banff, they really wanted to see the mountains and hoodoos, there was room in the Model A Ford. Couldn't they just hitch a ride? They'd be quiet. They wouldn't bother the lovebirds. But how can lovebirds love with six others in the tent? Ann laughs about it now.

Ann Smith and Raymond Clifford were married June 29, 1929, in Knox United Church, Calgary. Her white satin lace dress, veil and long white gloves were bought at Binning's Dress Shop in Calgary. The dress cost $35. Her sister Vi La France wore a coral satin dress. Both carried roses.

Waiting outside the church to transport the newly weds and family members to the reception were a big Nash and a big Packard, complete with chauffeurs. Lest you think Ann and Raymond had money, think again. They had a total of $80 between them that day. No, the cars were there courtesy of Pat Burns, the wealthy rancher, meat packer and businessman for whom Raymond served as chauffeur every day except his wedding day. Clearly some perks came with the job!

From chauffeur, Raymond moved on to become manager of the cattle operation at Burn's Bar U Ranch southwest of Calgary. As Ann said of her life from then on, **"Everything in these stories is big."** The ranch was huge—some 3½ townships big, there were as many as 8,000 cattle to keep track of and there were so many ranch hands at certain times of the year that a cow had to be butchered every week to provide meat for them. One year, 2,000 calves were branded in a single day using three corrals. It boggles the mind but somehow Raymond kept track of everything, even taking time occasionally to rub shoulders with the rich and famous. There's a picture in Ann's book that shows the Duke and Duchess of Windsor watching a branding demonstration. The Duke looks pretty calm but the Duchess, the former Wallace Simpson, looks like she'd rather be somewhere else. Paris maybe.

The group picture also includes Guy Weadick, the promoter who got the bright idea that Calgary—being in ranch country—should have an annual punch-up to be known as the Calgary Stampede. He was right too; it's been a feature of Calgary since 1912 (with a few years off during WWI.) Ann's book, incidentally, is called Ann's Story and is a wonderful record of many of those enormous ranches that ruled southern Alberta. They were like kingdoms of old—a small village in the center of miles and

Violet La France, J.R. Clifford, Raymond and Ann Clifford, 1929, Calgary, AB

miles of prairie, hills, coulees, fields and forest. You could spit in any direction and not hit a thing. As long as you were on a horse, that is. There were rules about behavior in any of the houses, especially the big house, although Ann did notice there were bullet holes in her living room walls, left there by earlier tenants on a tear.

All good things come to an end, however. In 1951, the Bar U was parceled up and sold to 29 different buyers. The ranch buildings are a national historic site now, complete with interpretive signs and paved paths and cutesy barbed wire wreaths which drive Ann crazy because no self-respecting cattleman could abide a barbed wire anything. Barbed wire was what farmers brought to the prairies when they fenced off their 160 acres. It was anathema to ranchers who needed land, lots of land, under starry skies above.

Raymond and Ann moved on to their own ranches. Stayed with the land to the end. There were no children. No complaining either. If you were lucky enough to have children in those days, fine. If you weren't, you didn't say anything about it. Just accepted. It wasn't anybody's business then, and it isn't now, she said with simple dignity.

1929...The Caribou Derby...

Women in the Caribou country of BC were as scarce as hens' teeth, acccording to Adam Coumine who worked as the foreman of a ranch in the Chilcotin River in the late 1920s. Single men, himself included, would think nothing of riding 50 or 60 miles to a barn dance in the hopes of meeting a girl. One day as he was riding along a ridge above the river, he saw a girl on horseback far below on the riverbank. Another cowboy saw the same thing.

"**This called for drastic action**," he wrote. "**The trail was steep and crooked. We jabbed the spurs into our respective horses and over the bank we went, taking all the short cuts. The other rider was close behind but to make a long story short, I reached my objective in a cloud of dust. The outcome was I married the girl two years later in the little Anglican chapel in Penticton.**"

THE 1930s

The Great Depression, hard luck weddings,
groom in the bushes, and more kids than most

The Wesko/Mackarinec wedding, 1931, Lethbridge, AB

1930...Marry Me, Please...

If all else fails, advertise. Why else would the single men of the Fort St. John area of northern BC wear hatbands that said loud and clear, **"Single, Willing To Be Married."** It was a bit of a surprise for Miss Monica Storrs when she arrived from England in 1930 to become the district deaconess. Here she thought her main task was the delivery of Sunday School lessons to the children of the remote area. Could it be that there were more important missions to be accomplished?

As it happened, she didn't fall for the hatband appeal, but she did stay in the north for years. Mostly she worked as a deaconess for the Anglican Church, but occasionally she joined Eva Hasell as a "van lady." They were an indomitable bunch of women who crisscrossed northern AB and BC in rickety motor vans in order to spread the Christian gospel.

1930...Happily Ever After...

Harry Stovel was certainly willing to be married, so willing, in fact, that he turned down the chance to go on an extended European trip with his parents and got married instead. He'd been keen on Edith Hardie for a long time; no way he'd go on a trip after she finally said Yes. So a wedding was quickly arranged, ostensibly so that his family could attend before leaving on their trip but also because Harry and Edith wanted it that way. Theirs was a love match. In among all the arranged and practical unions that occurred during the early years in the west, theirs stands out like an old movie where the newly weds walk arm in arm into the sunset and a happy-ever-after.

In spite of the rushed preparations, all the elements of a grand wedding were in place by March 5, 1930. The ceremony was held at the bride's home in Winnipeg, the living room decorated with banks of snapdragons, roses, tulips and ferns, while **"tall ivory cathedral tapers shed a soft glow throughout the room."** That's what the newspaper reported but someone forgot to light the candles, the bride remembered afterwards. Never mind. Wedding guests don't look at candles anyway. They look at the bride. **"The pretty bride...wore a becoming frock of madonna blue georgette made on princess lines; the bodice, having long sleeves and a round neckline, had a cape back and two scarf ends draped from the shoulders. The skirt was formed of cascade drapes which just escaped the ground, and gave a smart uneven hem. She wore matching blue brocaded satin shoes and a model felt cloche, drooping on the sides, and caught into tiny tuckings in the front with bandings of blue corded ribbon."**

The newspaper also reported that the bride carried a bouquet of lilies of the valley. Wrong again. Obviously wedding descriptions were written prior to the event for it turned out that Edith carried a large shower bouquet of many flowers, much bigger

Mrs. Harry Stovel, 1930, Winnipeg, MB

than the nosegay she had intended. Whenever she looked at her wedding pictures, she shook her head over that huge bouquet.

The newly weds left that night by train for a honeymoon in Minneapolis where they stayed two nights in the Nicollet Hotel for a total cost of $20.10. That's $10 a night plus 10 cents for a phone call. On the way back, they got food poisoning from the oysters served in the train dining car, or so they thought, but other than that, their married life started out happy and stayed that way.

The Stovel name was well known in Winnipeg by then as the proprietors of Stovel Co. Ltd., printers and publishers of newspapers and trade magazines. Harry went to work for the firm and stayed with them until the business was sold in 1948. He and Edith had three sons, James, Peter and Edward, and one daughter Bonnie, none of them named according to the system used by the first Stovel in Manitoba. That Stovel named his four sons alphabetically—the first son was A.B. (Augustus B.), the next one C.D. (Chester D.), the next two E.F.(Everett F.) and G.H.(Gordon H.) Maybe that's why he went into the word business—he liked his ABC's.

1930...The Bootlegger Connection...

How does a boy from Small Town, AB, end up marrying a girl from Big City, USA? Easy. He needs a job. His uncle in New York says he'll help him get one. While there, he meets Ann on a blind date and boom, it's the old story. They fall in love and marry soon after in her home city of Philadelphia.

How does a girl from Philadelphia end up in Camrose, AB, far from her family and Jewish roots? Not so easy. There were no other Jews in the area; it was a long way home. But Allan and Ann Schloss were a devoted pair and created their own Jewish home. As for the larger community, they joined most everything going and made a difference where they lived.

As for the wedding, it was memorable for the fact that Prohibition was in effect in the US when they were married. Liquor was not legally available, so you had to have a bootlegger connection or do without. Somehow, Allan made the right connections and was able to buy a number of small medicine bottles full of liquor. These he gave to his brother and Ann's brother who were told to hand one to every gentleman who came to the reception. They did so with great style. Because they were wearing the latest formal wear—white tie and tails—they had only to reach down into the deep pockets in the tails and bring out the necessary medicine.

1930...Society Girl Marries Home Town Boy...

Peter Whyte and Catharine Robb met at art school, courted at art school, filled their house in Banff with art and one day gave their art-filled house to the town of Banff to become the Whyte Museum of the Rockies. It goes without saying that the Museum includes an art gallery. It was their life.

Catharine was born to privilege and money in Concord, Mass. One of her beaus was John D. Rockefeller III, but somehow plain old Peter Whyte from a pokey little mountain town in Canada won her. Love conquers all. But just because it wasn't a high society wedding on both sides didn't mean it wasn't a splendid affair. Not at all. There's a letter in her records from Suzanne at 24 Place Vendome in Paris. Will she come for a fitting at 10 am instead of 11 am? the note asks. In other words, Catharine had her wedding dress designed in Paris and she was there to oversee the process. There was no Eaton's catalogue involved in these wedding arrangements.

That was the world she inhabited—Parisian designed dresses, travel, hobnobbing with the rich and famous. No wonder Peter Whyte's mother sounds a bit intimidated in the letter she wrote to Catharine a week before the wedding. Intimidated but determined to do the right thing. She will not be at the wedding.

"I know you and Pete are going to be happy together. You know things are so different out here in the West and in our little town and Banff but there is always one comfort. You and Pete can move around wherever your fancy takes you. We will be thinking of you both a week from tomorrow. I can feel with your mother who is losing her Daughter but gaining a son like I am losing a Son but gaining a Daughter. May you both be wonderfully happy and God Bless You both. Lovingly, Your Mother."

1931…What Did I Know Love?…

Anne Pieronek was 16 when Walter Chuchla said to her father, **"You know what, Mr. Pieronek, I think I'll marry your daughter. She's old enough now."** And so the deal was made between prospective groom and father of the bride. The bride had nothing to say about it but Anne remembered years later that she wasn't too upset. After all, it meant she'd get off her father's farm. Maybe she wouldn't have to work so hard in her own home.

Her own mother had married at age 14 and by age 18 had four babies. Anne was the oldest. **"At age 4, I worked like a 10 year old,"** she said, **"and when I was 10, I worked like an adult. I didn't know what was this thing called 'playing.'"** So she didn't object to marriage. It was what sensible Polish girls did. They got on with their lives.

"What did I know love?" she asked.

Walter Chuchla came to Canada from Poland in 1926. In search of adventure and a good living, he got his first job in Canada with a bootlegger in Edmonton who hid his illegal homebrew in a specially hollowed out shaft of a sleigh. It was Walter's job to drive to customers and fill their orders without arousing any suspicion as to why he had to adjust the sleigh's shaft so often. That was just a bit more adventure than he had planned, so he headed for the mines in the Crowsnest Pass.

He got to Coleman just in time to attend the funeral of eight men who'd been killed in an explosion in the mine. That was his introduction to mining, but what could he do? He had to make a living, so he became a miner. But he was a hard man to keep down, pun intended. Outside of the mines, he organized a fraternal club for miners, a youth club, an orchestra, a library. And then one day, when he had some spare time, he made a deal for Anne.

Anne's father was an old-timer in Canada by the time Walter appeared on the scene having come to Canada from Poland in 1907. At first, like so many of his countrymen, he worked in the mines in the Crowsnest Pass but he wanted to farm so eventually homesteaded in the Burmis area, still in the Crowsnest area. It was at this farm that the wedding of Anne and Walter took place. It was at this farm that Anne milked 16 cows the morning of her wedding, and then did the whole thing again that evening.

Anne and her mother made the wedding dress. The material cost $3.50. The veil came from Eaton's catalogue. It cost 39 cents. The three bridesmaids made their dresses—a similar price range. The mother of the bride wore her good dress, nothing new, and the flowers for the bouquets and boutonnieres came from neighborhood gardens. It was August 8, 1931.

After a proper Roman Catholic service conducted by Father O'Dea, the Polish three-day celebration began. Not that everyone stayed for three days but there was food and dancing and food again and music at various times for the next few days. Her mom made most of the food, her dad turned a stuffed pig on a spit over an outdoor fire, friends and family helped out. It was a good party. Anne and Walter got to sit at the only table available outside and she didn't have to do dishes for a change. It was more like a picnic, Anne remembered.

It wasn't a picnic for long. A year after the marriage, the miners went out on strike for better pay and safer working conditions, not unreasonable requests since the mines in the Crowsnest seemed always to be blowing up or bumping or caving in. It was desperately dangerous work, but the mine owners refused to budge for eight months during which time Walter occasionally played his saxophone at benefits for the unemployed men. That was enough to get him blacklisted when the strike was over. No job. It was 1933, the height of the Depression.

What to do? Well, they did whatever they could—Walter a little farm work here, odd jobs in construction there. For awhile he rode the rails through central Alberta in search of work but since many other unemployed men were also hopping rides on the trains, that didn't work. Anne stayed at home and did a little waitressing here, housework there, laundry for the miners now and then. She got 5 cents a shirt incidentally. Through it all, they never went on relief. Relief is the depression term for

social assistance. It was seen as a last resort then, almost a disgrace, and they were very proud to be able to manage without it, even though they were often down to their last dirty shirt, their last 5 cents.

Eventually, Walter got his mining job back but then he got injured. Anne had had enough. No more mining, she said. Let's move to Calgary. So they did. Walter worked as a caretaker, Anne worked in the Hudsons Bay cafeteria for some 20 years. Her starting wage was 20 cents an hour, but again she was very proud that they were able to make it without assistance. **"I was a hard worker,"** she said again and again. It defined her life, her work did. **"Work never hurts anybody,"** she said. **"Laziness hurts people."**

In 1936, Walter became a Canadian citizen, a big deal for him. **"I felt like I had the whole of Canada in my hand,"** he said. **"I was so proud."**

Anne and Walter Chuchla were honored during the 1980s for their work on behalf of Polish-Canadians, for their contributions to the history of the Crowsnest Pass area, and for their work in the Catholic Church. In fact, Anne made cabbage rolls and potato pancakes for the Cardinal of Cracow when he visited Calgary in 1969. **"Someday you'll be Pope,"** she told him.

"Oh, no, they would never allow a Polish Pope," he returned. (He was wrong. He became Pope a few years later.)

Walter died in 1987, aged 82. Anne is still making cabbage rolls for her church in 1998. Their daughter Claire lives nearby.

1931...High Time To Be Married...

The Wesko wedding was not arranged. Bill Wesko saw Marie Mackarinec at a local restaurant in Lethbridge, AB, and said, **"She's the one for me."** Whether he said those exact words in his first language Ukrainian or maybe English or Czechoslovakian or Hungarian or a combination of them all, we don't know, but he made his point. There were all kinds of languages around and about in southern AB in those days. Most everyone spoke bits and pieces of several.

The wedding wasn't hard to arrange. Marie came to Canada on her own; what little family she had was still in Czechoslavakia. Bill's folks were in the Lethbridge area alright but he was a grown man. High time he got married according to some of his friends, especially the joker in the back row of the picture who's holding up a watch to emphasize that very point.

The wedding day was Sunday, October 25, 1931; the church was the Greek Catholic Church in Lethbridge. Marie made her own dress of a cream colored silky material finished with hand done embroidery around the neck. She carried a bouquet of waxed flowers. There was a reception and a dance but by Monday morning, it was back to the real world which for Bill and Marie was his parent's home. That's where they lived for the first years of their married life. A good thing too since the depression hit and there weren't jobs for love nor money. Marie washed clothes for bachelors as a way of bringing in some income. They sold eggs, Bill worked when and where he could but they had to depend on relief for a large part of the depression years. $7.00 a month for many months.

As a young single man, he had been one of Picariello's rum running gang, picking up liquor in BC and Montana and bringing it across the mountains into dry AB and SK. For awhile, it was great fun—outwitting and outrunning the police. And the cars—how else would he get to drive a big powerful car? But one day, the police nearly caught him on a delivery between Hardieville and Lethbridge. If he hadn't turned into an auto wrecker's yard and lost the car among the other junk there, he would have been in jail for sure. So he swore off the trade. Then poor old Picariello shot a policeman one day and the jig was up entirely. Pick was hanged and prohibition was repealed. So there was no going back to that life.

Maybe it was remembering those exciting days, when money and fun could be had, that sent Bill back to the Crowsnest Pass, this time with wife and family. And from the time they unpacked and settled in Coleman, things went better for them. When oldest son Bill went to school, the teacher asked him his name. He said what

sounded like Wesko, she wrote down Wesko…which is how the Vesko family came to be the Wesko family. That wasn't the end of Bill's cross-cultural activities that day. When he got home that afternoon, his dad said, **"OK Bill, from now on we speak English and you have to teach us."** And that's about how it worked. There were six children in all. One died in infancy but the others grew up to be nurses and bookstore owners and farmers and housewives, all speaking very good English.

Bill and Marie died in a car accident in 1976. They were on their way home to Coleman.

1932…Two As Cheaply As One?…

If Ron Ratcliffe's real life story were made into a movie, no one would believe it. Even the wedding stretches credibility. Here are two young people with no money to speak of, no sure jobs, not even a bed to sleep on, but they get married anyway. Ron marries Doris Wintersteen on March 23, 1932, in St. Mark's Church in Nakusp, BC.

After the brief ceremony, they rowed down the lake to Ron's cabin and prepared for the two of them to live as cheaply as one. That's an old saying that must have been invented during the Dirty Thirties. It was an acceptable way of saying—We want to be married even though there's no money and no future. Therefore, we will tell you (and ourselves) that two can live as cheaply as one. It wasn't always a lie.

The picture of Doris and Ron was taken the day of the wedding in front of their cabin. They are still in their wedding outfits, the biggest concession to style being the kiss curl that Doris has coaxed into her hair. Once they get out of their good clothes, they'll get to work. There's no proper cookstove yet, just a heater, but Ron has a good woodpile beside the door. And when that's gone, he just has to go to the bush behind the cabin and chop some trees down. He's a logger, he knows how to use and axe and saw. He's also used to winter by now—witness the snowshoes on the wall. And soon, there'll be a wash tub hanging on the outside of the cabin as well. That will be Doris's job—to wash clothes by hand in a big washtub which, once the wash is done, will be hung beside the other tools of life on the outside of the cabin. Somewhere out back, there will be a clothesline.

You could tell a lot about people by the outside of their log shacks in those days. Were they careful with their tools, did they keep a good supply of wood on hand, did they arrange stuff on the outside walls with precision or with careless abandon, did they let the weeds grow? Live around log shacks for long and you could read them.

Ron came to Canada from England in 1923, thanks to the Salvation Army who brought young men to jobs in Canada, there being no jobs and no future for poor kids in England. He was 16. He knew nothing. For two years, he worked for a farmer/logger in Nova Scotia. No pay, no benefits. He knew enough by then to realize his debt to the Salvation Army must have been paid. Moved on to different work, some pay, enough indeed to buy a Model T Ford for $75. Figured he'd head north and go trapping. Knew nothing about trapping. Lost the traps under snowdrifts, ruined the car on terrible roads. Sold it for $18. Learned another lesson.

One fall, like thousands of other homeless hopeless men, he climbed on a harvest excursion train heading for western Canada where jobs awaited, or so they thought, but the jobs lasted only through harvest season and then winter came. Winter is no fun if you're living from hand to mouth so Ron hopped a train and headed west. "Hopping" a train meant sneaking onto or off a freight car without the police catching you. Drifters like Ron got very good at it. They knew, for instance, that the police at Field, BC, were particularly alert. **"It was a bad place to get into and a hard place to get out of,"** he wrote later, **"but I evaded them although one threatened to shoot me if I didn't stop."**

He got off alright but spent the night in the snowy bush near the tracks, then crept into a boxcar half loaded with coal the next morning. There were twenty other guys in the same boxcar, all of them heading west looking for work.

At Revelstoke, Ron was just too cold to go any further so he jumped out and stood for awhile by the heater in the train station. While there, a man who ran his own logging outfit in the bush south of Revelstoke approached him. Looking for a job? he asked Ron, and that's how Ron ended up in Nakusp as assistant to a "gyppo," the name given independent loggers. And that's where he met Doris.

It wasn't exactly happy-ever-after. Ron still had to take every kind of job he could get—road building, harvesting, logging, trapping until finally in 1942, he gave up on Nakusp and moved to Rossland and a job with Cominco. Then in 1955 he set up his own radio and television repair shop. In the meantime, Doris looked after the kids—a son and daughter, she sold cherries from the trees on their acreage, she raised chickens, milked a cow, planted a huge garden. They survived.

Years later, Ron wondered about it all in the Nakusp history book. **"I often look back in my life and wonder why we worked so hard because I haven't accomplished very much. The world doesn't seem any better off for my having been here. Is there any point in life? I doubt it."**

Maybe not, but what choices did he have? Life happens.

1933...Which Is It...Love or Money?

The hero of this story has to be Johnny Matson, the shy Norwegian prospector who moiled for gold for years and years on his claim in the Yukon. Never mind that his wife got all the headlines. He was sweet, kind, long suffering, loyal, and he loved Kate without reservation. Without much reward either, it must be admitted, but his love was so all encompassing that he asked no return.

Klondike Kate was lucky.

Kate Rockwell arrived in Dawson City in 1899 at the height of the gold rush when lonesome men were throwing gold around, literally. She made a ton of money as a dance hall girl and one night some of the boys took a notion to crown her Queen of the Klondike. To that end, they made a crown out of an old tin can, stuck candles hither and thither on it and placed it on top of Kate's red hair. What's more, they lit the candles. What's more, she wore the thing even though some of the candle wax dripped into her hair. She was gutsy, there's no getting around it, but she wasn't very wise. Who could be in such a crazy place where fortunes were made and lost overnight, where a fresh egg was more valuable than gold, where a fairly ordinary looking young woman could be transformed with a tin can into the Queen of the Klondike?

Kate's downfall began with one George Pantages, a waiter with big ideas. They should own a theatre together, he proposed, only he didn't have the money. Kate did.

Kate forked over. They left the north. Kate kept on forking out until George had a nice little theatre empire going—the Pantages Theatres. Then he dropped her on her head and married someone else. That hurt more than the burning candles on her crown.

She licked her wounds for awhile and then tried to get back on the stage, but what worked in Dawson City didn't work nearly so well in Seattle or New York or Podunk Corners. Kate had had her day. So what do Klondike Queens do after the party's over? They wait on tables, drink a bit too much, wash floors, wash clothes, drink a bit too much and maybe elope with a much younger Oregon cowboy. He was Floyd Warner, a handsome devil of a wrangler, but the marriage didn't last long.

It was back to square one for Kate—no money, no job, no prospects. She even approached Pantages and begged for a loan. He was Mr. Big by then with lots of money. He gave her a measly $6.

Meanwhile in the silent forest north of Dawson City, Matson continued his quest for gold. Day after day, all by himself, he dug into his claim, sluiced the dirt, watched for gold. Once a year, he hiked out to Dawson, sold his gold—if he'd found any, bought clothes, supplies and food, picked up his mail and headed back to his claim. People wouldn't even have known he was around except that he wore big boots and made a distinctive plopping sound as he walked. Must be Matson, they'd say.

In his cabin one day, he unpacked some supplies that had been wrapped in three year old newspaper. There on a crumpled page, he saw a face he recognized—the Queen of the Klondike, the beautiful woman who'd worn candles in her hair. And apparently she was in trouble, something about a lawsuit and Pantages and Kate who had no money. Summoning more courage than he knew he had, he wrote to her: **"I have always been in love with you, Kate, and all these years I never had the courage to tell you before. I have heard that life has not been too good to you. You have had lots of hardship. I would like to take care of you. I would like to have the right to take care of you as my wife."**

Whether Kate even remembered Johnny Matson is debatable, but she saw her chance and took it. Her letters were polite, not too forward, but she let him know she'd be glad to marry him but in the meantime, she had a few immediate expenses. She needed a new coat, a garage for her car, living expenses, and apparently Johnny came through. There is reference to a bank account and the new garage. As for the wedding, that took a bit longer. Johnny didn't respond to her letters for nearly two years. She thought she'd lost him, but in the fall of 1932, he finally emerged from the bush, read all her letters and wrote to say he'd be out in Vancouver next summer. They could be married then.

Sure enough, Johnny made his second trip to the outside in 35 years. He was 70 years old but strong and muscle hard. In a new suit, he cleaned up very well and in their wedding pictures they look very pleased with one another. Kate is 57; she too is in pretty good shape, and manages to get the story and picture into most newspapers.

"Klondike Kate" and Johnny Matson wedding, 1933, Vancouver, BC

She was media wise even when there was just one medium. Her wedding ring was made of gold nuggets; so was a necklace that Johnny gave her. It all made wonderful copy…the happy ending of a dream born under the midnight sun.

For a honeymoon, they went to—where else—Dawson City. Johnny was used to the new/old Dawson but Kate couldn't believe her eyes. The stores and dance halls were boarded up, the place was dead compared to its heyday in the early 1900's. She could barely look at the old Orpheum Theatre where she'd been the toast of the town. It was just too sad, and whether it was sadness or calculated forethought but Kate was back home in Oregon within a few weeks. No problem, she told newspaper reporters. Johnny will live in the north, I will live here and we'll see each other every summer.

That's what they did for the next 13 years. Every summer, Johnny came out to Dawson, Kate went into Dawson, they saw one another, lived in separate hotels, and then returned whence they had come. Oldtimers said she just went in to get his money and furs every summer; others were kinder and said Johnny had never been happier. Why question the arrangement?

In 1946, a passing prospector found Matson dead in a trapper's cabin. **"There's only one thing to do now,"** Kate told reporters, **"Mush on and keep smiling."**

Two years later, she married again, this time to W.L. Van Duren, and nine years later, she died at 77 years of age. The Flame had gone out.

1934…Goods Satisfactory or Money Refunded…

If one were to write a play about western Canada in the 1930s, Eaton's would have to be a real live character. The catalogue, the company, was so much a part of prairie life that a Martian, hearing the name Eaton's constantly, would have to conclude that Eaton was a brother, a kind uncle perhaps.

You wanted a new house? Contact Eaton's. They'd send all the makings to the nearest train station. All you had to do was put it together like a giant construction set.

Snowsuits for winter? Get out the Eaton's catalogue. Let the kids pore over the pictures. Decide which ones you can afford. Then fill out the order form, order everything two sizes too big so there will be room to grow, enclose a money order and send it off. Wait to see if the real thing looks at all like the picture. Hope for substitutions because they were often better than the original.

You wanted new boots but had no idea of your size? Stand on a blank piece of paper, trace the outline of your foot, enclose it with the order. Somebody at Eaton's would figure out the size.

The school wanted small gifts for the children's Christmas party? Give Eaton's the details—ages, numbers, money available. Eaton's would look after it.

A wedding coming up? Tell Eaton's about it. Their personal shoppers would pick out a dress, hat, shoes, gloves, whatever. Just tell them your size, your preferences, your budget.

Anna and Roy Keedian, 1935, Winnipeg, MB

Sending an order to Eaton's was like writing to a friend. Who but a friend would fiddle around with personal shopping and Christmas gifts for school kids and the like?

Even the catalogue was an old friend. Known as the Prairie Bible, it was read in some homes more than the real Bible. Kids used it as fodder for games—if you could have anything on this page, what would it be? Girls made cutouts from old catalogues. Homemakers used it as a guide to current fashions, made their homemade dresses like the ones shown in the catalogue. Everyone checked out the underwear pages—the only sex education available at the time. Indeed, if Eaton hadn't thought of that catalogue, someone would have had to, it fit so perfectly into the culture of the prairies at that time.

And, it must be mentioned, a catalogue continued its usefulness even after a new one replaced it. Then the old one became toilet paper in the biffy, the john, the little house, the back house, whatever the outdoor facilities were called. By that stage, the black and white pages were preferred. They weren't as stiff as the colored ones.

The first Eaton's store was opened in Toronto in 1869, which makes Eaton's almost as old as Canada. The mail order service was launched in 1884, and in 1905 that part of the business moved to Winnipeg and got bigger and bigger. Both in 1916 and 1921, new and larger office buildings were added to the Winnipeg operations. It was a huge service and a huge employer.

Thus, it is fitting that one of the 1934 weddings is that of Anna Daman who worked for years at Eaton's in Winnipeg. She was one of the legion of women who took the personal requests and turned them into reality. If a woman asked for a wedding dress, preferably in blue, with matching gloves and shoes—diagram of foot included—it was Anna who went first to the dress department, then to gloves and shoes looking for the right combination for the money provided. Every request represented a different story. It was like working in a dream factory; she was making dreams come true, or not, as the case may be. Not that she carried on in such a fanciful way. It was an 8:30 a.m. to 5 p.m. job and she worked hard. But she felt she was part of a family—at the store and beyond. It was never just numbers or names. The requests came from real people with real needs, and her work made a difference.

She got her own wedding dress at Eaton's, of course, a floor length gown of pink mousseline de soie, frilled in tiny ruffles from the knees to the hemline. Her picture hat was of pink mohair, her gloves and shoes were pink, and she carried pink roses and lily-of-the-valley. She was, as the newspaper reported, **"a picture in pink."** The date was August 4, 1934.

The groom was Roy Keedian, and if Anna brings to mind Eaton's and its part in western history, then Roy has to carry the can for curling, another important part of Winnipeg's history. He wasn't all that keen on curling himself but his dad was. Say "Keedian" in the early 1900s in Winnipeg and everyone knew you were talking Jimmy

Keedian and curling. A charter member of the Thistle Curling Club, he won numerous trophies through the years and when he wasn't on the ice, he was making the ice.

Son Roy preferred baseball and was much in demand by various provincial teams for his pitching ability. In the 1930s, he built Roy's Garage in Bird's Hill, a community just south of Winnipeg, and it was there that Eaton's catalogue orders were dropped off and picked up. You see? Eaton's was everywhere.

After a two-day honeymoon in Minnesota, Roy went back to work at the garage and Anna became a housewife and mother to two children, Jackie and Gary. Married women didn't work outside the home in those days but she did go back to Eaton's years later after the war. But it was different by then, she said. No longer a big family at work, no longer a member of the family for customers.

There's one more character that must be mentioned in this story—Dr. Curtis James Bird for whom Bird's Hill is named. We Canadians sometimes think our history is pretty bland compared to that of the USA, but here's proof to the contrary. Dr. Bird was part of an illustrious group of men assigned in 1870 to come up with a Bill of Rights for the new province of Manitoba. He then became an MLA in the first provincial election and then Speaker of the House. He had influence, power, a name, but when he voted against the incorporation of Winnipeg as a city, there were those who thought he had too much of the above. In fact, somebody was so mad at him that he arranged to have him tarred and feathered on a lonely road one dark and stormy night. Sounds like a bad movie, doesn't it, but it really happened in boring old Canada.

Dr. Curtis survived. His attackers were never found.

1934...The Dog Who Ate the Wedding Presents...

At her wedding shower, Maggie Medernach got several hand painted dishes and framed pictures of the Blessed Virgin and Sacred Heart.

At the wedding itself, Maggie and Gerhard Leiffers got one pig, one cookstove, one feather bed and pillows plus $30 to have their wedding picture taken. That came from Gerhard's family. From Maggie's family came 30 chickens and two cows. For 1934, that was a pretty good start. Mind you, the dog ate all but six of the chickens soon after Maggie and Gerhard moved to their own farm, but they still had enough to give them some eggs and some new chicks the next spring.

It was more than their folks had had when they came to the Cudworth area of SK, the Lieffers in 1904 and 1905, and the Medernachs in 1902. They didn't even have the English language when they arrived, which was why Anna Lieffer almost didn't find her husband when she first arrived. No one understood her German, couldn't help her, until a settler who could speak some German was found. Yes, there was a new settler nearby but he was tall with a full flowing beard. No, no, Anna said, her husband was tall alright, but he did not have a beard. And so on it went, with Anna getting

more and more frightened all the time. It was only when one of the neighbors mentioned that he'd seen dark blue striped underwear on the line at this newcomer's house that she believed it might possibly be her Gerhard. Gerhard, she knew, had blue striped underwear.

It wasn't the first time that underwear saved a new settler. In fact, there should be statues to underwear and the lives it saved in the Canadian west.

On July 31, 1934, Maggie and Gerhard were married at the Medernach farm. Maggie wore a long white satin dress, her bouquet was pink and white satin roses, her veil a long net panel gathered to a seed pearl headdress. During the wedding dance, she changed to a long mauve dress, her going-away dress, although they didn't go far. Just down the road to their own place. Their honeymoon was spent doing the harvest.

The harvest must have been pretty good; that fall they bought a Ford truck for

$175, three horses and a binder for $350.

Maggie always worked alongside Gerhard—in the winters gathering and cutting wood, in the summers helping with the fieldwork and animals. Even when the first baby came along, she continued to help out in the fields. They made a box for Joseph and, with the dog left as guard, checked on him every time they made a round of the field. When the next baby came, they just made a bigger box. Eventually, there were seven children in all, and no, they didn't all go into the box. The girls all went on to Catholic boarding school, however, a fact that made Maggie very proud. She still had on her walls the set of framed pictures of the Blessed Virgin and Sacred Heart that she had received as shower gifts so many years before. She still had the hand painted dishes as well. They were too precious to actually use.

In 1957, a reunion of the Medernach family was held. Maggie and Gerhard were there with their seven children. Her 16 brothers and sisters were there too with their children, and when a count was taken, the total came to 100 grandchildren for the first Medernachs in Canada. Add that number to the 46 that the first Lieffer family produced (less the seven that overlap) and you'll see why these stories should be called How the West was Won. The West was won by big families and small who did what they had to and what they could to survive. It's just as amazing every time it's told.

1935…No Lurking For Grant MacEwan…

Grant MacEwan believed in conservation. Even before conservation was a fashionable concept, he believed in it. Even after he left home and didn't have to hear his Scottish mother saying, **"Waste is a sin; thrift is a virtue,"** he believed in it. It defined his life.

He didn't even waste words. In his journal on June 30, 1935, he recorded, **"Phyllis and I decided finally to get married about July 26."** That's Phyllis Cline, his school teacher friend of some five years. Does he wax lyrical about her beauty, her charm? He could have. She had both. No, ever the sensible frugal Scotsman, he simply records the facts. Just the facts. A week later, he wrote, **"Phyllis Cline got her Bluebird, reg. #70193."** Again, he might have given us some romantic details about the engagement ring—did he present it on bended knee, did she cry tears of joy, all that stuff? But no, he records the registration number. Who even knew engagement rings *had* registration numbers?

A practical Scotsman, that's who, an agriculturist who was used to statistics about crop yields and farm animal prices, one who knew the value of a dollar and an hour, one who noted in his journal that on April 10, 1935, **"I consumed half a pumpkin pie and a quarter of an apple pie….at the Knox Church Men's banquet."** It is not surprising, therefore, that he wrote about his wedding as if reporting a horse show: **"Phyllis Cline and Grant MacEwan were wed. The place was the Saskatoon Forestry Nursery, the day was excellent and Dr. John Nicol officiated. About 50 people were** present, among them Hon. Robert Weir who just arrived from Ottawa today. Phyllis and I left at 5 p.m. amid a small hurricane of excitement and devilment. To Rosetown by train."

Fortunately, the Saskatoon and Winnipeg newspapers had a bit more to say about the wedding which was, after all, an important social event in the summer of 1935. Phyllis Cline's family was well connected in Saskatchewan. Her father was a stationmaster in Churchbridge, Uncle John Nicol was the minister who married them, and Uncle James McLean was director of the Forestry Farm where the wedding took place. Phyllis herself had taught school in Saskatoon for a number of years and was well known. For his part, MacEwan was by then a professor in the department of agriculture at the University of Saskatchewan. They were somebodies in their own world and could have enjoyed star treatment for a few days at least, but it just wasn't MacEwan's style. As the wedding hour approached, for instance, best man Al Ewen couldn't find the groom. He wasn't lurking in the bushes, staying out of sight like good bridegrooms are supposed to do. Instead, he was out front welcoming all the guests as they came through the gates to the farm. Ewen had to tell him he was supposed to wait behind the hedge until the music started.

The wedding was held outdoors, **"in a veritable Garden of Eden,"** the Free Press gushed. The setting should have relaxed MacEwan, the outdoorsman, but in the pictures he still looks as if he'd like to get out of his suit and into old clothes. Phyllis had no such trouble. She looks entirely comfortable in her long ivory satin gown with matching train. Her veil was an embroidered silk net held in place by a Juliet cap, and her flowers were calla lilies.

According to the newspaper account, tea honors at the reception were performed by Mrs. A.M. Shaw and Miss E. Stormont while the ices were cut by Mrs. James McLean and Mrs. J.L. Nicol. In other words, tea and ice cream were served. Thus fortified, the newly weds left on their honeymoon. This is where the story gets really interesting.

They took the train from Saskatoon to Rosetown, some 90 miles. Spent the night in the Rosetown Hotel and then boarded a bus. A bus? You could hear the tea pouring matrons catching their breath. Even on a honeymoon, he's so stingy that he takes a bus? Unbelievable. But a bus it was and led to one of the most memorable moments of the honeymoon. While on a bus from Spokane to Vancouver, they met fellow traveler Will Rogers, the American humorist and social critic. The man who said, **"I never met a man I didn't like."** MacEwan liked him enormously, never forgot the thrill of meeting him. Never forgot either that Rogers was killed in a plane crash just days later in Alaska.

As for the choice of a bus honeymoon, Phyllis explained years later that it had nothing to do with economics but everything to do with space. MacEwan was over six feet tall. He couldn't fit into a railway berth at the best of times and certainly couldn't fit into one with a new wife. Thus, it was easier to travel by bus during the day and

stay at hotels each evening. Mind you, it also gave her new husband a chance to work on his book manuscript. **"I did more work on the manuscript during the honeymoon than I had a right to, but come hell, high water or matrimony, I was resolved to finish it and get it off to the publisher,"** he apologized later.

That was his first book, The Science and Practice of Canadian Animal Husbandry, a title that could only come from Grant MacEwan. It is what it is. This is the man who went on to write many more books about agriculture and eventually western Canadian history, none of which got fancy titles. One of his best selling histories is called simply Fifty Mighty Men. It is what it is.

The closest he ever came to patting himself on the back is in his note about the birth of their only child on May 3, 1939. **"Phyllis to hospital at 11 am. Heather MacEwan born at 11:45 pm. Length 23", head 14½", hair black and lots of it. Disposition good. Proof that a good sire pays."**

MacEwan's life touches on all three prairie provinces. He was born in Manitoba, moved with his folks to Saskatchewan, became a professor at the University there, and then moved back to Winnipeg in 1946 to be dean of agriculture at the University of Manitoba. In 1951, he left university life and moved to Calgary where he became a full time writer, full time politician and mayor, full time environmentalist and farmer. Calgarians got used to seeing their mayor taking the bus back and forth to city hall, walking whenever possible, generally underusing the resources of the modern world. Just as his father worked to leave his farm better than he found it, so did MacEwan want to leave his piece of the world better than he found it. If that meant using less gas, polluting less, eating simply, wearing old but good clothes, then that is what he'd do. And he did. Even when he became Alberta Lieutenant Governor in 1966 and looked like a million bucks in his cocked hat and gold trimmed uniform, he managed to avoid the traps of consumerism and affluence. He was always that same down-to-earth guy that greeted the guests at his own wedding.

When interviewed in 1998, he gave this advice for modern couples: **"Be practical, live simply, be spiritually alert and be open about feeling."** He was in a longterm care facility by then. Phyllis predeceased him in 1985.

1935…Summer Weddings in York Factory…

Luckily, the Hudson's Bay Company trader at York Factory in northern Manitoba had a small camera, and luckily he was there the day that Jeremiah and Rebecca Stoney got married. Otherwise, we wouldn't have this amazing picture of a native wedding. The bride and groom, right and center of the picture, are holding a narwhale tusk. It's their wedding gift and a very valuable one. Narwhale tusks even then were pretty rare.

Flora Beardy guesses it was a gift of the Hudson's Bay Company and its man-in-charge, Ralph Ingram, the aforementioned photographer. She also guesses that the material for the dresses, the lace trimming and the new shawl came from the HBC store, not as a gift perhaps but as regular purchases. Ditto for the bridegroom's suit and spanking new hat.

Flora Beardy is the co-author, along with Robert Coutts, of a book published in 1996 called *Voices from Hudson Bay, Cree Stories from York Factory*. It's an oral history that covers the years from 1920-1957 when York Factory was closed. Everything changed for the northern natives during those years—airplanes brought medical care and groceries, government people brought social services and schools, radio brought news of a crazy outside world. At the same time, nothing changed. Traditional ways

Jeremiah and Rebecca Stoney (centre front), 1935, York Factory, MB

persisted…which meant that every summer when families returned to York Factory to sell the furs they'd trapped through the long winter, there were weddings. And weddings meant good parties.

By and large, the marriages were arranged by the parents, by the women mostly. A first marriage was easy, simply the selecting of two young people, but a second or third was harder. If a man were killed on a hunting expedition, for example, the families would have to find another husband for the widow, and so on. Some years, the turnover would have been such that there'd be several marriages at once. One of the elders told Flora Beardy that there were lots of weddings. **"Sometimes at one wedding there would be ten couples getting married. Oh, yes, they would dress up. The men wore suits and hats, straw hats. The women sewed their own dresses. They also wore shawls."**

There was a fairly substantial church in York Factory then, the Church of St. John. It would have had a short aisle for the bridal procession but the northern natives liked a longer approach. They'd line up outside—bride and groom followed by their attendants followed by the next bride and groom, and so on. This is what one native remembered about that scene: **"Then they would all walk in a line to the church. It used to look so nice. The area they would leave from was nice. It was all clearing, no trees. Anyway, the church was quite a ways, especially from Mr. Faries' house. But they all walked the distance…Behind these people there was usually someone playing music. Most of the time it was my dad and he would be playing the instrument that you stretch—the accordion."** (Rev. Richard Faries served as minister in the York Factory area for 53 years.)

The best part was yet to come—the dancing. The brides would take off their store bought shoes, put on their moccasins and dance the night away. Sometimes part of the next day too. There'd be food breaks— bannock, fish, wild game—but it was the dance that mattered for once it was over, so was the party. Time then to get back to work.

1936…Amazing Ordinary Lives…

Art Ford and Isabel Tyner had a pretty ordinary wedding. No guns boomed. They had pretty ordinary lives too. No fireworks, no medals, no visits from the Queen. Just one year after another year, ordinary piling on ordinary, or so it would seem.

So it would seem wrong. No life is ordinary. No combination of lives is ordinary.

Take 1913 when Isabel's mother in Ontario decided to join her husband in the west. She knew he was seldom home in the log cabin he'd built for them near South Fort George, now Prince George, so she bought a padlock and two keys. The padlock and one key, she sent to Tom. The other key she kept. Just send me a map, she said, and I'll find the place. If you're not there, I have a key. And so it was. She traveled by rail and river across the country with four little kids, aged 15 months to five years. In

Art and Isabel Ford, (couple on left), 1936, Prince George,BC

South Fort George, she dragged bags, kids, feet and water up a hill to the locked log cabin, unlocked it, and called it home.

Amazing. Her husband didn't even know she was there until several neighbors told him there were people in his cabin.

Isabel, born 1909, was the third of the seven Tyner children. The seventh was Margaret born in 1918 in Prince George. There were two epidemics scourging the countryside that year—whooping cough and influenza. She died at three months of age from one or other of the terrible diseases. Nothing could be done. The family carried on. Amazing.

After an on-again, off-again school career, due to moves and changes in family fortunes, Isabel finally graduated from high school and looked around for career choices. There were three—stenography, teaching and nursing. She chose nursing because it didn't cost much to enter the three-year training course. In fact, the student nurses were a handy source of cheap labor. Didn't matter to Isabel. She got her R.N. and then she got tuberculosis. Happened to a lot of student nurses because they were constantly exposed to live TB germs. Back into hospital, this time as a patient at the Tranquille Tuberculosis Hospital near Kamloops. Fortunately, she recovered. Others didn't. Amazing.

In the spring of 1936, Arthur Ford came courting. He was a shy Englishman who wanted to propose to Isabel in the privacy of her folks' living room, but other family members kept interrupting. Then Art asked her to go for a walk. Not right now, she said, so poor Art had to blurt out his proposal in front of half a dozen family members. **"I should have gone for that walk,"** Isabel says now, **"but I didn't know."**

Art was a Morse operator for Canadian National Telegraph. That is, he sent and received messages in Morse code, the only way that news got in or out of Prince George. In fact, he was the equivalent of an old-fashioned town crier. He'd translate messages received through the dit dots that came over his machine, then he'd take the bulletins down to the newspaper office. He got the news before the newspaper did. Eventually, Prince George got all the bells and whistles of modern communication but for awhile Art was it. Amazing.

The wedding on May 9, 1936, was quiet. Isabel's sister was the only one with a job right then so she bought the wedding outfit—a swagger suit of red-flecked brown travel tweed with a matching red felt hat and brown gloves. Art's brother in Edmonton sent red roses for the bridal bouquet; it was too early for garden flowers. And that was pretty well that. A reception was held at the Tyner home after the ceremony. On top of the wedding cake was an ornament that had been used by Isabel's maternal grandmother for her wedding in 1879. How did that fit itself into the luggage when Isabel's mother packed up to come west? Amazing.

After marriage, Isabel didn't work outside the home, of course. Women didn't then. They were expected to keep the home fires burning, to have children and to work for the church and community. Isabel did all those things except there were no children. It would have been nice to have a family, she says now, but when it didn't happen in those days, you accepted your fate. God's will. She looked after the children of family and friends and eventually worked into a job with the local Health Unit.

After 48 years with CN Telegraphs, Art retired. He got a watch. Amazing. And in 1992, he died. Not amazing but not unexpected either. He was 81 years old.

Isabel, in the meantime, continued with her care of church and community as a result of which she was named Local History award winner in 1990. With great amazement, she said on that occasion, **"People tell me my life has been interesting. To me, it's not really. Back in those days, it was day-to-day living, nothing special."**

Wrong, Isabel. It was amazing.

1936...Almost An Operatic Tragedy...

The Pocaterra story is much more exciting. It's an amazing story, one might almost say, but in the end, it too was day-to-day living. Is that how the world ends, not with a bang but with day-to-day living? Looks that way.

Norma Piper was a rising opera star when she and George Pocaterra were married in Milan, Italy, on June 18, 1936. In fact, she was known as Norma San Georgio by then, no more the cute blond from Calgary whose dentist father wanted his little girl to have the very best music training possible. Thus, the apartment in Milan and the voice teachers and language coaches and letters of introduction from such notables as the Canadian prime minister of the time, R.B. Bennett. No effort was spared to launch Norma's singing career but the biggest boost came from George Pocaterra.

The son of a well connected family in Italy, he did the adventure thing in the early 1900s—left behind privilege and money and came to Canada to prove himself. The proving ground ended up at the foothills of the Rockies west of Calgary. There, he set up the Buffalo Head ranch on the Highwood River, a sort of dude ranch, but mostly it was a base from which Pocaterra explored the mountains around him. As a result of his ramblings, there's a Pocaterra Creek, Pocaterra Valley and Elpoca Mountain in the Kananaskis region, all found by the young adventurer from Italy with help, it must be admitted, from the Stoney Indians.

But along came some of that day-to-day living. George's father was dying in Italy. Would he come home? And by the way, would he look up young Norma Piper when he was there? She'd love to see someone from home.

"I guess it was love at first sight," Norma said years later, but it was also about the best thing that could have happened to her career. Before George got involved, it was stuck. She had a voice; all the experts agreed, but it needed training. Thousands of North Americans were in Milan trying to find music teachers. How could Norma compete? Enter George with his family connections, and soon after enter Riccardo Pettinella, a noted voice

Norma and George Pocaterra, 1936, Milan, Italy

teacher and conductor in major European opera houses. It was the boost she needed and she trained night and day. Maybe that's why she isn't at all dressed up on her wedding day. An opera star ought to be able to come up with a tiara or a feather boa or a gilded dress or something, but not Norma. It was music that mattered, not fashion.

By 1939, her work had paid off. She was known, she was getting work. But life intervened again. This time, it was war. Who could care about Lucia de Lammermoor when bombs were falling all about? Norma and George headed back to the foothills of Alberta.

And that was that for Norma's singing career. She ended up training young students at Calgary's Mount Royal College, and George ended up building—by himself—a house in the foothills. It was wonderful, they loved it, but eventually they had to move into Calgary and then they had to die, and there's that day-to-day stuff again.

It's amazing.

1937...Bride Servant No More...

It was theatre, pure and simple. No wonder it was hard to let go of the Braut Diener wedding tradition.

A Braut Diener was a bride servant. That is, he was someone that the bride or groom picked out to a) deliver wedding invitations in person, b) act as master-of-ceremonies at the reception and c) just generally keep the party alive. A good Braut Diener made all the difference, and the Werner brothers were often selected for the job because they were good at it.

However, by 1937 when Adolph Werner and Elsie Gruntman were being married, the world was changing. The pictures tell the story. Robert Werner looks like the Braut Dieners of old—he's dressed in his best suit, the red and white banners are arranged diagonally across his chest, the horse is shined up and decorated with flowers and ribbon, even the whip is properly finished with red and white ribbons. Red for love, white for purity. Mind you, Robert doesn't look thrilled to death with the assignment ahead of him but he certainly looks the part.

Edward Werner, on the other hand, is setting off on his rounds with a car. He's wearing the right stuff but the car was never part of the script. Even if it's got a token ribbon or two, it's just not traditional. How do you gallop to the front door of each invitee and stop just in time to avoid hitting the door? How do you take a car

right into the house, for that matter, and recite the traditional verses? That was always fun on horseback and scared the wits out of the people inside. How do you do that with a car?

And how do you drink all the Schnapps that went with each stage of the party and still drive that car? The parties were often two or three day events with food and drink, song and dance, at every stage. How do you do that if you have a 9-5 job, for that matter?

There were other reasons for the demise of the Braut Diener tradition, of course. Second and third generation Canadians didn't want to keep up the old country ways; they wanted to be like everyone else. There were phones and printed invitations; who needed personal invitations? And who, for that matter, could recite all the German or Russian verses of the official Braut Diener invitations?

So, with one thing and another, Adolph and Elsie had about the last wedding in the area south of Edmonton that involved Braut Dieners. They were married April 1, 1937 and lived in the Edmonton area until 1942 when they pulled up stakes and moved to Vancouver. There, Adolph worked in construction and Elsie looked after their five children.

1938...All Because of Bacon and Eggs...

Memories are like images that fade at the edge with no beginning or end. That's a line from Mary Smith's memoirs, the Mary Smith in the picture, and it's exactly right as a description for 1938. By 1938, you see, things were picking up in western Canada, but you couldn't see the beginning or the end. Farmers were getting better prices for their produce, there were more jobs available, there were fewer men riding the rails of desperation, and in Alberta there was an oil industry just waiting to boom.

Unfortunately, there was also a war just waiting to boom, and that too—in an awful way—contributed to the beginning of the end of the Dirty Thirties, the Great Depression.

In 1938, in other words, things were better but they weren't always good.

Mary Smith was a good example of that. She grew up south of Calgary around Okotoks and got herself a job soon after she'd finished school. That was the good part. The bad part was that she worked as a telephone operator from 9 p.m. to 9 a.m. on weekdays and noon to 4 p.m. on Sundays. For that, she was paid $36.50 a month to begin with, $46.50 four years later. Not that she ever complained. She liked her job, felt fortunate to have it.

One of her frequent visitors was the local RCMP officer, Cpl. Jim Smith. He had to work at night too, so he needed company, but he spent a fair amount of his time singing the praises of his brother George. You'd like him, he'd tell Mary. He's a roughneck on an oil rig. I'll get you two together someday.

Oh, yes, he also visited Mary's mother to tell her to pull up the spiky green plants she had as background in her flower garden. The seeds were called "common hemp" and were readily available from seed catalogues but turned out they were marijuana. The world was just becoming aware of the narcotic properties of certain plants.

One day Cpl. Jim made good on his threat. He came in with two tickets for the St. Patrick's Day Dance in Turner Valley, one ticket for Mary, one for the elusive George. No way, Mary said. If he wants to take me to the dance, he has to ask me himself. Which is how George finally got up the nerve to ask Mary out and how Mary bought a dress that made her feel like a million bucks. **"I didn't often feel pretty,"** she said in an interview, **"but I did that night. The dress, my hair, everything cooperated."**

And Cpl. Jim was right. She and George got on like a house on fire and decided to marry December 8, 1938. The community rallied with four, count them, four bridal showers: a linen shower put on by the women of four rural telephone lines; a pantry shower of jams, pickles and baking supplies put on by friends; a general shower put on by neighbors, and a personal shower—underwear, silk stockings, perfume, that sort of thing—put on by fellow telephone operators. A bridal shower accomplished two things in those days—they were a welcome social occasion but they also helped set up new couples with household and personal goods that they would not have been able to afford otherwise.

Once married, the couple followed the oil boom from town to town—from Turner Valley to Little New York (later known as Longview) to Little Chicago (later known as Royalties) to Okotoks and finally to Peachland, BC, where they ended up with a dairy. It was a long way from the excitement of gushing oil wells but it was stable, in more ways than one! And once the two children were grown, Mary became the artist and writer that she'd always been but never had the time for. Sometimes, life works out.

There's a great story about the discovery of oil in the Turner Valley area. Seems that area rancher Bill Herron brought some investors to his place one day and took them out to a certain rock formation. Because he knew that gas escaped through the fissures of this formation, he lit a match and held it to a crack in the rock. The escaping gas caught fire, Herron whipped out a frying pan and made bacon and eggs for everyone. What a great promotion, and apparently it worked for gradually more and more money was invested in the exploration for oil and gas in the Turner Valley area. And that's why George met Mary, and that's where this story started.

1938...Polygamy and Population...

Marguritte Peterson must have wondered—for the briefest moment possible for she is such a loyal soul—if she really wanted to marry a Leavitt. There were more Leavitts in southern Alberta than any other family name. There was even a town called Leavitt full of Leavitts. They were everywhere.

Mind you, the Leavitts were a fine upstanding Mormon family so Marguritte, herself a fine upstanding Mormon, would not have wondered long. Devere Leavitt proposed to her in June 1938, they were married in November of that year.

Devere's grandfather, Thomas Rowell Leavitt, has to take most of the responsibility for the preponderance of Leavitts in southern Alberta. He was a polygamist in Utah back in the days when that practice was encouraged for Mormon men and more or less ignored by the US government. Thus, he had a total of 26 children: 12 with his wife Ann Eliza, nine with Antoinette and five with Harriet Martha. Four died as babies so that left 22. However, things started to heat up for Mormon men in

the US when the government changed its mind about plural marriages and passed legislation outlawing the practice. That's when a group of Mormon men headed by Charles Ora Card headed for Canada to check out land and climate. The land was good, so was the climate as far as rain and sunshine was concerned, but the Canadian government was not too keen on plural marriages either. You can come—and welcome—they said as long as you bring only one wife.

That's more or less what happened. In 1887, Leavitt brought his third wife Hattie with him to Canada and left Ann Eliza behind with 19 children, Antoinette having died by then. After a few years, Hattie went back to the States and Ann Eliza had a turn in Canada. Meanwhile, most of the children were growing up and 20 of the 22 ended up in Canada. That's how the Leavitts came to be so plentiful, which isn't even taking into account the Leavitt nieces and nephews who also found their way north.

Alfred Leavitt was the son of Thomas Rowell and Antoinette Leavitt. He followed his father to Canada in 1897 and with his brothers helped dig the irrigation canals that Card had promised the Canadian government in exchange for more land for more Mormon settlers. Once that was done, he took out a homestead and with his wife Mary raised nine sons and two daughters. One of those sons was Devere.

Marguritte Peterson's folks were Mormon as well and came to the Welling area near Cardston to be with others of their faith. John Christian and Genevra Peterson had 14 children, the last one born to Genevra when she was 47. Marguritte, born in 1916, was the second youngest.

Marriage in the Mormon church is a very important sacrament, not to be taken lightly, as they say in marriage ceremonies, since the marriage is for eternity. Not just for this life or until something better comes along, but forever. That's why Mormons refer to being "sealed" in matrimony. If they believe in life after death, and they do, then a marriage will continue after death too. Devere and Marguritte received their endowments and were married for all time and eternity by Pres. E.J. Wood in the Alberta Temple at Cardston on Nov. 9, 1938.

She wore a soft white voile dress with a gathered skirt, demure gathered neckline and long sleeves. By the time the wedding picture was taken a month later, the long sleeves were short so that, as Marguritte explained, **"I could get some more wear out of the dress."** It was 1938, after all. Money still did not grow on trees.

The newly wed Leavitts moved to the Leavitt Sr. farm and farmed there until they had two crop failures in a row. That was more than enough for Devere—he got a job in town and stuck with it until retirement. Ever and always, he and Marguritte worked within the organizations of the church. They had five children—two daughters who are married with jobs and families, three sons who have all done their duty as missionaries overseas for the church. As soon as the youngest was married, Marguritte and Devere took their turn as missionaries, spending a year and a half in Malaysia, India and Sri Lanka. They were both in their sixties but the church encourages retired couples who have the health and means to carry the Mormon message to the larger world. So they did.

The present generation hasn't kept up with their Leavitt forefathers and mothers as far as family size is concerned, but they're ahead of the national average nevertheless. The five of them have a total of 29 children.

Polygamy is no longer practiced by faithful Mormons but there's always great curiosity about how that must have worked. In a journal kept by Charles Ora Card in 1886, he tried to explain it. He felt no favoritism toward any one wife or family, he said. **"I praise the name of the Lord for a quorum of good faithful wives. I feel I could wade through much affliction for them."**

Mind you, he was divorced from his first wife. About that, he wrote, **"How sad to contemplate such a thing as the parting of man and wife, a circumstance I have always abhorred from my youth…"**

1938…Who Knew War Was Out There?

Was it an omen that one of the prized white sweet peas dropped out of the wedding bouquet as the bride stepped out of the wedding taxi? Could her husband-to-be, so gallantly helping her to the sidewalk, have picked it up and stuffed it back into the bouquet? Would that have made a difference?

Of course not, but it's typical of the questions asked about WWII then and now. What could have been done to avoid the human tragedy that followed? Why didn't the world see it coming? Was it the white sweet pea?

The last is the easiest to answer. No, WWII did not start because of a lost sweet pea but it changed forever the lives of these two, not to mention their daughter who became a Canadian citizen and continued to look for reasons. For understanding of what happened to their family.

Dory Alers and Frits Wijbrans were married May 11, 1938, in a civil service in the city hall of The Hague in Holland. That night, they left for the Dutch colony known as the Dutch East Indies, now a part of Indonesia, where Frits had a job as a chemical engineer on a sugar plantation. Lots of young professionals from the Netherlands had to seek jobs outside their small country. It was not at all unusual.

What was unexpected was the Japanese entry into the war, first with the bombing of Pearl Harbor in 1941 and then with the subsequent attack and occupation of many of the islands near Japan including the Dutch East Indies. By March, 1942, it was entirely under Japanese control, and "whites" were rounded up and interned in camps throughout the area. Dory and three-year-old Marijke ended up in Java in a camp for women and children. Frits was sent to various work camps near Singapore. For four years, they had no contact with one another, no idea whether the other lived or died.

The camp experiences were the stuff of movies—not enough food, no space, no privacy, no medicines, cruel treatment, hopelessness, although Marijke says now that the mothers in the camp held onto hope. They had to. They had the children. Books have been written about the internment experiences, so suffice it to say here that Dory and Marijke survived the experience and were reunited with Frits in Holland in March of 1946.

It was like a bad dream, Marijke remembers now, especially since Holland was so full of its own suffering in the years following the war that they couldn't make room for the suffering that happened outside their borders. The Wijbrans were expected to get on with their lives and be quiet about it, so they did. Dory had another baby girl in 1947, then suffered with various ailments until her early death in 1960. And as the world turns, Marijke in 1963 married a geologist who couldn't find work in Holland so sent applications to Australia, South America, the USA and Canada.

Canada, it was, and they've been here ever since. There are many paths to Canada.

1939…Chinese Family, Canadian Wedding

1939 was a very big year. Esther Chan and Roy Mark were married in February, the King and Queen came to Canada in May, Hazel Mahon and James Robinson were married on September 2, Great Britain declared war against Germany the next day and Canada followed suit a week later.

If you think that's a mixed bag, it is. If you question putting the personal events in the same list as the political as if they were equal, they were. Depends on your point of view. Nobody knew in September of 1939 how long and bloody that war would be. Home by Christmas, the politicians and military leaders reassured their armies and one another. Thus, war news was more exciting than frightening, a change from the depressing stuff about grain prices and unemployment. Ditto with news about weddings. A change from doom and gloom.

By far, the most exciting news in Canada in 1939 was the Royal Visit. Capital letters— The Royal Visit. Canadians flocked to get a glimpse of the very first reigning monarch to ever set foot in the country. We'd had the Prince of Wales and the Princess Louise Caroline Alberta and such but never the heads that wore the crowns. A Winnipeg man who had fled Russian pogroms in 1906 couldn't believe the freedom that the royal

visit represented. That a former Russian peasant with no rights would be allowed to stand a few feet from an unguarded King and Queen blew his mind. **"Such a thing I have to see once more,"** he said and rushed to another vantage point.

The visit reinforced Canada's ties with Britain, our status as a loyal colony. Things British counted—British roots, traditions, laws, royal families. Canadian equalled British, more or less.

Which is why Esther Chan and Roy Mark chose to have a "Canadian" wedding rather than a more traditional Chinese one. It was a time when Canadians were seeking ways to be the same. Being "different" was out—been there, done that. Being "the same" was in.

The marriage was more or less arranged—that much adhered to old Chinese customs. Roy lived in Winnipeg. There weren't many single Chinese women there so a friend in Victoria recommended Esther Chan, also of Victoria. Professional matchmakers used to be called in to arrange marriages but in this case, it was a friend who acted as matchmaker and persuaded Roy to come to Victoria. Esther said of that first meeting, **"When I saw him, he seemed alright."** She also said she wasn't upset that she barely knew the man who was to become her husband. **"We listened to our parents in those days. They said it was a good choice."**

So the deal was made. There was the usual exchange between families of courtesies and gifts, but when it came time to buy the wedding dress, Esther decided against the traditional red skirt and black top. She opted instead for a long white chiffon dress with short puff sleeves, a sweetheart neckline, seed pearl tiara, pearl necklace and long white gloves. To add to the whole 1939 wedding look, it was an Anglican minister who conducted the ceremony on Feb. 11, 1939.

Back in Winnipeg, Esther quickly adopted another Canadian tradition—woolen underwear. "**It always itched though**," she remembers. She wasn't outside that much, however, since husband Roy had a restaurant on Main and Logan called The Exchange Café. Both worked there. Roy died in 1961 and Esther continued to work there. The four children carried on the Canadianization process, one son marrying a woman of Icelandic origin, another a woman of Japanese origin. And speaking of Canadianization, four of Esther's brothers served in the war that started in 1939. All four came back safely.

It's no wonder that Esther and Roy wanted to fit in, to have a wedding like other Canadian couples. From the very first moment that Chinese men appeared on Canadian soil during the Cariboo gold rush, they were, as a race, separated and segregated in such blatant ways, it's hard to understand now. Certainly, Great Britain, she whom we all wanted to emulate, has to take a lot of the blame. British politicians, and therefore Canadian politicians, referred to Chinese people as "the yellow hordes" or "the heathen peril." Editorial writers opined that the Chinese could never integrate into Canadian society; they were too different, somehow suspect. Even by the 1940s when the Marks ran their Winnipeg restaurant, Chinese people were still referred to as "Chinks" and the restaurant was simply "The Chink's."

The Chinese were the only ethnic group assessed a head tax. That is, most Chinese immigrants had to pay between $10 in 1886 to $500 in 1903 in order to enter Canada. After 1923, the Exclusion Act barred Chinese people from entering the country, period. No wonder there were so many unattached Chinese men in Canada. If they had wives and families in China, they couldn't afford to bring them here. If they weren't married, they couldn't afford to bring a potential wife over or weren't allowed to. And mainstream Canadians saw nothing wrong in these attitudes. A Royal Commission set up to examine the Chinese 'problem' concluded in 1902 that Asians were "unfit for full citizenship...obnoxious to a free community and dangerous to the State."

In fact, it was the other way around. Canada was dangerous to the Chinese, especially the men who were hired to push the railway lines through the dangerous mountain passes of Alberta and BC. So many died in accidents and explosions that it is said, "**for every foot of railroad through the Fraser Canyon a Chinese worker died**." Still, for all the awful parts of the Canadian experience, Chinese still wanted to come to the Gold Mountain, their name for Canada. Esther's mother was born in Hong Kong, eg, and her father in China. They came to Canada with their parents and were among the Chinese who persevered and prospered eventually.

1939...Standing on Guard in Regina

King George VI and Queen Elizabeth came to Canada in May, 1939, partly because they were conscientious royals who didn't mind waving at strangers in formerly British colonies, partly because they were expected to cement British/Canadian ties in case of war. If war was declared, Britain needed all the friends it could get. The King and Queen made friends. It was part of their job and they were good at it.

In Regina, they visited the RCMP chapel and were photographed leaving through the front door under the arched portico, the Queen carrying a splashy bouquet of flowers and looking very bride like. That picture and their visit added even more luster to the old chapel and it became a popular place for RCMP weddings. Take Lance Corporal James Robinson and Hazel Mahon. They were married there on a beautiful late summer day, September 2, 1939.

The newspaper described the wedding as **"charming,"** the chapel as **"picturesque,"** and the bride as **"lovely."** She wore a Jean Patou designer dress of imported all wool Swiss lace over a taffeta slip, her hat was a pillbox with satin flowers on the crown, a net bow on the back, and her bouquet was shaggy asters. The groom wore full dress uniform, of course, as did the guard of honor. How could you get more colorful, more Canadian, than a wedding in September with designer dresses and RCMP red coats in attendance? As the newly weds left the church, and this is the best part of a military wedding, the men of the honor guard snapped to attention and crossed their lances over the path of the bride and groom. Perfect.

Britain declared war on Germany the next day. Nothing was ever perfect again. The newly weds had to cancel their honeymoon.

Robinson, known always as Robbie, served with the RCMP in Alberta, the NWT and in the crime detection lab in Regina. He retired in 1967, died in 1986. There are two sons, one daughter.

THE 1940s

War again, Elsie the Ironworker, a famous trial, and playing chicken on the rocks

Ekvana and Steve Angulalik, 1941, Cambridge Bay, NWT

1940...Before The Flood and After The War...

"My wedding dress?" Margaret Brown said, **"oh, it went in the flood."**

Everywhere in Manitoba, you hear about the flood. Just "the flood." No adjectives, no introduction to the subject. People in the north have 14 words, it is said, for snow, their most notable weather feature. People in Manitoba have only two to describe theirs—the flood—and that's all they need. There is so much history, so much understanding invested in those two brief words that additional words would only get in the road.

"The flood" has occurred in the Red River valley of Manitoba since time began, but since time has been measured it has happened in 1776, 1826, 1852, 1861, 1916, 1950, 1979 and 1997, and every time the reasons are the same. Lots of snow the winter before, a sudden spring thaw, unusually heavy spring rains, and overnight the shallow basin of the Red River overflows its banks. It doesn't help that the river is flowing north into land and lakes that aren't thawed yet and can't receive the extra waters. It's a flood asking to happen every spring, and every spring Manitobans begin the flood watch.

The flood that took Margaret Brown's wedding dress was the 1950 one that drove some 100,000 people from their homes and inundated 15,000 farms and businesses. It's the big one in current memory, the one that's marked with a line on kitchen walls all over the Red River valley with the words: **"This is where the flood reached."**

They nearly had another of "the floods" in 1997, but as bad as it was for areas south of Winnipeg, it never reached the proportions of the 1950 one. But the meaning of the word came back with a vengeance.

However, it's hard to be sad when looking at the wedding picture that fortunately did survive the flood. It's a group picture taken at the community of Bird's Hill, just east of Winnipeg. The sun is shining, the bride is beautiful, the groom handsome, the wedding guests in their places with pleasant faces, the trees and grass and flowers suggesting that all is well with the world and who's to say naught. It's June 1, 1940. Margaret Lough is marrying Edward Ross Ransby.

She's wearing a gown of white suede lace over satin, the frock styled with a sweetheart neckline and a skirt that flares into a full circular train. Her flowers are Adeline roses and lilies of the valley. Six of her friends carry tall white staffs tied with blossoms and thus arrayed, form an aisle as the bride makes her way up the aisle on the arm of her father.

Not that Margaret remembers any of these details in 1998. Hers has been a long life and she can barely believe that, according to the newspaper write-up, she had six bridesmaids all done up like Little Bo-Peep. Nor has she looked at the precious scrapbook saved from the flood that contains the clippings of all the bridal showers held for her. There are 14. Daughter Lynn Ransby is amazed. **"How come you had so many showers, mom?"** she asks.

Her mom shrugs. **"That's just how it was then,"** she says. And the Winnipeg papers covered every one of them—the handkerchief shower hosted at Mrs. Morrison's residence on Garfield Street, the crystal shower hosted by Mrs. Harry Smith of Waterloo Street, a luncheon at the University Women's Club, the kitchen shower hosted by Miss Sylvia Washington, a bridge party at Miss Ringer's home, tea parties galore. There's even an account of the stag dinner for Mr. Ransby at which **"a presentation was made to the guest of honor on behalf of the 25 guests present."**

Newspapers in the 1940's took the local and social news of the day seriously, gave it equal play with national and international news. For instance, when Mrs. Douglas Andrew held a tea for Margaret, the Winnipeg newspaper reported that: **"Iris were combined with daffodils as a center for the table. They were flanked by blue tapers."** Now there's a piece of news that brightens up your day. Ditto with the description of Miss Washington's shower: **"A silver bowl holding yellow and Talisman roses made a pretty floral center for the tea table which was lighted by ivory tapers in silver candlesticks with tulle bows."**

Weddings got the same detailed attention on the social pages. Here's the description of Margaret's going away ensemble: **"For travelling, the bride wore a printed sheer crepe frock in tones of chartreuse, navy blue and ivory, with square neckline, puff sleeves, and a wide soft girdle of the navy providing an interesting color contrast. Her hat was a white straw off-the-face model with touches of blue, and she wore a coat of navy crepe with long full sleeves held by broad close fitting cuffs, and with circular neckline, full bodice and skirt joined by a broad close fitting girdle. She wore gardenias."** You'd have to be marrying royalty to get that much written about a wedding dress in a newspaper nowadays.

However, all the flowery words in the world couldn't guarantee a happy ending. Ross worked for the Rupertsland Trading Company, a subsidiary of the Hudson's Bay Company, before and after serving with the RCAF in WW11. Part of his war years were spent in Burma where he helped liberate Prisoners of War and Margaret still wonders if that experience might have contributed to his illness. He was never very well after the war and died in 1957 of cancer.

What do you do when you've got three children and no husband? Well, for one thing, you go to the baseball games and the soccer games that the kids play in, you go out hunting for them when they don't come home from the park, and eventually you meet a widower who's doing the same thing. In 1961, Margaret married Ed Brown and his two children Ned and Nancy. Thus did their household become Yours, Mine and even though they didn't have any children of their own, the blended family became Ours. They were ahead of their time. No one was using the term Blended Family then, but that's what it was.

And so life went on. Ted, Ken and Lynn Ransby moved on to their own homes and lives, so did Ned and Nancy Brown. Then Eddie died in 1984. Margaret was alone again, left with scrapbooks about a life and time she could barely remember and certainly couldn't believe. Shaking her head over the fairy tale picture taken in 1940, she said, **"Was that really me? It was all so long ago."**

1941...Falling In Love With Love...

Picture this: a beautiful young woman in a white net evening gown, a lonely young airman in uniform, the dining room at the Royal York in Toronto, a big band orchestra that played dreamy falling-in-love songs, two people whose steps match one another perfectly on the dance floor. **"We floated across the dance floor,"** Ruth Moore said later about her first date with Guy Moore.

Sounds like a movie right out of the 1940's, Fred Astaire and Ginger Rogers maybe, falling in love with love on the dance floor. But this is not a movie. This is the real life story of Ruth Hall and Guy Moore, a story that begins with romance and ends with romance. Not all wedding stories do.

It was a blind date and Ruth was beginning to regret it. Her date was a bit grumpy in the car enroute to the hotel, but he cheered up when he saw Ruth in her evening gown. Then they danced and that clinched it. The attraction was so great that Ruth allowed a kiss on the way home. On the first date. It just wasn't done. She worried later that he would think she was a **"loose sort of girl**."

That was Christmas Eve 1940. By New Year's Eve, they were an item although Guy was taken aback when he saw his beloved perform in a New Years Eve kick line. Wearing one of her skating costumes, Ruth showed a fair amount of leg. Nothing new for her since she was a championship figure skater but Guy was from a small town in Alberta that had neither skating shows nor kick lines.

What Beaverlodge did have was country dances that turned out good dancers. Once Ruth was back into her evening gown, they danced the night and any doubts away.

He was stationed in Brantford for part of his training.

Could Ruth come there to see him get his wings? No, she could not. Mr. and Mrs. Hall did not approve of unattended young girls travelling on their own. Could she come to Trenton for a special mess dinner? Only if a properly married chaperone could be found. Ruth was an only child, 19 years old. Her folks were not about to let her follow her fellow unless the proprieties were observed. And the proprieties were such that a single woman could not ever stay with a single fellow, could not even stay in a hotel by herself *near* a single fellow. Period. Marriage was the only option if togetherness was the object.

So Guy asked Ruth's folks for her hand in marriage. They could see the stars in her eyes, they knew she was head over heels, what could they say? So they started marriage arrangements. The only trouble was that Guy had no idea when he would get a five day pass in the coming months. They had to arrange as much as could be arranged and then wait. For Ruth and Guy, it was misery because they wanted to be together. For Ruth's folks, it was misery because they couldn't send out proper invitations, they couldn't book a church or a hall or a minister, they couldn't entertain and be entertained in traditional ways.

On March 26, Ruth got the telegram. **"Have five days leave. Call Ed, get marriage license. No more leave till Calgary."** By March 28, all was accomplished: Ed got the license (Ed was Guy's cousin), the Commanding Officer came through at the last minute with permission to marry, Ruth's mother and aunt stayed up half the night arranging goodies for a reception, Ruth's dad bullied a florist into last minute flowers, and Guy got his friends and comrades in arms to put on their uniforms and fill St. George's United Church in Toronto with pomp and ceremony. It was done. It was fine. Who needs months and months to arrange a wedding?

And while the older folks put up their feet and called it a day, Ruth cut the train off her wedding dress, hemmed it up and went—you guessed it—dancing at the Royal York Hotel. That's where they met, that's where they spent their two-day honeymoon.

Two weeks later, they were posted to Calgary and Guy began training pilots at the Commonwealth Airforce Training School. A precarious existence, Ruth remembered of that time—Guy never sure of the weather, the planes, the young men under his wings; Ruth never sure of her role as homemaker. Her thing was skating. Before she married, she practiced five hours a day to be ready to compete in the 1940 Winter Olympics. That plus school plus a lively social life plus a mother who indulged her left the newly married Ruth wondering just how the heck you make a pie or boil an egg for that matter. It was lucky in a way that the 1940 Olympics were cancelled. Ruth had to put that part of her life on the back burner and learn how to use the front burners.

When the war ended in 1945, they headed back to Ontario, Guy as Squadron Leader Moore, winner of the Air Force Cross, and Ruth Moore as pretty darn good cook and mother of three. Guy worked from then on in the civil service of both Ontario and Manitoba governments, serving as deputy minister of various portfolios in both provinces.

When he died in 1994, Ruth took his ashes and scattered them on Forget-Me-Not Mountain along the Monkman Pass west of Beaverlodge. It was an area that Guy had explored as a young man, an area that he loved. His wife, a romantic to the end, knew he'd want to be there.

Their story ends as it began—with a lovely romantic gesture, with a slow waltz, with a sunset over a mountain peak, a final dip.

1941...Stupid Question...

Then there's the story about Father John Paul Tanguay and the long distance wedding. Both the bride and groom had to walk a long way to get to the nearest Catholic Church in a remote area north of Whitehorse, YT. The bride had the furthest to walk; she was some 75 miles away. However, they finally made it and stood before the priest.

Fr. Tanguay asked the groom if he'd take Sarah to be his lawful wedded wife? The groom said yes. Father Tanguay asked the same question of Sarah. She said nothing. He repeated the question. She said nothing. Language wasn't the problem; the priest had been in the north long enough to be able to conduct a wedding service in the native tongue. He asked a third time and Sarah still stood silent. Finally, the priest turned to the groom and said, What's the problem? The groom spoke to his intended and they had a quick conversation in their own tongue, quicker than Father Tanguay could pick up. Finally she spoke, **"Why do you think I walked all this way here if I wasn't going to marry him?"**

Stupid question, in other words.

1941...A Northern Wedding and A Famous Trial...

Steve and Ekvana (Mable) Angulalik were married at St. George's Anglican Church in Cambridge Bay on Victoria Island in the Northwest Territories on August 11, 1941. It's one of the white parts of Canada—look north, look way north. For the occasion, the bride wore white, the groom wore brown. Furs, that is. There were two reasons for the beautiful fur outfits: 1) it's the north—even in the summer, it isn't all that hot, and 2) Angulalik was a fur trader. He had access to the best furs in the whole Cambridge Bay, Perry River area. Why wouldn't he save some of the best skins for the wedding outfits?

Mable was Angulalik's third wife. She was a teenager when they married; he was almost 50, but the union was a strong one. She bore him 12 children, eight of whom survived infancy. His first marital arrangement had included two wives at the same time. He was a polygamist, in other words, but that sort of arrangement was fairly common in the north and generally ignored by Canadian law. It was only after Koloahok and Kuptana died in 1938 and 1939 respectively that he met Mable and set up a one-woman household.

Angulalik was a bit of a legend in the north. He was such a canny trader that one of the local missionaries said he would have been an industrial tycoon had he lived in the south. This in spite of the fact he couldn't speak English or read or write Inuktitut. How he ordered supplies from the Hudson's Bay Co. was always a mystery, but he improvised well, getting others to do the book work or simply copying the names of the supplies straight off the boxes they came in. Occasionally, this ordering method led to requests for "5 cases of This Side Up" or "One Box of Fragile." Didn't matter.

His suppliers knew what he meant and since he always paid his bills, they sent the goods.

His good fortune took a turn at a New Years party on January 1, 1957. He drank too much, an old enemy drank too much, and they fought in the course of which Angulalik "poked" Otoetok. It wasn't a bad wound but Otoetok died four days later. In the confession that Angulalik dictated to a friend, he said, **"He caught me and I poked him...when I got sober, I like to kill myself. I was think about my family. Got nobody to watch for them and nobody to keep them."**

The trial was not your typical down south spit and polish performance, which was just fine with Judge Jack Sissons. The first judge of the North West Territories, he made sure that justice prevailed but didn't worry too much about court decorum and procedures. Thus, there was constant conversation and movement in the courtroom as the attending Inuit discussed the finer points of the testimony and translated for one another. But the trial proceeded as most trials do. In the end, the jury found Angulalik not guilty, and he went back home to Perry River.

Ten years later, he and Mable moved to Cambridge Bay and schools for the children. There, Steve died in 1980, a respected elder among the Copper Eskimos, a fond parent and a good husband. It is said that Mable still smiles when she says his name.

1942...The Drill Team Guard of Honor...

Members of the Victoria Girls' Drill Team normally performed at parades and civic events, but on June 17, 1942, they expanded their repertoire to perform as guard of honor at the wedding of one of their ex-members, Elsie Edwards. Elsie was "ex" the minute she said "I do" to Bill Watson that balmy evening in June. Rules were rules. Members of the Drill Team had to be single. Also had to be slim, good looking, willing to practice drills and precision routines for long hours every week and had to be willing to finance costumes, trips, whatever, themselves. They were a little army all to themselves.

A very popular army, mind you, one that was asked to attend most important functions in the vicinity of Victoria. Even went to the San Francisco World's Fair in 1939. By the time, the group disbanded in the 1970's, some 1,000 young women had been through the ranks.

But their most important record may have been set when members and ex-members became the first women's unit to go into war work, which is why Bill Watson bought his new wife steel-toed boots as a parting gift. He was going overseas with the Seaforth Highlanders; she was going to work at the Victoria Machine Depot, the VMD. In the US, Rosie the Riveter became famous, but Canada during the war had lots of women in non-traditional jobs as well. Elsie, for one. She became Elsie the Iron Worker, dealing with huge plates of steel laid out flat into which she had to cut a pattern. Like cutting a dress out of fabric except that she was working with steel and blowtorches and heavy machinery. Loved it, felt she was doing real work, helping the war effort.

Of course, Elsie and her female companions at the VMD left the shop floor as soon as the men came home from the war. They put on their aprons and returned to traditional roles. Bill

bought the English Sweet Shop in downtown Victoria, Elsie went to work with him and there they stayed for 33 years. Bill died in 1990, and Elsie remarried a few years later.

1942...His Head in the Chandelier...

Obviously it was another happy occasion, this wedding in Saskatoon on July 11, 1942, of Winnifred Blakeley and Dave Williamson. After all, the sun is shining, the guests are smiling and the horses are in fine form.

Not that Dave and Winnie had planned on horses for their wedding. They had planned for a quiet wedding at Winnie's house, dignified but simple. The wedding ceremony would be followed by a wedding luncheon, delicious but simple, for a few friends and family at home. Then they'd get into their car—hidden away from pranksters all the while—and they would drive to Emma Lake, safely and simply, for a brief honeymoon.

None of the above.

Oh, the ceremony itself was fairly simple and somewhat dignified. The only trouble was that Dave was too tall for the chandelier and that's where he was supposed to stand, right under the chandelier. Consequently, he said his vows with his head in the crystals, as it were, trying not to move and cause undue tinkling. He looked good in his new suit, mind you, even though there was no matching vest because material was scarce in the war years. Nor were there cuffs on the pants. The men's wear store told Dave he couldn't have cuffs because of the war. There was enough length on the pants to make cuffs but they still insisted there couldn't be cuffs because of the war. It didn't make sense then and doesn't now, but there was nothing Dave could do but take them to Winnie who made cuffs.

Winnie got her dress, a white Bembrook sheer, off the rack at Eaton's. No big fuss about the dress, she said. She just got one that fit.

Eaton's also supplied the fancy sandwiches for the wedding reception, and cousins baked angel food cakes. Tea and coffee. Nothing complicated.

But then Dave left to get the car from its hiding place and suddenly life got complicated. Waiting outside the house was Pat Lundy on the seat of a splendid carriage drawn by two splendid horses. Your carriage awaits, Pat Lundy said, and off they went for a tour of Saskatoon, stopping at various pre-arranged places to have pictures taken. Everybody, it seemed, knew about the prank and was out to take pictures and wave. **"We might have been the King and Queen,"** Winnie says now. Along the way, they learned that their friends had tried to arrange a donkey and cart but couldn't so settled for the carriage from the Exhibition Board and Pat Lundy's horses. Thank goodness for small mercies.

It was tons of fun but Dave did begin to wonder what awaited him in the supposedly

safe place he'd left the car. Had that security been breached also?

Of course. Great attention was paid to wedding day pranks in those days. Nothing seemed amiss when Winnie and Dave got to the car, but when they finally got to Prince Albert that night, they discovered that their suitcases were full of confetti, their clothing hopelessly jumbled. They trailed confetti wherever they went, like Hansel and Gretel leaving breadcrumbs in the forest, until finally they stopped near some bush by the side of the road and shook out every piece of clothing they owned.

The rest of their lives was fairly tame compared to the wedding day. Dave worked in a lumber yard, Winnie worked as a bookkeeper. There were no children.

1944...War Brides To Canada...

So many stories of weddings in the years 1939-1945 start with the words, **"It was wartime."** It seems as if those three words explained everything, and they did. With daily bulletins about battles won and lost, with casualty lists in every newspaper, with fear and pride and anger and despair all competing to own the hearts and heads of Canadians, there was no ordinary life anymore. Everything was heightened by the passions of war.

So speaking of passions, why not get married? Thousands did—Canadian servicemen married women in Great Britain and Europe, Canadian women married servicemen from other parts of the world, men in other parts of the world married women in other parts of the world. It was an occupational hazard, this marriage business, and those in the know have tried to explain it in psychological terms. It was a way to ensure some normality, it was hope in a hopeless world, it was honest-to-goodness love, etc. etc., but also it was a way to have sex without breaking the taboos of the day. It was easy to fall in love—a cheek to cheek dance, a kiss or two on a quiet lane—but it wasn't easy to fall into bed. It wasn't done in those days. Well, it was done but there was great shame if the inevitable happened, if a baby came sooner than the requisite nine months, so most couples went the marriage route and then had a baby nine months later.

Which is how come 48,000 war brides and their children came to Canada at the end of the war. Ursula Surtees was one of them. She and 16 month old Patricia boarded a train dubbed "The Bride's Special" which took them from London, England, to Southampton where the Queen Mary waited to take them and other war brides to Canada. Of Canada, she knew nothing except that it was a huge patch of pink on a map of the world.

"It is hopeless," she wrote later, **"to describe the peculiar feelings that inhabit the mind and heart at a crossroad such as this. Part of you yearns to stay with the old and loved ways, the dear familiar things, the families who love you and whom you may very possibly never see again. The other part of your mind is projected into the future. What is it like? Will his family like me? What kind of home will we make? Is it really as cold as they say in winter?"**

When the huge ocean liner finally docked in Halifax, a band welcomed them to Canada with *Here Comes the Bride*. It was a kind gesture, Ursula wrote, but a little off the mark since most of the women had children with them. Never mind, they were at least on land, but that was the first thing Ursula learned about Canada. It's a lot of land. She was on the bride train five days to get to Sicamous, BC. She had been on the Queen Mary only four days.

In Calgary, she watched as one of their number got off the train to be greeted by her husband. Instead of a handsome man in uniform, she saw an ordinary working man in cowboy clothes, and she refused to believe the change. This undistinguished person couldn't be her husband. The last Ursula saw of the drama, the Red Cross had been called in to mediate.

There was no such problem for Ursula. Her husband was waiting at the station in Sicamous, and Ursula noticed neither the wonderful scenery nor the terrible mosquitoes that she'd been told about. She was home.

1944...War Brides From Canada...

Dawn Sharp grew up in Nelson, BC, and was teaching school there when she met George Penniket, an airman from New Zealand who was training in Canada. A Kiwi, they called him. Two weeks after they met, Dawn and the Kiwi were in love and determined to marry.

"You don't even know him, let alone anything about his family," Dawn's mother said when she heard the sudden plans. **"I was engaged to your father for five years before we married."**

Dawn's answer was typical of those war years. **"Oh mum, things were different way back in 1912 when you and dad decided to marry. Things are different now. The whole world is different."**

She was right. The war made all the difference. Engagements that might have lasted months and years now lasted weeks and days. Weddings that used to take months to arrange were arranged overnight. As Dawn explained in her memoirs, the motto for both men and women in those crazy war years seemed to be, **"Live today for we know not what the morrow will bring."**

She and George were a great example of that. He was in Canada as a flying instructor with the British Commonwealth Air Training Plan whereby would-be airmen from all over the British Commonwealth came to western Canada to learn how to fly—the west because there were lots of wide open spaces for flying, flying because flying was the glamour boy of war. Thus did places like Fort Macleod and Claresholm in AB have more young men than usual which is why Nelson, BC, invited a batch of them for a weekend's R&R in their town. They rolled out the carpet, got dates for all of them...and you can see what's coming. Dawn Sharp was home in bed when a girlfriend called her and said, **"Come on over to Gordon's. There's a bunch of airmen here and it's going to be fun."**

There wasn't time to paint her legs brown with the goop called Liquid Stocking, nor was there time to put a dark line up the back of her legs to simulate nylons. She just threw on a dress, her spectator pumps, some lipstick and went to the party. And there was George. One more 48 hour pass a few weeks later and a week long pass after that, and they were engaged. No wonder Dawn's father wrote her a letter at summer school asking the following:

1. There has been no mention of a ring or don't they do it that way any more?
2. Why do you have to get married in war time?
3. Why did you have to fall in love with a flyer? (Her dad hated flying and planes.)
4. Are you strong enough to cope with the fact he might not come back or be maimed for life?
5. Are you old enough for the responsibilities of marriage?
6. Will you finish your summer school courses and keep your head out of the clouds?

Apparently, Dawn was able to answer his questions satisfactorily for she and George were married one week after the conclusion of her summer school courses on August 23, 1944. It was a typical wartime wedding, she wrote later. Groom and best man were in their summer issue uniforms. The bride wore her $11.98 Bembrook sheer wedding dress with a veil and headpiece that cost more than the dress and **"looked dumber"**— Dawn's words. It was called a Mary Queen of Scots headpiece, sort of a crown affair, but Dawn's mother took it apart, reattached the veil and her almost hysterical daughter decided she would wear it after all. The bride's bouquet was three dozen pink roses, a gift of the groom. And the wedding cake was a sight to behold but tasted like sawdust because sugar was rationed in those days.

Who noticed? It was a wedding, after all. And they left the next morning for Fort Macleod. Time to get back to the war business. Packed among her trousseau was a book called Love, Marriage and Sex, a very daring book in those days when men were expected to administer sex and women were expected to accept sex. In fact, the word 'sex' was seldom used except as a way of differentiating between the female sex and the male sex. If couples figured out how to enjoy 'sex,' they were expected to be quiet about it. If they didn't, they were also expected to be quiet about it.

Mind you, that's one of the things that the war helped to change. Turned out that some countries were far more open about sex than prudish young Canada. Turned out also that some countries enjoyed wine and liquor without its people turning into degenerate criminals. The men who survived the war brought home some expanded ideas of how to live.

Two months after their marriage, George was posted to England to begin training for low level day raids in Harvard and Hurricane airplanes, but he never saw action before the war was over, May 8, 1945.

The rest of the story should be simple. Soldier reunites with wife and new baby girl, they live happily ever after. Except.

George had to go to New Zealand—not via Canada, by the way—to wait for Dawn there. She meantime had to wait in Canada for a boat that would take her and 35 other Kiwi wives and families to join their husbands. While waiting, the Canadian grandparents get awfully fond of Penny, the new baby. In fact, grandpa Sharp got out an atlas and measured the distance from Nelson, BC, to New Zealand. **"If you went any further away, you'd be coming closer to home,"** he announced after he'd finished with the ruler. Good thing that the Love, Marriage and Sex book had emphasized that a husband and wife belong together, come what may. Dawn hung on and finally got on the boat—a tub, she called it—that would take them to New Zealand. Five weeks later, they were there.

Thus did Dawn reverse the 1945/1946 flow of war brides and babies. Not for long though. They were back in Canada for good by 1947.

1944...But Where Is the Bathroom?

War was awful, but what was Canada? That's what a lot of the British and European war brides asked themselves when they got on the ships that brought them here.

It was the distances that overwhelmed them first. Then the differences, especially the differences in expectations. Somehow a Canadian farm sounded grander when it was described in England on a moonlight night on a country lane. When it turned out to be a subsistence farm with barely a granary to live in, there was some surprise, to put it mildly. Add to that the differences in the language, the cookstoves that had to be constantly fed with wood, the plumbing that wasn't there, the in-laws that weren't always thrilled to have a daughter-in-law land upon them, the jokes that were made at their expense, and it's easy to see why some 10% of the war brides went back home, wherever home was.

The ones who stayed coped, just like new Canadians had been doing for decades. Kay Garside came to live on a farm in Saskatchewan. She explained how she was able to make that huge adjustment in Ben Wicks' book, *Promise You'll Take Care of My Daughter*: **"We were young; the idea of going to another country was exciting. At the time of my marriage, there seemed no end to the war and Canada was a far-off place. Most of us lived for the day and didn't look very far ahead into the future. There might not have been a future, for all we knew."**

That too was a major reason for all the wartime weddings. The future was now.

1944...Newly Weds on the Rocks...

There's more than one way to fight a war. Try being a lighthouse keeper. Try being his wife, for that matter. Try living on a pile of rocks in Brown Passage west of Prince Rupert, BC, known officially as Triple Island but unofficially as Alcatraz. And know that if you don't live there in the teeth of every storm that comes along, in almost complete isolation, a whole lot of lives will be lost.

Gordon Odlum was assigned to Triple Island in November 1942, and he did fine. He liked the isolation, except that he did yearn for a certain young woman who worked in a Vancouver bakery. He knew her name but not her home address. Did he dare write her c/o the bakery, or would that seem too forward? Could he wait until his next leave and go speak to her in person, but that could be a year away? Too long. What to do?

Finally one day while making a batch of bread in the concrete kitchen of his concrete bunker, he found himself forming a teeny tiny loaf of bread. Why not bake it and send it to Jean—in a matchbox maybe? Nobody could criticize the gift of a tiny loaf of bread, and if she didn't like it, she could pitch it.

She didn't. She sent him a thank you note instead and included a return address. Courtship by correspondence began, Gordon taking pains to explain just why a man would live as he did. **"I like it here on my inhospitable rock pile, especially on these wild winter nights when the tower shakes and roars with the force of the gale and to go outdoors is to risk being blown overboard, and when the huge storm swells sweep in from the open sea and send spray shooting up 100 feet into the beams of the light as it sends its piercing beams through the night."**

Doesn't sound like heaven on earth but Jean was fascinated and then convinced. They were married September 20, 1944, in Vancouver. She was 18. When they returned to Triple Island, they had their picture taken beside the one measly miserable spruce

Gordon and Jean Odlum, 1944, Triple Island, BC

tree that grew on the rock. It could have been an omen of tough times ahead, but the pair of them made that old rock pile sing. They played chicken with the wind and waves on the top floor of the lighthouse, they played chess until they could do it in their sleep, Jean played her reed organ and sang, Gordon banded birds during their migration periods, Jean helped him and cleaned up the kitchen after 200 or so birds spent the evening with them, Jean learned Morse Code. They were an irrepressible pair, and it was only when Coral was born that they decided to transfer to a more accessible lighthouse on Atkinson Point.

Speaking of Coral, she might have been called Joseph P. Schwelenbank if Gordon had stuck with his original plan to name the baby for the first boat that passed. Such was the fun that the pair of them created in the lives around them. Sort of like the yeast in certain bakery products, or is that taking a metaphor too far? The Odlums wouldn't have minded.

1945...Gone But Not Forgotten...

1945 was a wonderful year. The war in Europe was declared over and done with on May 8, 1945. The war with Japan ditto on August 15, 1945. People celebrated; they danced and kissed and cried. **"The war is over,"** they said again and again as if the words might make it so. But the war didn't end just like that.

1945 was an awful year. The killing was done but the dying went on. People in concentration camps or prisoner of war camps left their camps and captors behind, but never left the experience behind. How could they? The war in Japan ended with the help of the first atomic bomb. The first atomic bomb led to a second and then to a hydrogen bomb and then to such sophisticated war machines that the very planet is threatened. How come all those words said in 1945, over and over again, that the war is over, didn't make it so?

Just over 1,000,000 Canadian men and women performed full-time duty in the three military services in WWII. Of that number, 42,000 died in the service. That's 42,000 families and communities changed forever.

Still, the war *was* over. Once the ships and planes and tanks went back to wherever ships and planes and tanks go after a war, once the men and women came home, once the economy turned out washing machines and nylons instead of guns and khaki uniforms, once there was a semblance of domestic order, the world changed. Couldn't help it. Everything was different, weddings included. So that's why the book ends at this point. It was a new world making new history from then on.

Mind you, the new world didn't happen overnight. When Evelyn Grace Harris married William Arnold Edwards on September 12, 1945, in Saskatoon, SK, her own mother said to the groom, **"Now, don't let her boss you."** That's very pre-war advice. For their honeymoon, the newly weds boarded a train for Banff but were delayed all along the way by troop trains—trains full of men coming back from Europe or Asia. Troop trains had priority over regular domestic runs. Evelyn, by the way, served on hospital boards and committees, various community boards, then on city council, then as Liberal MLA for Saskatoon. The only defeat she suffered in her political career was when she ran for mayor. The people of Saskatoon just weren't ready for a woman to be mayor. Too many changes at once.

Annie and Walter Hess met overseas so their 1946 wedding was a direct result of the war. Ontario born, Annie was a member of CWAC, Canadian Women's Army Corps, working in a military laundry in Borden, England. Walter, from Alberta, was also working at Borden, mostly in maintenance. They met and courted there, then corresponded after the war and married June 8, 1946 in Westlock, AB. Theirs was the usual story of life on a farm—lots of work, tough years, etc.—but they've come out on top. Now, their RV says, **"Too old to work/ Too young to die/ So here we go/ Just ma and I."**

The Jensen wedding in 1947 was also war related. 19 year old Earl Jensen from BC met 15 year old Betty at a dance in Tunbridge Wells, England, in 1945. **"I just kind of liked the look of her,"** Earl explained, **"and I guess she liked the uniform."** Whatever the reason, Betty joined him in BC in 1947 and was married in a borrowed dress, veil, shoes and country. When she wasn't smiling, she was crying. What a culture shock. But the wedding took. They were one of the couples that the Queen invited to a garden party in the summer of 1997 to celebrate with her and Prince Phillip their 50th anniversary. Betty had a new hat, nothing borrowed this time around.

And when Gwen Hooks got married in 1947, she and her new husband had their wedding pictures taken in a photographer's studio. Her parents and other blacks from the Southern US who had immigrated to western Canada in 1910 and 1911 never had enough money for a wedding picture, or they were too far from photographers' studios to get pictures taken. For Gwen and Mark, it was different. He had served in the Canadian army for five years. He had a job after the war ended. Things were looking up economically and socially.

Talk of "the war" gradually gave way to talk of peace and the United Nations…which is why Helen Matheson and Ken Sisson got into a heated argument at a Manitoba folk camp about nationalism vs. internationalism. How to have an ideal world, one that would never let wars happen again. The answer, they decided, was cooperation. To that end, they married in 1948 and a few years later set up a cooperative farm with four others. As a symbol of their earnest intention to live communally rather than individually, the women put all their spice cans together, the men named the farm dog Co-op. It was such a brave plan and might have worked if Ken hadn't been injured in a farm accident. He could never work the same again. The dream died. Peace doesn't guarantee good luck.

Nor does it guarantee prosperity. When three members of the Kiemele family in southern Alberta married in a triple ceremony in the fall of 1949, they did so out of a consideration for money. Three weddings for the price of one preacher and one reception. No fussing about flowers and hairdos. Margaret married Paul Ost. She remembers that she curled her hair the night before the wedding—put it up in rags and hoped for the best the next day. Her sister Hazel married George McDonald and brother Delbert married LaRene Vance. After the wedding, they got on with their lives.

By 1950, that's what was happening—people were getting on with their lives. Certainly, Joan Murray was. She was getting married on June 6 in Winnipeg. The sensible blue suit was bought, the arrangements made, except that the Red River flooded. The 1950 flood, so deep that water came to the ceiling of the main floor of her parent's house. A local newspaper talked her into faking a picture. With a headline that said something like….Local Bride Rescues Her Wedding Dress…the picture showed Joan hauling a white dress out of the upstairs window. Told a great story except that Joan didn't have a white wedding gown. Never mind. She and Arlington Dixon (known forever after as Dix) made it to St. Paul's Anglican in Fort Garry on the designated day, and the ceremony took place to the tune of pumps emptying the church basement. One thing's sure; she wasn't thinking about the war.

In the next 50 years, weddings changed almost completely (except for the parts that didn't change at all.) They got bigger, more expensive. Brides arranged their own weddings and their fathers didn't 'give them away.' Churches weren't necessary. Marriage vows didn't promise 'til death us do part;' they promised companionship as long as it was mutually satisfying. They didn't mention obedience and fidelity; they promised friendship and equality under the law. *Here Comes the Bride, Big, Fat and Wide* lost out as processional music. In came flautists and violins playing *The Ode To Joy* or *Pachelbel's Canon*. Soloists sang *Feelings* instead of *O Promise Me* or *Because*. Ring bearers didn't wear Little Lord Fauntleroy outfits. They wore jeans. The wedding cake because a photo prop made out of Styrofoam instead of a rich fruit cake. And the wedding day of choice became almost exclusively Saturday in spite of the old ditty that said:

> **Monday's for health;**
> **Tuesday's for wealth;**
> **Wednesday's the best day of all;**
> **Thursday's for losses;**
> **Friday's for crosses;**
> **Saturday's no day at all.**

But among all the major changes, one thing did not change. The dress. The all-important wedding dress that will for one day make an ordinary woman into a princess. For one day, she will be the star, the most important thing in the room. Whether that's a sad commentary on the lives of girls and women, or whether that's so much part of our history and culture that it doesn't carry a lot of significant baggage is hard to know, but there you are. The dress is the bride. The bride is the dress. Indivisible. No wonder young women shop for their wedding dress months in advance, years even. If this is her one chance at glory, she'd better make it good. And more than likely, she'll make it white, just as the old poem suggests:

> **Married in white, you have chosen aright;**
> **Married in gray, you will go far away;**
> **Married in black, you will wish yourself back;**
> **Married in red, you will wish yourself dead;**
> **Married in green, ashamed to be seen;**
> **Married in blue, he will always be true;**
> **Married in pearl, you will live in a whirl;**
> **Married in yellow, ashamed of your fellow;**
> **Married in brown, you will live out of town;**
> **Married in pink, your heart will sink.**

University of Manitoba Associate Professor Cecile Clayton-Gouthro got to thinking about the evolution of colour in wedding dresses. It was a natural for her since she taught in the Human Ecology faculty and worked with the wedding dresses in their collection—most of which were white or ivory or cream. Why not the occasional dark colour, she wondered. Why not black, for that matter? Her questioning led to a research paper entitled, **" Does black stand a chance at the altar?"**

After much analysis and cultural study, she predicted that brides would sooner or later be wearing black for their weddings. After all, hadn't black made it into bridesmaid ranks? she asked. And wasn't black a power color? Women were into power in the 1980s and 1990s. Of course, brides would wear black. But that research paper came out in 1990 and time has not proven the professor right…yet.

So, white still rules the wedding day, but it's mostly a fashion statement. It's no longer an indication of virginity. That's the biggest change of all in the last 50 years. A bride before 1950 was supposed to be pure, ie, she was supposed to be a virgin. If she were a widow or, heaven forbid, a divorcee, she was expected to wear gray or navy or a nice print perhaps. If she were pregnant, heaven forbid, she was supposed to wear whatever was handy and get married as quickly as possible.

All of that is gone. Some say good riddance; some regret the loss of innocence that's involved.

Then there are those who say the heck with the whole rigmarole. Why get married at all? That too is a change from the earlier part of the century when common law relationships were most often called "shacking up" and decent people wouldn't countenance such an arrangement. However, it's done all the time now in spite of old mothers who keep murmuring about the "M" word. Marriage is just a piece of paper, the common law couples say, and besides there are laws about common law now. It isn't a gamble; it's a commitment made without the expense and phoniness of a wedding, they say.

Thus, with one thing and another, weddings as a social and cultural benchmark lost ground in the late 1900s. They weren't a once-in-a-lifetime thing. They became big parties, period, without the overtones of innocence so they weren't news anymore. Pretty soon, wedding write-ups on the social pages were replaced by hard news—how to lose weight and how to impeach a president and how to deal with economic cutbacks. Wars even. How did they sneak back onto the world's agenda? Bring back the weddings, some old mothers murmured. Give us a rest now and then from the hard news. Even if weddings are an elitist competitive show of money, let us see them. Even if we can't afford silver salvers, whatever they are, let us know that someone can. Tell us about real people at real weddings. They are at least beautiful and interesting and happy. And now and then, they are magic. Like other rituals that have been around for a very long time, weddings can transcend all their baggage and live up to that most wonderful dress, those most solemn words, the most beautiful music.

They can be, as poet W.J. Lampton said, **"Same old slippers, same old rice, same old glimpse of Paradise."**

Acknowledgements

Books Used in Preparation of Once Upon A Wedding

Airforce magazine, Summer 1998

Andersen, Doris. Evergreen Islands. Vancouver: Gray's Publishing, Whitecap Books Ltd., 1979.

Backhouse, Frances. Women of the Klondike. Vancouver/Toronto: Whitecap Books, 1995.

Bayley, Denis. A Londoner in Rupert's Land. Chichester, Eng: Moore and Tillyer, 1969

Beardy, Flora and Coutts, Robert, ed. Voices From Hudson Bay, Cree Stories From York Factory. Montreal and Kingston: McGill-Queen's University Press, 1996

Bird, Shawn L. Isabel Tyner Ford, A Woman in Early Prince George. Unpublishedpaper.

Black, Martha Louise. Martha Black. Alaska Northwest Books, 1980.

Bowen, Lynne. Three Dollar Dreams. Lantzville, BC: Oolichan Books, 1987.

Bowering, George. Bowering's B.C. Toronto: Penguin Books, 1996.

Bronfman, Sadye Rosner. My Sam, A Memoir. 1982

Byfield, Ted, editor. The Great West Before 1900. Edmonton: United Western Communications Ltd, 1991

Cantwell, Sister Margaret SSA. North To Share. Victoria: Sisters of St. Ann,

Carpenter, Jock. Fifty Dollar Bride, Marie Rose Smith. Sidney, BC: Gray's Publishing, 1988

Carter and Akili. The Window of our Memories. St. Albert, AB: B.C.R. Society of Alberta, 1981

Chafe, J.W. Extraordinary Tales from MB History. MB Historical Society, 1973

Chan, Anthony. Gold Mountain, The Chinese in the New World. Vancouver: New Star Books, 1983

Clifford, Ann. Ann's Story. Forever in Memory, 1995

Corbett, E.A. McQueen of Edmonton. Ryerson, 1934.

Cormack, Barbara Villy. Perennials and Politics. Sherwood Park, AB: 1968

Dafoe, Christopher, ed. The Beaver. February/March 1995

Dempsey, Hugh, ed. The Best From Alberta History. Saskatoon: Western Producer Prairie Books, 1981

Dempsey, Hugh, ed. The Rundle Journals, 1840-1848. Calgary: Historical Society of AB, 1977

Duff, David. Victoria and Albert. NY: Taplinger Publishing Co. Inc., 1972.

Duffus, Maureen, ed. Beyond the Blue Bridge, Stories From Esquimalt, Victoria: Esquimalt Silver Threads Writers Group, 1990

Duncan, Joy, ed. Red Serge Wives. Centennial Book Committee, 1974.

Ewanchuk, Michael ed. Pioneer Profiles. Winnipeg: 1981

Farrell, Ann. Grace MacInnis: A Story of Love and Integrity. Fitzhenry and Whiteside, 1994

Findlay, Nora. Jasper, A Backward Glance. Jasper, AB: Jasper Yellowhead Historical Society, 1992

Flanagan, Thomas, ed. The Diaries of Louis Riel. Edmonton: Hurtig Publishers, 1976.

Flanagan, Thomas. Louis 'David' Riel, Prophet of the New World. Universityof Toronto Press, 1996.

Foran and Jameson, ed. Citymakers. Historical Society of Alberta, 1987.

Foran, Max, ed. Grant MacEwan's Journals. Edmonton: Lone Pine Publishing, 1986

Friesen and Parsey. Manitoba Folk Schools, The First Ten Years.

Fryer, Harold. Alberta, The Pioneer YearsLangley, BC: Sunfire Publications, 1984

Gaudin, Samuel. Forty-four Years with the Native Crees. Toronto: Mundy-Goodfellow Printing Ltd., 1942.

Gerrard, Nelson. Icelandic River Saga, 1985

Gould, Ed. All Hell For a Basement—Medicine Hat, 1883-1983. City of Medicine Hat, 1981

Gould, Jan. Women of British Columbia. Vancouver: Hancock House Publishers Ltd., 1975.

Graham, Donald. Lights of the Inside Passage. Vancouver: Harbour Publishing Co., 1986

Gutkin, Harry. Journey Into Our Heritage. Toronto: Lester and Orpen Dennys Ltd., 1980

Hamilton, Bea. Salt Spring Island. Vancouver: Mitchell Press Ltd., 1969.

Harris, Lorraine. Halfway to the Goldfields, A History of Lillooet. Vancouver: J.J. Douglas Ltd. 1977.

Harvey, Dr. Robert. Pioneers of Manitoba. Winnipeg: Prairie Publishing Co., 1970.

Healy, W.J. Women of Red River. Winnipeg: Peguis Publishing, 1977.

Historical Society of AB. Alberta History, 1955, 1963, 1977, 1987, 1988, Calgary.

Hudson, A. James. Charles Ora Card, Pioneer and Colonizer. 1963

Hughes, Katherine. Father Lacombe, The Black Robe Voyageur. Toronto: McClelland and Stewart, 1920

Jalink-Wijbrans, Marijke. A Forgotten War. Personal memoir.

Jewish Historical Society of Southern AB. Land of Promise. Calgary: The Society, 1996

Johnson, J.K, ed. Affectionately Yours, The Letters of Sir John A. Macdonald and his Family.
        Toronto: Macmillan of Canada, 1969.

Kennedy, Liv. Coastal Villages. Madeira Park, BC: Harbour Publishing, 1991.

Koester, C.B. Mr. Davin, MP, A Biography of Nicholas Flood Davin. Saskatoon, SK:
        Western Producer Prairie Books, 1980

Konantz, Gail. Edith Rogers, Manitobans in Profile. Family memoir.

Krupp, Lillian. Life and Legends, A History of High River. Calgary: Sandstone press, 1982.

Large, R.G. Prince Rupert. Vancouver: Mitchell Press, 1960.

Lefebvre, Marie Rose Gisele Therese. Listen, The Wind is Rising.

Leven, Esther. The Wedding Ceremony in the Jewish Tradition. Winnipeg: An unpublished paper, 1981.

Lewis, S.P. Grace. Madeira Park, BC: Harbour Publishing, 1993

Lloyd, Lewis. Memories of a Co-operative Statesman. A memoir.

Luchkovich, Michael. A Ukrainian Canadian in Parliament. Toronto:
        Ukrainian Canadian Research Fdn., 1965

Lucia, Ellis. Klondike Kate, Queen of the Yukon. Toronto: S.J. Reginald Saunders, 1962

Macdonald, R.H. Grant MacEwan, No Ordinary Man. Saskatoon: Western Producer Prairie Books, 1979

MacGill, Elsie Gregory. My Mother The Judge. Toronto. Peter Martin Associates Ltd, 1981.

MacGregor, J.G. Edmonton Trader. Toronto: McClelland and Stewart Ltd, 1963

MacLaren, Sherrill. Braehead. Toronto: McClelland and Stewart, 1986.

Manitoba Historical Society. Manitoba History Magazine. Winnipeg:
        Spring 1986, Spring 1994, 1983 and 1991.

Marrus, Michael. Mr. Sam. Winnipeg: The Peguis Group, 1991

Mayer, Melanie J. Klondike Women. Swallow Press, Ohio University Press, 1989.

McDonald, Donna. Lord Strathcona, A Biography of Donald Alexander Smith. Toronto:
        Dundurn Press, 1996

McKillop, Ingibjorg Sigurgeirsson. Mikley, the Magnificient Island. 1979

McWilliams, Margaret. Manitoba Milestones. Toronto and London: J.M. Dent, 1928

Moore, Ruth. Personal Memoir.

Morrow, J.W. Early History of Medicine Hat Country. Medicine Hat Historical Society, 1923.

Nesbitt, James K. Album of Victoria, Old Homes and Families. 1956

Nisbet, Jack. Sources of the River, Seattle: Sasquatch Books, 1994

Norris, Pat Wastell. Raincoast Chronicles 16, Telegraph Cove. Madeira Park: Harbour Publishing, 1995

Palmer, Howard and Tamara, ed. Peoples of Alberta. Saskatoon: Western Producer Prairie Books, 1985

Palmer, Howard. Alberta, A New History. Edmonton: Hurtig Publishers Ltd., 1990.

Patton, Brian. Tales From the Canadian Rockies. Edmonton: Hurtig Publishers, 1984

Penniket, Dawn. I Was a War Bride and the Sharp-Penniket Story. Personal memoirs.

Peterkin and Shaw. Mrs. Doctor. Winnipeg: Prairie Publishing Co., 1976

Pigott, Peter. Flying Canucks, Famous Canadian Aviators. Toronto: Hounslow Publishers, 1994

Rasmussen, Rasmussen, Savage, Wheeler. A Harvest Yet To Reap. Toronto. Women's Press, 1976.

Reid, Sheila. Wings of a Hero. St. Catharines, ON: Vanwell Publishing Ltd., 1997

Reksten, Terry. More English Than the English. Victoria: Orca Publishers, 1986.

Reksten, Terry. Rattenbury. Victoria: Sono Nis Press, 1978

Reksten, Terry. The Dunsmuir Saga. Vancouver: Douglas and McIntyre, 1991.

Riber, Barbara. The Life and Times of Mary Elizabeth Bettinger Barton. Seattle: Unpublished manuscript on Sister Mary of the Cross

Robertson, Heather. More Than A Rose. Toronto: A Seal Book, 1991

Saskatoon Women's Calendar Collective. Herstory 1980, 1987. Saskatoon: Coteau Books.

Scott, Andrew. The Promise of Paradise. Vancouver/Toronto: Whitecap Books, 1997

Shipley, Nan. Anna and the Indians. Toronto: Ryerson Press, 1955.

Siggins, Maggie. Riel, A Life of Revolution. Toronto: Harper Collins Publishers Ltd., 1994

Sismey, Eric. Pioneer Days in British Columbia, vol. 2. Vancouver: BC Outdoors Magazine

Sissons, Jack. Judge of the Far North. Toronto/Montreal: McClelland and Stewart Ltd., 1968

Smith, Dorothy Blakey. James Douglas, Father of British Columbia. Toronto: Oxford University Press, 1971.

Smith, James K. Wilderness of Fortune, The Story of Western Canada. Vancouver: Douglas and McIntyre, 1983

Smith, Marie Rose. Fifty Years on the Plains. Edmonton: Canadian Cattlemen Magazine

Smith, Mary E. A Family Saga. Personal memoir.

Sound Heritage Series, ed. Sound Heritage, Voices From British Columbia. Vancouver: Douglas and McIntyre, 1984.

Stewart and Antonson, ed. Great Stories From the Canadian Frontier. Antonson Publishing, 1979.

Storrs, Monica. God's Galloping Girl. Vancouver: University of BC Press, 1979

Surtees, Ursula. A War Bride Story. Personal memoir.

Susan Riley. Political Wives. Toronto: Deneau and Wayne, 1987

Sykes, Ella. Home Help in Canada. London: G. Belt and Sons, 1912.

Thomas, Dr. Saskatchewan History Magazine. Saskatoon, SK: Saskatchewan Archives Bd.

Trafford, Tyler. Toole Peet 1897-1997. Calgary

Von Hauff, Donna. Everyone's Grandfather, the Life and Times of Grant MacEwan. Edmonton: Grant MacEwan Community College Fdn., 1994

Voth, Norma Jost. Mennonite Foods and Folkways from South Russia, V. 2. Good Books, PA

Wetton, C. The Promised Land. Lloydminster: Lloydminster Times, 1979.

White, Howard, ed. Raincoast Chronicles, Eleven Up. Madeira Park, BC: Harbour Publishing, 1994

Wicks, Ben. Promise You'll Take Care of my Daughter. Toronto: Stoddart Publishing Co. Ltd., 1992

Woodcock, George. The Century That Made Us Canada, 1814-1914. Toronto: Oxford University Press, 1989.

Museums, archives and libraries across Western Canada that provided information and assistance— thanks to all!

Alberta Provincial Archives, Edmonton
Barr Colony Heritage Cultural Centre, Lloydminster, AB/SK
British Columbia Archives, Victoria, BC
Bulkley Valley Museum, Smithers, BC
Calgary, AB, Public Library and Local History Room
Campbell River Museum and Archives
Campbell River, BC, Museum
Canadian Sikh Centennial Museum, Vancouver, BC
City of Edmonton, AB, Archives
City of Victoria Archives, BC
Courtenay and District Museum and Archives, Courtenay, BC
Dawson City Museum and Historical Society, YT
Dugald, MB, Costume Museum
Glenbow Museum and Archives, Calgary, AB
Grande Prairie, AB, Museum
Hay River, NWT, Museum
High River, AB, Museum and Archives
Historic Costume Collection, University of AB, Edmonton
Jasper Yellowhead Museum and Archives, Jasper, AB
Jewish Historical Centre, Vancouver, BC
Jewish Historical Society of Western Canada, Winnipeg, MB
Kaatza Station Museum, Lake Cowichan, BC
Kamloops, BC, Museum and Archives
Kamloops, BC, Museum and Archives
Kootenay Museum and Historical Society, Nelson, BC
McBride Museum, Whitehorse, YT
Medicine Hat, AB, Archives
Mennonite Heritage Centre, Winnipeg, MB
New Westminster, BC, Museum

NWT Archives, Northern Heritage Centre, Yellowknife, NWT

Peace River, AB, Museum

Penticton, BC, Museum and Archives

Prince Albert, SK, Historical Society

Prince Rupert City and Regional Archives, BC

Provincial Archives of MB, Winnipeg

Quesnel and District Museum and Archives, BC

Red Deer and District Archives, Red Deer, AB

Salvation Army Heritage Centre in Toronto, ON

Saskatchewan Archives Board in Regina and Saskatoon, SK

Sir Alexander Galt Museum and Archives, Lethbridge, AB

Vancouver, BC, Public Library

Vernon, BC, Museum and Archives

Western Development Museum, Saskatoon, SK

Whyte Museum and Archives, Banff, AB

Yukon Education, Archives Branch, Whitehorse, YT

Individuals who provided stories, pictures and support for the book—thanks to all!

Adamson, Elsie, Coquitlam, BC

Aebli, Lynwyn Foran, Calgary, AB

Arcand, George and Alice, Shaunavon, SK

Askin, Florence, Arcola, SK

Backhouse, Frances

Banda, Kay, Regina, SK

Barnett, Ruth, of Comox, BC

Beardy, Flora, Churchill, MB

Bennett, Elva, Dodsland, SK

Billard, Georgette, Shaunavon, SK

Bizon, Lorraine, St. Albert, AB

Biscoe, Frederick, Crofton, BC

Bjerkey, Irene, of Hope, BC

Brown, Carol, St. Albert, AB

Brown, Margaret, Winnipeg, MB

Buckles, Agnes, Edmonton, AB

Burger, Mrs. M.E., Calgary, AB

Burtonshaw, Geoff, Calgary, AB

Chuchla, Annie, Calgary, AB

Clayton-Gouthro, Dr. Cecile, Faculty of
    Human Ecology at U of Man.

Clifford, Ann, High River, AB

Coonen, Father Tim, Dawson City, YT

Coutts, Bob, Winnipeg, MB

Davies, Shirley, Nelson, BC

Dawe, Michael, Red Deer, AB

Dawn Brashear, Auburn, CA, USA

Dawson, Millie, Saskatoon, SK

Dixon, Joan, Spruce Grove, AB

Dykes, Marjorie, Calgary, AB

Evans, Annabelle, Bow Island, AB

Ford, Isabel, Prince George, BC

Frejd, Margaret, Regina, SK

Fuller, Donald, Calgary, AB

Goertzen, Eleanor, Kyle, SK

Gottschlich, Hilda, Lacombe, AB

Gould, Madeleine, Dawson City, YT

Goulet, Agnes, Winnipeg, MB

Gramms, Beverly, Beiseker, AB

Grise, Rosella, Saskatoon, SK

Guidinger, Vera, Eatonia, SK

Guynn, Vivian, Three Hills

Hall, Mary Elizabeth, Herbert, SK
Harrison, David, Tobago, West Indies
Hess, Walter and Annie, Clyde, AB
Hitz, Josephine, Dixonville, AB
Iwaasa, Clara, Brooks, AB
Jalink-Wijbrans, Marijke, Calgary, AB
Jensen, Earl and Betty, Port Coquitlam, BC
Jordan, Norma, Saskatoon, SK
Keedian, Anna, East St. Paul, MB
Kerr, Edna, Port Moody, BC
King, Eleanore, Regina, SK
Knelsen, Jean, Abbotsford, BC
Knight, Leith, Moose Jaw, SK
Krahn, Anne, Niverville, MB
Leavitt, Devere and Marguritte, Leavitt, AB
Lien, Emma Brick, Sherwood Park, AB
Lloyd, Jack, Beechy, SK
Luchkovich, Sophie, St. Albert, AB
Lupton, Kate, Saskatoon, SK
MacEwan, Grant, Calgary, AB
Mark, Esther, Winnipeg, MB
Mary. E. Smith, Peachland, BC
McDougall, John, Edmonton, AB
McKinnon, Donna, Vancouver, BC
Moffat, Bill, Vancouver, BC
Moffat, Kathryn M., Quesnel, BC
Moore, Ruth, Winnipeg, MB
Moyles, Dr. Gordon, Edmonton, AB
Newton, Mrs. T.D., Guelph, ON
Nissen, Brenda Edwards, Saskatoon, SK
Odlum, Jean, Vancouver, BC
Ost, Margaret, Lomond, AB
Pallister, Carey, Victoria, BC
Paton, Adrian, Arcola, SK
Popoff, Eli A., Grand Forks, BC
Ransby, Lynne and Ted, Winnipeg, MB
Rasmussen, Pat, Drumheller, AB
Ratcliffe, Ron, Nakusp, BC
Rex, Marion, Edmonton, AB
Riber, Barbara, Seattle, WA
Roberson, Gerald and Eunice, Parksville, BC

Royan, Don, Calgary, AB
Rushton, Ruth, Kelowna, BC
Sandhu, Daljit Singh, Vancouver, BC
Schloss, Sondra, Vancouver, BC
Schumacher, Marguerite, Calgary, AB
Schuster, Eileen, Regina, SK
Senda, Florence, Lethbridge, AB
Shail, Donna, Hythe, AB
Sharman, Bill, Calgary, AB
Sigurgeirsson, Binnie, Winnipeg and Hecla Island
Simbrec, Rose, Grand Forks, BC
Sisson, Helen, Winnipeg, MB
Smith, Shirley, Fort Saskatchewan, AB
Sovereign, Dr. A.E., Vernon, BC
Stokes, Kathleen, Winnipeg, MB
Stovel, Bonnie, Winnipeg. MB
Surtees, Fran, Kelowna, BC
Tanguay, Fr. John Paul, Whitehorse, YT
Tellier, Corinne, Winnipeg, MB
Tomyn, Michael, Vegreville, AB
Toole, William, Calgary, AB
Turner, Peggy, Lloydminster, AB/SK
Van Ruskenveld, Yvonne, and Sheila Daly,
    Old Cemeteries Society in Victoria, BC
Verigin, Mike and Doris, Cowley, AB
Waddell, Jackie, East St. Paul, MB
Werner, Gail, Powell River, BC
Wesko family, Cochrane and Calgary, AB
White, Donny, Medicine Hat, AB
White, Linda, Winnipeg, MB
Whyte, Anne, Winnipeg, MB
Williams, Billie, Kamloops, BC
Williamson, Dave and Winnie, Saskatoon, SK
Zetaruk, Eugenia, Winnipeg, MB
Zimmerman, Sheila, Sechelt, BC

Credits for pictures throughout Once Upon A Wedding...

1878, the Douglas wedding—BC Archives, A-01236

1889, the White wedding—Donny White, Medicine Hat Museum, AB

1890, the Moffat wedding—Quesnel and District Museum, BC

1892, the Bomford wedding—Medicine Hat Museum, AB

1895, the Gaudin wedding—Dugald, MB, Costume Museum

1896, Brick wedding—Provincial Archives of AB, B 7410

1898, Rogers wedding—Provincial Archives of MB

1899, Gottschlich wedding—Hilda Gottschlich, Lacombe, AB

1900, Sr. Mary wedding—Yukon Archives/Barbara Riber Collection 96/23 #1

1901, McGee wedding—Yukon Archives/Beverly Gramms 83/59 #3

1902, Cataline wedding—Irene Bjerky, Hope, BC

1903, Prairie wedding—Provincial Archives of AB, A1631

1905, Sacret wedding—City of Vancouver Archives PORT. P314

1907, Young wedding—Glenbow Archives, Calgary, AB, NA 2755-20

1908, Pidcock wedding—Courtenay and District Museum, BC, D 127

1911, Hume wedding—Kootenay Museum Assn., Nelson, BC

1912, Biscoe wedding—Courtenay and District Museum, BC, P225-1651

1912, Nanton/Cameron wedding—Elspeth Mary Newton, Guelph, ON

1912, Crowchild wedding—Glenbow Archives, Calgary, AB, NA 192-17

1913, Hironaka wedding—de Jourdan Studio and City of Lethbridge Archives, AB

1913, Sovereign wedding—Dr. A.E. Sovereign, Vernon, BC

1914, Gregoire wedding—George Arcand, Shaunavon, SK

1915, Toole wedding—Glenbow Archives, Calgary, AB, NA 2788-70

1917, Jordan wedding—Western Development Museum, Saskatoon, SK

1917, Kerr wedding—Shirley Davies, Nelson, BC

1918, Tom Thumb wedding—Kootenay Museum Assn., Nelson, BC

1920, Henderson wedding—Elva Bennett, Dodsland, SK

1920, Askin wedding—Adrian K. Paton, South SK Museum, Arcola, SK

1921, Mills wedding—Jasper Yellowhead Museum, AB, PA 92/19

1922, Lagimodiere wedding—Agnes Goulet, Winnipeg, MB

1922, Taylor wedding—Bettie Hall, Herbert, SK

1924, Double wedding—Shirley Smith, Fort Saskatchewan, AB

1924, Shatz wedding—Medicine Hat Museum, AB

1925, Moffat wedding—City of Victoria Archives, BC

1925, Moody, Pearson, etc. wedding—Sheila Zimmerman, Sechelt, BC

1925, Sigurgeirsson wedding—Provincial Archives of MB

1926, Husak wedding—Provincial Archives of MB

1926, Cuica wedding—Eileen Shuster, Regina, SK

1927, Church wedding—Medicine Hat Museum, AB

1927, Stratton wedding—Clara Iwaasa, Brooks, AB

1927, Anderson wedding—Glenbow Archives, Calgary, AB, NA 2574

1928, Verigin wedding—Michael Verigin, Cowley, AB

1928, Wastell wedding—Pat Wastell Norris, Vancouver, BC

1929, Airplane wedding—SK Archives Bd. R-B 4085

1929, Luchkovich wedding—Carol Brown, St. Albert, BC

1929, Clifford wedding—Ann Clifford, High River, AB

1930, Stovel wedding—Bonnie Stovel, Winnipeg, MB

1931, Chuchla wedding—Glenbow Archives, Calgary, AB, NA 3091-30

1931, Wesko wedding—City of Lethbridge Archives/ de Jourdan Studio P1991000618-GP

1932, Ratcliffe wedding—Ron Ratcliffe, Nakusp, BC

1933, Klondike Kate wedding—Vancouver Public Library, Vancouver, BC, 6632

1933, Keedian wedding—Anne Keedian, Winnipeg, MB

1934, Lieffers wedding—Rosella Grise, Saskatoon, SK

1935, MacEwan wedding—Lynwyn Aebli, Calgary, AB

1935, York Factory wedding—Ralph Ingram

1936, Pocaterra wedding—Glenbow Archive, Calgary, AB, PA 695-70

1936, Ford wedding—Fraser-Fort George Regional Museum, BC, P986.45.27

1937, Werner wedding—Gail Werner, Powell River, BC

1938, Leavitt wedding—Devere and Marguritte Leavitt, Leavitt, AB

1938, Wijbrans wedding—Marijke A. Jalink-Wijbrans, Calgary, AB

1938, Smith wedding—Mary Smith, Peachland, BC

1939, Mark wedding—Esther Mark, Winnipeg, MB

1939, RCMP wedding—RCMP Centennial Museum, Regina, SK

1940, Ransby wedding—Margaret Brown, Winnipeg, MB

1941, Moore wedding—Ruth Moore, Winnipeg, MB

1941, Angulalik wedding—Archibald Lang Fleming/ NWT Archives

1942, Watson wedding—Victoria City Archives, BC

1942, Williamson wedding—Dave and Winnie Williamson, Saskatoon, SK

1944, Odlum wedding—Jean Odlum, Vancouver, BC

1944, Pennikett wedding—Dawn Pennikett, Nelson, BC

1949, Triple wedding—Margaret Ost, Lomand, AB